A BOOK OF JEWISH CURIOSITIES

D1115802

DAVID M. HAUSDORFF

A BOOK
OF
JEWISH
CURIOSITIES

BLOCH PUBLISHING COMPANY, INC.

NEW YORK, NEW YORK

Library of Congress Catalog Card Number: 55-11366

Second Printing, February, 1956

First Paperback Printing, 1979

ISBN 0-8197-0466-0

To my darling granddaughter,
Debra Jane,
and to her dear parents, her devoted uncles,
and, naturally, her
ever-loving grandmother

Manufactured in the United States of America

CONTENTS

INTRODUCTION

This collection of strange items from ancient and traditional Jewish writings, such as the Talmud and the *Midrash,* is not a book of theology. The selections have been chosen purely because they are unusual; their ethical or theological teachings have been deliberately by-passed.

It is only natural, however, that some religious elements appear. Because of the integration of religion with every phase of life in Judaism, it is as impossible to divorce religious significance from Jewish thought and writings as it is to separate action from energy.

Many of these curiosities, though they may seem perfectly ordinary to the modern reader, acquire uniqueness in their expression many centuries ago when such ideas were uncommon. Quite a number of them are thus also prophetically prochronistic—far ahead of their time.

We must bear in mind that the Talmudists touched upon scientific problems only in so far as they related to the religious questions under discussion. Hence many of these oddities are merely fragmentary, yet they afford a keen and deep insight into the profound, comprehensive, and well-nigh unbelievable knowledge of these ancient sages in an age when such was the exception rather than the rule among the world's nations.

Many more complex sciences are dealt with in talmudic literature in addition to mathematics and geography, such as

~§ ANATOMY

There are 248 members (bones, joints) in the male body and 252 in the female; 365 chords (sinews, tendons, muscles, arteries). The 248 "members" are as follows: 30 in each foot, 10 in each ankle, 2 in each lower leg, 5 in each knee, 1 in each thigh, 3 in each hip—11 ribs on each side—

30 in each hand, 2 in each forearm, 2 in each elbow, 1 in each upper arm, 4 in each shoulder—101 on each side, for a total of 202, plus 18 links in the spine, 9 members in the head, 8 in the neck, 6 in the breast, and 5 in the apertures.

✍ EMBRYOLOGY

The child of a pregnant woman whose steady diet includes mustard will be greedy (gluttonous); small fish—it will have small eyes; strong drink—red and ruddy complexion; meat and wine—it will be healthy and strong; eggs—large eyes; fish in the *cauf* (corf)—charming; parsley (celery)—noble and worthy; coriander—fleshy; *ethrog* (citron)—pleasant (no bodily odor). If a woman gives birth before the age of twenty, she is capable of bearing children until sixty; from twenty to forty, until she is forty; after forty—she will never again give birth.

✍ HYGIENE

Kissing on the lips is dangerous, as one may thereby transmit or contract disease.

✍ THERAPY

One who is suffering from heart ailments will find hot rich milk every morning beneficial.

✍ PSYCHOLOGY

Excessive self-pride (an overbearing attitude) is an indication of an inferior mentality. Forbidden things are the only ones that are susceptible to temptation. Repetition of wrongdoing convinces the culprit of its permissibility. Women have more understanding than men.

✍ ZOOLOGY

The hide of a black ox is excellent; the flesh of a red ox is preferable; a white ox is excellent for ploughing. It is the nature of the horse not to sleep but to nap. Pigs are more serious carriers of plague than any other animal.

ᴇᵹ ICHTHYOLOGY

Certain species of fish do not have scales in their infancy but grow them as they mature; others lose their scales when drawn from the water. All fish that have scales have fins, but some with fins have no scales.

ᴇᵹ BOTANY

If flaxseed is put into water, even though no earth is there it will sprout roots. A southern field will yield better crops than one at any other point of the compass. The flavor of large mountain-grown fruit differs from that of fruit grown in a valley.

ᴇᵹ GEOLOGY

Sand will continue to heat a hot substance placed in it, and will cool a cold one. In the depths of the sea are some stones so soft that they ooze water, and one called *geta*, which repels, in contrast to the lodestone, which attracts.

ᴇᵹ ASTRONOMY

The solar year is longer than the lunar year by 10 days, 21 hours, 11 minutes, and 20 seconds. The distance traversed by the sun in a week is covered by the moon in one day, and the distance traveled by the sun in a year is covered by the moon in fifty days.

ᴇᵹ METEOROLOGY

Wind from the south brings devastation; from the north, cold; from the west, barrenness; from the east, rain. There is danger in an individual white or green stroke of lightning, and from clouds surging from due south to due west, and from two thunderclouds meeting.

ᴇᵹ CHEMISTRY

Deep stains in a flaxen material are worse than in a woolen one, and more difficult to eradicate. Anything boiled after baking will never re-ferment. If water is placed in a clear, transparent glass and set in the blazing sun, flax can be ignited from the rays.

The quotations given in the following pages naturally do not include all of the unusual passages of the Talmud, *Midrashim,* and other Jewish literature. Nor do they attempt to prove anything one way or another.

These selections do, however, afford a fairly comprehensive glimpse of the vast panorama of Jewish thought, particularly the Talmud, about which one talmudic sage, Jochanan (a descendant of proselytes) said in *Pirkei Ahvoth* V, 25 (Ethics, or Chapters of the Fathers), "Turn it and turn it over and over again, for everything is in it."

This modest volume is dedicated to that premise, for knowledge leads to understanding, and understanding leads to peace.

PREFACE

■ brief outline of the history and contents of the sources of the oddities contained in this book will be helpful to those unacquainted with Hebrew lore and literature.

First and foremost, of course, is THE TORAH—the Five Books of Moses, or Pentateuch. This consists of

> Genesis—*B'reishith*
> Exodus—*Sh'moth*
> Leviticus—*Va'Yikrah*
> Numbers—*Ba'midbar*
> Deuteronomy—*D'vahrim*

The Torah is the Written Law, transmitted to Moses on Mount Sinai together with the Oral Law, later committed to writing. Every rule and regulation of Jewish law and life, in order to be traditional, must be traced either directly or indirectly to the Torah, which is God's Word.

Revelation at Sinai occurred over 3,300 years ago (some chronologists, curiously enough, fix the date of the Exodus from Egypt, seven weeks before Revelation, as 1492 B.C.E., which by an amazing coincidence brings to mind the exodus from Spain in 1492 of the Common Era). Traditionally the entire Torah was written by Moses, so that its contents were recorded over thirty-three centuries ago (although there is a saying in Jewish lore that the Torah was composed by the Almighty two thousand years before the creation of the world).

The Torah is the first of the three sections of Scripture, followed by *N'viim* (Prophets) and *K'subim* (Writings, or Hagiographa)—the trilogy forming the word *T'nach* from the initial Hebrew letters of these three words.

Prophets consists of the Books of Joshua, Judges, Samuel, Kings, Isaiah, Jeremiah, Ezekiel; the Twelve Minor Prophets—

Hosea, Joel, Amos, Obadiah, Jonah, Micah, Nachum, Habak-
kuk, Zephaniah, Chaggai, Zechariah, and Malachi. The Hagiographa consists of Psalms, Proverbs, Job, Song of Songs, Ruth,
Lamentations, Ecclesiastes, Esther, Daniel, Ezra, Nehemiah, and
Chronicles.

The Book of Joshua was written approximately 3,220 years
ago; the period of the Judges comprised about 350 years;
Samuel lived about 2,800 years ago; King David wrote the
Psalms in the days of Samuel; and his son Solomon, author of
Proverbs, Song of Songs, and Ecclesiastes, reigned after him.
The Book of Kings contains data concerning a period of some
three hundred or more years—2,670 to 3,000 years ago; the
Book of Chronicles, a history of the Temple and its priesthood
as well as of the House of David and the Kingdom of Judah,
is more or less contemporaneous with Kings.

Isaiah lived about 2,700 years ago; Ezekiel about 2,550 years
ago; Jeremiah about 2,500 years ago. The time of the Twelve
Minor Prophets was from about 750 to 450 B.C.E. The Book
of Esther was written about 2,400 years ago, and the Books of
Ezra and Nehemiah a little over 2,300 years ago. Lamentations
was written by Jeremiah, and the Book of Ruth was composed
in the days of the Judges. As for the Book of Job, its authorship was attributed to various individuals in various periods
of time, as mentioned in the section of this volume entitled,
"People."

For the purposes of identification of passages cited, quotations from the *T'nach* show chapter in Roman numerals, with
verses in Arabic numerals.

THE *MISHNAH* is the Oral Law and teachings, traditionally transmitted to Moses on Mount Sinai together with the
Written Law—the Five Books of Moses. It is considered an
integral part of the Torah.

The *Mishnah* consists of *Halachoth*—legal traditions, practices, customs, usages. These were learned orally, from teacher
to pupil, down through the ages: "From Moses at Sinai to

Joshua, Joshua to the Elders, the Elders to the Prophets, and the Prophets to the Men of the Great Synagogue" (*Pirkei Ahvoth* I, 1).

There had always been a prohibition against committing them to writing, possibly because writing would have given the traditional law a permanence which would have precluded elasticity, and detracted from the authority of the teachers. Discussions were therefore conducted without the aid of written copies, yet keen memories would cite the teachings verbatim in the name of the sages who had received the traditions from their predecessors.

It is interesting to note that in the third century of the Common Era, Rabbi Judah bar Shalom (in *Midrash Tanchuma, Ki Sissa* 34) stated: "When The Lord told Moses to 'write down' His words, Moses asked permission to record the *Mishnah* as well. But the Almighty foresaw that the nations in the future would translate the Torah into Greek and read it in Greek, and then claim that they were 'the children of Israel.' To which He would reply: Only they who know My secrets are the distinguished ones; and these 'secrets' are the *Mishnah,* to be transmitted, learned, and studied by word of mouth."

So vehement was the opposition to writing down the Oral Law, that Rabbi Jochanan bar Nappacha, in the third century, declared that "he who writes down *Halachoth* is like one committing the Torah to flames."

Despite the age-old and vociferous objections, there is talmudic and midrashic record of various scrolls in use by individual teachers or in academies as guides or curricula.

The early teachers of traditional law were called *Tannaim* (plural form of the word *Tanna,* meaning "teacher"). Of these, one of the pioneers was Rabbi Hillel, who lived at the end of the century preceding the Common Era and the beginning of the first century of this era—a little less than two thousand years ago. He was a descendant of King David through his mother. Born in Babylon, he migrated to Judea, and was one of the foremost scholars of his time, renowned alike for his erudition, practicality, humility, and patience. His followers, all recognized sages, were known as *Beth Hillel* (The House of Hillel), and they had many learned discussions and scholarly disagreements on points of law with *Beth Shammai* (The House of Shammai)—talented disciples of Rabbi Shammai, contemporary of Hillel. More than three hundred points of divergence are mentioned in the Talmud, but in practically all instances the more lenient (yet truly traditional) interpretations of *Beth Hillel* prevail.

The period of the *Tannaim* began about the year 10 B.C.E. and ended around the beginning of the third century of the Common Era.

Altogether, there were 277 of these profound thinkers and interpreters of Jewish Law, and the Talmud and *Midrashim* are replete with their sayings, as well as with anecdotes concerning their lives and personalities.

Among the more prominent were the following:

Jochanan ben Zakkai, Hillel's youngest yet most distinguished disciple who, at the destruction of the Temple by the Romans, had himself carried out of the besieged city in a coffin; when he made his way to the Roman camp, he succeeded in obtaining one favor from its commander, Vespasian—permission to dwell in the tiny village of Jabneh. There he established a school which became the center of Jewish life and learning—the nucleus of Jewish survival.

Ishmael ben Elisha, later martyred in the Hadrianic persecution, who placed the learning of Jewish Law on a scientific basis by outlining thirteen rules or principles of interpretation, and who coordinated rabbinical decisions by attaching them to the Biblical texts from which they were deduced. His commentary on the Pentateuch—of which only a fragment is in our possession, and after which many later commentaries were modeled—is known as the *Mechilta* (measure).

Akiba ben Joseph, one of the most outstanding sages in Israel's endless honor roll of piety and intellectual prowess, who is called "the father of rabbinical Judaism." Born mid-

way in the first century of the Common Era, he suffered mar-
tyrdom at the hands of the Roman torturers and executioners
in the eighth decade of his life. Of humble parentage, illiterate
until the age of forty, he attended school at the insistence of
his wife, Rachel, daughter of a wealthy Jerusalemite who dis-
inherited her when she became the wife of this ignorant peas-
ant. Assiduous and inspired study transformed the lowly Akiba
into a veritable intellectual giant—and the greatest *Tannaim*
of the middle of the second century came from his school. He
was distinguished by his excellence of character, modesty, benev-
olence, and piety. It was Akiba who definitely fixed the canon
of the Sacred Scriptures, known to non-Jews as the Old Testament, and who systematized and brought into methodic arrangement the multitude of legal dicta which had accumulated
up to his time. His was the groundwork or foundation upon
which the *Mishnah* was finally built.

Meir, one of Akiba's brilliant disciples, details of whose birth
are cloaked in legend. According to one version, he was a
descendant of the Emperor Nero who escaped death when de-
posed and subsequently became a convert to Judaism. Along
with his deep learning he had a prodigious memory. The Talmud relates that once on the Feast of *Purim* (Feast of Lots),
when he was in a small community which did not possess a
copy of the Scroll of Esther, which must be read at that time,
he wrote the entire book from memory without a mistake.
Well-versed in Greek and Latin literature, he would quote
fables, parables, and maxims in his lectures, so that he always
had an appreciative audience. He was known for his humility,
love of peace, and tolerance, and because of certain miracles
attributed to him, earned the title of *Meir Ba'al Ha'Nes* (Meir
the Miracle-Worker). Meir continued the work begun by Akiba
of arranging the Oral Law according to subjects, paving the
way for the compilers who followed him.

Simeon ben Yochai, one of Akiba's principal pupils, and also
reputed to have performed many miracles. It was he who, accompanied by Elazar ben Jose, went to Rome on a successful

mission to have abolished the decree against certain vital observances of the Jewish religion. His *Halachoth* are exceptionally numerous, encountered in all but six talmudic treatises.
Like his teacher, he was extremely systematic, but differed by
combining mysticism with his rationalistic interpretations. To
Simeon ben Yochai is attributed authorship of *The Zohar*—a
mystical commentary on the Bible and a partial basis for
cabala, Jewish mystical philosophy.

There were many prominent *Tannaim* whose words and
deeds are recorded in the Talmud and *Midrash,* including
such personalities, to mention just a few, as Akabyah ben
Mahalaleel, Rabban Gamaliel the Elder, Chanina, Simeon ben
Gamaliel, Rabban Gamaliel II, Zadok, Dosa ben Harkinas,
Eliezer ben Jacob, Eliezer ben Hyrcanus, Joshua ben Cha-
naniah, Eleazar ben Azariah, Judah ben Bathyra, Tarfon, Jochanan ben Nuri, Jose ha-Gelili; Simeon ben Nanos, Judah
ben Baba, Jochanan ben Baroka, Judah ben Ilai, Jose ben
Chalafta, Eleazar ben Shammua, Jochanan ha-Sandalar, Eleazar ben Jacob, Nechemiah, Joshua ben Karcha, Nathan ha-
Babli, Symmachus, Jose ben Judah, Eleazar ben Simeon, Simeon
ben Eleazar. Naturally it would take volumes to describe their
lives and works.

But this brings us up to Judah ha-Nasi, Judah the Prince,
born in the year 135 of the Common Era. Great-grandson of
Gamaliel I, he was given a liberal education which included
Greek and Latin, and his learning and social status gave him
a position of unquestioned authority. For more than fifty years
(until his death in the year 219 or 220) he was the "Nasi"
(Prince, or Patriarch) of his community.

It was Judah ha-Nasi (known throughout the Talmud as
"Rabbi" without need for any further designation) who committed the Oral Law to writing. While in all probability most
of the *Tannaim* who preceded him had composed written col-
lections of *Halachoth* to use as notes in preparing their lectures, there was no comprehensive anthology. Using the works
of Akiba and Meir as his model, Rabbi compiled the *Mishnah,*

to be used (as it is to this very day) not as a law book, but
as a uniform code, guide, or textbook for further study and
discussion. His purpose was to facilitate the study of the Law,
not to fix it arbitrarily. The *Mishnah* does not include many
legal opinions which were *Tannaite* traditions—and these are
known as *Baraithoth* (singular, *Baraitha*)—"external."

The language of the *Mishnah* is a terse, concise, vernacular
form of Hebrew, distinguished from biblical Hebrew by less
rigid conformity to grammatical rules, and the occurrence of
Greek and Latin words and expressions. The *Mishnah* is arranged in six "orders" (*Sedarim*), each consisting of tractates
(*Mesichtoth*) which total sixty-three. Each tractate is divided
into chapters and subdivided into paragraphs. There are 523
chapters in all (524, if the sixth chapter of *Ahvoth,* a later
addition, is included).

The six Orders of the *Mishnah* are as follows:

Zera'im (Seeds)—11 tractates, as follows: on rules and regulations on blessings; the corners of the field not to be har-
vested; doubtful cases as to fruit-offerings; forbidden mixtures;
the seventh year when the land is to lie fallow; offerings to
be given to the priests; the first tithe; the second or supple-
mentary tithe; the heave-offering; prohibitions against fruit before its tree reaches a certain age; and first-fruits.

Mo'ed (Festivals)—12 tractates: on the Sabbath; methods of
complying with certain Sabbath regulations; *Pesach*—Passover
and the paschal sacrifice; poll-tax for Temple expenses; *Yom
Kippur*—Day of Atonement; *Succoth*—Feast of Tabernacles;
feast days; *Rosh Hashanah*—New Year; fasts; *Purim*—Feast of
Lots, and the Scroll of Esther; intermediate and minor days
of holidays; and the three "pilgrimage festivals."

Nashim (Women)—7 tractates: on widows and levirate marriages; marriage contracts; vows; Nazirite vows; divorce; infidelity; betrothal.

Nezikin (Injuries, or Damages)—10 tractates: on injuries and
compensation; sales, leases, found objects, usury; real esate and
inheritance; judicial procedure and criminal law; legal pun-

ishment; oaths; testimony; idolatry; maxims and aphorisms (*Pirkei Ahvoth*—Chapters or Ethics of the Fathers); erroneous religious and legal decisions.

Kodashim (Holy Things)—11 tractates: on sacrifices; meal-offerings; slaughtering; first-born; redemption of those dedicated to the Almighty; exchange of a dedicated animal; excommunication, trespass in dedicated objects; the daily sacrifice; the Temple; the dove-offering.

Tohoroth (Purifications)—12 tractates: on uncleanness of utensils; defilement; leprosy; the red heifer and its purificative ashes; minor defilements; ritual baths; menstruation; defilement of wet items; uncleanness because of bodily discharges; uncleanness through physical contact; uncleanness and cleansing of the hands; uncleanness of fruit affecting its stems, skins, and seeds.

Quotations from the *Mishnah* show chapter in Roman numerals, section or paragraph in Arabic numerals.

There are several other works of post-mishnaic age (around the third century), which include *Ahvoth d'Rabbi Nathan,* an elaboration of the *Pirkei Ahvoth; Sopherim* (Scribes) on liturgical matters including the writing of scrolls; *Ebel Rabbathi* (The Great Mourning—known euphemistically as *Semachoth,* meaning "joys"), on burial and mourning customs; *Kallah* (Bride), on chastity; *Derech Eretz Rabbah* and *Derech Eretz Zuta* (Behavior, greater and minor, respectively), on prohibited marriages and behavior; *Perek Shalom* (Chapter on Peace); *Gerim* (Proselytes), on conversion to Judaism; *Kuthim* (Samaritans), on practices of Samaritans in relation to Jewish Law; *Avahdim* (Slaves), concerning Hebrew slaves; *Sefer Torah, Mezuzah, Tephillin,* and *Tzitzith,* on the rules for Scrolls of The Law, Sign on the Doorpost, Phylacteries, and Fringes, respectively.

Mention must also be made of the *Tosefta* (Supplement)—a systematic arrangement of laws often paralleling those of the

Mishnah, attributed to Rabbis Rabbah and Oshaya of the third century.

THE *MIDRASH* (plural, *Midrashim*) is the term for those literary works, some of them quite ancient, which contain scriptural interpretation of Haggadic, and at times Halachic, character. *Midrash* in this sense means "to search out a scriptural passage, expound it, and derive a result from this exposition."

The *Midrashim* consist of "religious truths, maxims of morality, colloquies on just retribution, inculcation of the laws which mark off national coherence, descriptions of Israel's greatness in past and future, scenes and legends from Jewish history, parallels drawn between the institutions of other nations and those of Israel, praises of the Holy Land, edifying accounts, and all kinds of consolation. These expositions were delivered in academy, synagogue, or private and public gatherings on various occasions."

Many of the *Midrashim* were composed in the days of the *Tannaim* (from about 10 B.C.E. through 220 C.E.), as the *Sifra, Sifre,* and *Mechilta* on various books of the Pentateuch. The authors of the sayings contained in these works are for the most part *Tannaim,* but the final compilers were *Amoraim.* Of the *Midrashim* composed during the period of the *Amoraim* (from about 220 C.E. through the year 500), the most prominent are *Pesikta, Midrash Rabbah, Tanchuma* (or *Yelam'deinu* as it is also known), *Shochar Tov,* Samuel, *Seder Olam, Pirkei d'Rabbi Eliezer, Sefer Ha'Yashar, Derech Eretz.* While some of these were not compiled until later periods during this era, they contain for the most part sayings of the sages of the first and second centuries.

Quotations from the *Midrashim* give the name of the *Midrash* followed by the section in Arabic numerals.

The Talmud is the commentary which accumulated around the *Mishnah.* It is an exhaustive record of the discussions of the sages on all matters and phases of Jewish Law. *Talmud* means "learning," and is a contraction of the phrase, *Talmud Torah,* "learning Torah." It is also known as *Gemarah* ("completion" and also "learning"), as it completes the *Mishnah.*

The Talmud is one of the monumental works of the world's literature. Next to the Bible itself, it is the supreme product of the Jewish mind, and throughout the centuries has exercised an influence on the life of the Jewish people not inferior to that of the Bible.

Many erroneous impressions have existed concerning the Talmud and its contents. The Dominican Friar Henricus Synensis in the Middle Ages thought it was the name of a Rabbi, and he introduced a quotation with the words, "As Rabbi Talmud relates"!

A nineteenth-century theologian ridiculed the Talmud because he thought the lengthy tractate called *Beitzah* dealt entirely with the subject of eggs. He was woefully ignorant of the elementary fact that it is a Hebrew custom to designate a book or section by its opening word. For instance, the first of the Five Books of Moses is called *B'reishith,* "in the beginning," as that is the first word of the Bible.

Others have felt that the Talmud is a "secret" book, containing information exclusively for adherents of Judaism. The truth is that nothing is hidden except from the individual who cannot read and understand the text.

For one reason and another, the Talmud was "persecuted," like the Jewish people themselves. Prohibitions against its study were proclaimed throughout history, copies were confiscated and burned, and its students tortured and martyred.

Among the many definitions of the Talmud, the description offered by the famous scholar, Emanuel Deutsch, deserves quotation:

◄§ "The Talmud is the work which embodies the civil and canonical law of the Jewish people, forming a kind of supplement to the Pentateuch—a supplement such as took one thousand years of a nation's life to produce. It is not merely a dull treatise, but it appeals to the imagination and the feelings, and to all that is noblest and purest. Betwcen the rugged boulders of the law which bestrew the path of the Talmud there grow the blue flowers of romance—parable, tale, gnome, saga; its elements are taken from the heavens and the earth, but chiefly and most lovingly from the human heart and from Scripture, for every verse and every word in this latter became, as it were, a golden nail upon which to hang its gorgeous tapestries. The Talmud taught that religion was not a thing of creed or dogma or faith merely, but of active goodness."

And as another scholar, A. S. Rappaport, declares: "The Talmud is an inexhaustible mine, embodying the purest of gold and the most precious of stone; its maxims and its ethics instil the teachings of religion and morality of the very highest order."

It is only natural and significant, therefore, that the majority of the items in this *Book of Jewish Curiosities* has been quarried from the rich lodes of talmudic literature.

While the Talmud itself is comprised of many huge volumes, printed with the original text and hundreds of commentaries—some of which are essential for an understanding of the meaning, and others of which are required for deeper insight, it would take a volume in itself merely to describe this monumental work. Sufficient for present purposes is the following excerpt from *Vallentine's Jewish Encyclopaedia:*

"The Talmud consists of the two lengthy, encyclopaedic works which have come down under the name of the Palestinian (less correctly: Jerusalem) and the Babylonian Talmud respectively. The word *Talmud* means study, studying, teaching. It forms an extensive literature reflecting the religious way of thinking and the mental activity of the Jewish scholars of Palestine and Babylonia, in the period from the third to the sixth centuries. It treats in the first place the laws and the ethics contained in the *Mishnah*. Further, it deals with everything that has in any way to do with Jewish life and the lives of the Jews, so that all kinds of subjects of a scientific, ethical, social, and folklorist nature are discussed, even if only indirectly. Although the Talmud gives the outward impression of a commentary on the *Mishnah,* and although it is one to a certain extent, in reality it is far more. The *Mishnah* for the most part forms the starting point for the detailed dissertations, of which the Talmud gives the minutes, so to say.

"Neither the date at which the Palestinian Talmud was concluded nor the name of its editor is known. Some Jewish writers assume that Rabbi Jochanan ben Nappacha was the editor, but he died in 279 C.E., whereas many scholars mentioned in the Palestinian Talmud lived later. But it was probably finished around the year 425. Of the Palestinian Talmud, there survive only 39 of the 63 *Mishnah*-treatises.

"The Babylonian Talmud has been of far greater importance for the doctrine and the life of Jewry than the Palestinian. It was provisionally concluded around 500, while the definite conclusion was in the middle of the sixth century. Two scholars, Rab and Samuel, were the organizers of the Babylonian schools, and consequently the founders of the Babylonian Talmud. They had both studied at Sepporis with Rabbi Judah ha-Nasi, but about the year 220 they returned to their native country—Rab to Sura, and Samuel to Nehardea, where their schools attracted hundreds of disciples. In these schools and in some others (Pumbeditha, Mechuza) the Babylonian Talmud came into being. In it more than 2,200 scholars—technically called *Amoraim*—are mentioned by name."

The *Amoraim* (singular: *Amora*), as distinguished from the *Tannaim,* previously mentioned, were "speakers" or "interpreters," who were the bearers of the traditional Oral Law active in Palestine and Babylonia from the time of the completion of the *Mishnah* until the redaction of the Babylonian Talmud. Those ordained at the law court of the *Nasi* (Prince, or Head) in Palestine bore the title "Rabbi," and those ordained at the Babylonian academies had the title of "Rab" or "Mar." Their principal task was to explain the traditional material contained in the *Mishnah* and *Baraithoth* and to derive from it, with the help of a dialectical system of discussion, the Halachic inferences.

As is the case with the *Tannaim,* many references occur in the Talmud to the personalities, activities, and sayings of the *Amoraim.* Prominent among them were Chiyyah and his sons, Judah and Chizkiyah, Oshaya, Bar Kappara, Bar Padda (Judah ben Pejayah), Jochanan and his disciple and comrade Simeon ben Lakish, Eleazar, Joshua ben Levi, Ammi, Assi, Chiyya bar Abba and his son Abba, Isaac Nappacha, Chanina bar Pappa, Zera, Abuha, Jeremiah, Jonah and his son Mana, Chizkiyah, Berechiah, Tanchuma bar Abba, Nisa—in Palestine. In Babylonia, mention must be made of Rabbis Chuna ha-Nasi, Shila, Abba bar Abba and his son Samuel, Levi bar Sisa, Rab (Abba Areka), Chuna, Mar Ukba, Adda bar Ahaba, Sheshet, Chisda, Rabba bar Nachman, Huna bar Chiyya, Abbaye, Raba (bar Joseph bar Chama), Rabba bar Chuna, Rabba bar Nachman, Pappa, Chuna ben Josua, Nachman ben Isaac, Mar Zutra, Ashi, Rabina, Mar bar Rab Ashi, Mar bar Rabina, Aha of Difta, Maremar (Rab Yemar), Rabina bar Chuna.

"Rab Ashi was head of the academy at Sura around the year 367. He set himself the task of collecting the voluminous material that had gathered around the *Mishnah* in the course of years. He was engaged for thirty years in this work. Next he revised the compilation, which took another thirty years. The collection of Rab Ashi in this second version is in the main the Talmud of today. The final version, however, was not established before the time of his successors, Rabbina and Jose, around the year 500.

"Some scholars of the sixth century—called *Saboraim* (singular: *Sabora*) because they 'reflected' and 'rendered decisions' on unsettled discussions of the *Amoraim*—made small additions and gave the whole work a definite form.

"Of the 63 tractates or treatises of the *Mishnah,* only 37 survive in the Babylonian Talmud. All editions have the text divided the same way, with the same page numbers, so that in quoting, reference is always made to the treatise and the page.

"Two currents are distinctly discernible in the Talmud: the *Halachah* (legal element) and the *Agada* or *Haggadah* (homiletic-didactic element). The former is the outcome of the attempt to elaborate the religious laws in connection with the *Mishnah*, the latter paying more attention to the religious and ethical aspects of life. The *Haggadah* is really popular sermonizing. Mostly it starts from a biblical text and interprets it, not according to the requirements of a logical, natural, historical exegesis, but freely, often wittily playing with the words and attaching to them all kinds of subjects of a religious, pedagogic, or moral tendency. *Halachah* and *Haggadah* occur side by side in the Talmud.

"The influence which the Talmud has exercised on the spiritual life of the Jews throughout the ages is immense. It has been their teacher not only in all matters of religion and morals, but also in the wide field of thought and science. In the worst times of persecution and humiliation it has prevented their minds from being blunted and saved them from ruin."

Chief commentary on the Talmud, without which its study today is impossible, is that of Rabbi Shelomo Yitzchaki (Solomon, son of Isaac, known as "Rashi" from the Hebrew initials of his name), who was born in Troyes, France, in 1040, and died in 1105. He is said to have founded his first Talmud school at the age of twenty-five. Dissatisfied with the inadequacy of the commentaries then in existence, he wrote one which superseded them all, but which itself has never been even rivaled. It is written in terse and lucid language which is a model of Hebrew style, is accurate and reliable, and gives the student sufficient aid to make the text clear and interesting. This indispensable commentary by Rashi is printed alongside the talmudic text in every edition.

As a document of religion, the Talmud acquired that authority which was due it as the written embodiment of the ancient tradition. Those who profess Judaism feel no doubt that the Talmud is equal to the Bible as a source of instruction and decision in problems of religion, and every effort to set forth religious teachings and duties is based on it. This does not, however, affect or lessen the authority of the Bible itself as the primal source of religious and ethical instruction and edification. The Talmud expounds, expands, and explains its teachings, and rules supreme over Jewish religious practice. It has thus served, throughout the centuries and despite the most unfavorable external conditions, to foster the spirit of deep religion and strict morality.

Perhaps the best illustration of how all of the various elements (Torah, *Mishnah,* and Talmud) discussed in the preceding pages are considered traditional to the Orthodox Jew, is expressed in the words of Rabbi Simeon ben Lakish (also known as "Resh Lakish" in the Talmud), one of the most prominent of the third-century Palestinian *Amoraim,* and brother-in-law of Rabbi Jochanan ben Nappacha, in his comment on Exodus XXIV, 12: "And I will give thee the tables of stone, and the Law, and the Commandment which I have written, to teach them." Says Resh Lakish: "The tables of stone" are the Decalogue (Ten Commandments); "and the Law"—that is the Scriptures; "and the Commandment"—that is the *Mishnah;* "which I have written" refers to the Prophets and Hagiographa; "to teach them" refers to the *Gemarah* (Talmud). Thus we are instructed that all of these were given to Moses from Sinai. (*Berachoth* 5a)

Quotations from Talmud Babli (Babylonian Talmud) show page in Arabic numerals, followed by either "a" or "b," designating the left-hand and right-hand page respectively. Quotations from Talmud Jerushalmi (Palestinian, or Jerusalem Talmud) show chapter in Roman numerals, section or paragraph in Arabic numerals. In each instance, the name of the tractate appears before the page and folio number.

As mentioned earlier, the Talmud consists of the text of the *Mishnah* and commentaries (glosses) thereon emanating from the academies where it was discussed. Neither the Baby-

lonian nor the Palestinian Talmud consists of a complete
Gemarah, the Palestinian covering 39 of the *Mishnah's* 63
tractates, and the Babylonian 37, despite which the latter is
seven to eight times the size of the former. A complete list of
the mishnaic treatises (tractates) follows, and in each instance,
the letters "P" and/or "B"—representing "Palestinian" (Talmud
Jerushalmi) and "Babylonian" (Talmud Babli) respectively—
are given in parenthesis, indicating that there is *Gemarah* to
such tractate:

FIRST ORDER—*Zera'im* (Seeds)
   Berachoth (Benedictions)—concerning prayers and benedic-
       tions ("P," "B")
   Peah (Corner)—on laws regarding the corner of the field and
       other obligations toward the poor ("P")
   Demmai (Dubious)—on produce concerning which it is doubt-
       ful if the tithe and heave-offering were given ("P")
   Killaim (Mixtures)—unlawful mingling of plants, animals,
       clothing ("P")
   Sheviith (Seventh Year)—concerning the sabbatical year ("P")
   Terumoth (Heave-Offerings)—on heave-offerings for the
       Priests ("P")
   Maaseroth (Tithes)—on tithes for the Levites ("P")
   Maaser Sheini (Second Tithe)—which, or whose equivalent
       in money, was to be utilized in Jerusalem ("P")
   Challah (Dough)—on the portion from the dough given to
       the Priests ("P")
   Orlah (Uncircumcision)—regulations concerning the first four
       years after a tree's planting ("P")
   Bikkurim (First-fruits)—brought to the Temple ("P")

SECOND ORDER—*Mo'ed* (Season)
   Shabbath (Sabbath)—on the labors prohibited on the Sabbath
       ("P," "B")
   Eirubin (Blendings, or Amalgamations)—on Sabbath bound-
       aries as to walking, carrying ("P," "B")
   Pesachim (Paschal Lambs)—on Passover regulations ("P," "B")

Shekalim (Shekels)—on the annual tax for maintenance of the Temple ("P")

Yoma (The Day)—on *Yom Kippur,* The Day of Atonement ("P," "B")

Succah (Booth)—on the Festival of *Succoth* (Tabernacles) ("P," "B")

Beitzah (Egg)—on labors permitted and prohibited on Festivals ("P," "B")

Rosh Hashanah (New Year)—on observance of this holiday ("P," "B")

Taanith (Fast)—regulations concerning public days of fasting ("P," "B")

Megillah (Scroll)—on *Purim,* Feast of Esther, Feast of Lots ("P," "B")

Mo'ed Katan (Minor Feast)—on the intermediate days (*Chol ha-Mo'ed*) of *Pesach* and *Succoth* ("P," "B")

Chagigah (Festival Offering)—on observances during the three "pilgrimage" festivals (*Pesach, Shevuoth, Succoth*) ("P," "B")

THIRD ORDER—*Nashim* (Women)

Yebamoth (Levirate Marriages)—regulations concerning marriage with a childless sister-in-law and prohibited marriages ("P," "B")

Kethuboth (Marriage Settlements)—on marriage documents and dowries ("P," "B")

Nedarim (Vows)—laws on the making and annulment of vows ("P," "B")

Nazir (Nazirite)—laws concerning this special vow ("P," "B")

Sotah (Suspected Adulteress)—regulations concerning a wife suspected of infidelity ("P," "B")

Gittin (Divorces)—on divorces and annulments of marriage ("P," "B")

Kiddushin (Sanctification)—marriage laws and betrothals ("P," "B")

Fourth Order—*Nezikin* (Damages, Torts)

Baba Kama (First Gate)—on injuries, damages, and compensation ("P," "B")

Baba Metziah (Middle Gate)—on found objects, bailments, buying and selling, leases, rentals, hiring, wages, interest, pledges ("P," "B")

Baba Bathra (Last Gate)—real estate and inheritance laws ("P," "B")

Sanhedrin (Court of Justice)—judicial procedure and criminal law ("P," "B")

Makkoth (Stripes, Lashings)—regulations on punishment for perjury; cities of refuge; lashings ("P," "B")

Shebuoth (Oaths)—laws concerning private oaths and those administered in court ("P," "B")

Eduyoth (Testimonies)—a collection of testimonies on the part of later teachers on statements of earlier authorities

Avodah Zarah (Idolatry)—on idol worship and practices ("P," "B")

Ahvoth (Fathers)—a collection of ethical maxims known as *Pirkei Ahvoth,* Chapters or Ethics of the Fathers

Horayoth (Decisions)—on decisions in religious law made in error ("P," "B")

Fifth Order—*Kodashim* (Sanctities)

Zebachim (Sacrifices)—regulations concerning the Temple sacrificial system ("B")

Menachoth (Meal-Offerings)—on the meal and drink offerings ("B")

Chullin (Things Profane, Unhallowed)—on ritual slaughter and dietary laws ("B")

Bechoroth (Firstborn)—regulations concerning the firstborn of man and animals ("B")

Arakhin (Estimations)—on amounts to be paid because of vows to the Temple ("B")

Temurah (Substitution, Changing)—on exchanges of animals dedicated as sacrifices ("B")

THE UNIVERSE

The Heavens and Their Hosts

Like philosophers of all nations and times, Jewish thinkers devoted thought and study to that fascinating trilogy:

> *Cosmogony—the creation or origin of the world or universe*
> *Cosmography—a description of the constitution or struc-
> ture of the world*
> *Cosmology—metaphysical speculation on the character of
> the world as an orderly system, with its funda-
> mental causes and processes.*

They never lost sight of the fundamental principle of Judaism:
that the Almighty is the Creator, as described in Genesis, who
created the universe out of nothing (*creatio ex nihilo*).

Inasmuch as the Bible begins with this very same subject, it
is the natural and logical starting place for this treasury of
Jewish curiosities. The biblical text is terse and concise, and
lends itself to countless explanations and interpretations. For

instance, the very first sentence reads: "In the beginning, God created the heavens and the earth."

Immediately, talmudic speculation dealt with the order of creation. Rabbi Hillel (in the first century of the Common Era) argued that the earth was created before the heavens, as (based on Amos IX, 6), "No architect, in building a house, begins with the upper story." Rabbi Shammai, contemporaneous with Hillel, replied (based on Isaiah LXVI, 1) that the heavens were created first, as "no artificer makes a footstool first, and then the throne." Their differences were reconciled by Rabbi Simeon ben Yochai (in the second century) who (referring to Isaiah XLVII, 13) declared that heaven and earth were created simultaneously, the former being placed on top of the latter like a cover upon a pot. (*Chagigah* 12a, Talmud Jerushalmi *Chagigah* II, 1, and *B'reishith Rabbah* 1 and 12).

Undoubtedly the words of King David, inscribed in the immortal Psalms (Psalm XIX) some twenty-eight centuries ago, offer the best descriptive introduction to a chapter on the Universe, the heavens, and their hosts:

> *"The heavens relate the glory of God, and the sky reveals the work of His hands . . . there is no speech, nor are there words—their voice is not heard . . . yet their voice goes forth through all the earth, and their words to the end of the world."*

(Here, incidentally, and in keeping with our theme of oddities, is a hint of the man-made "miracles" of wireless telegraphy, radio, and television.)

The following sources are quoted—with approximate dates of their origin:

APPROXIMATE DATE	SOURCE
1st-5th Century, C.E.	*Mishnah* and *Talmud* (*Rosh Hashanah, Berachoth, Avodah Zarah, Tamid, Baba Bathra, Yoma, Horayoth, Sanhedrin, Pesachim, Succah, Taanith, Eirubin*)

APPROXIMATE DATE	SOURCE
1st-3rd Centuries, C.E.	*Midrashim (Midrash Rabbah, Yalkut Shimoni*—13th century collection of ancient *Midrashim*)
2nd Century, C.E.	Wisdom of Sirach (Ben Sira)
Ancient commentary on Psalm CXXXVI	*Siddur* (Hebrew Prayer Book)
12th Century, C.E.	Maimonides (Moses ben Maimon)

&ed; When the Lord created His works in the beginning, He fixed their various divisions after He had made them. He organized His works in a system forever, and their divisions for all their generations. They do not grow hungry or tired, and they do not cease working. None of them crowds his neighbor aside, and they never disobey His command.

Wisdom of Sirach XVI, 26-28

&ed; Members of the British Association for the Advancement of Science were shown samples today of a superfluid whose qualities, described as six-dimensional, may exist naturally only in the stars.

The New York *Times,* September 7, 1954

&ed; The heavens are fluid and in it are stars composed of fire, yet neither element damages the other.

Talmud Jerushalmi, *Rosh Hashanah* II, 4

&ed; When the Almighty declared (Genesis I, 6): "Let there be a firmament in the midst of the fluid, to be a division between one type of fluid and another," He caused it to coagulate, congeal, solidify.

Talmud Jerushalmi *Berachoth* I, 2

&ed; The Almighty took two coils—one of heat [fire] and one of cold [snow]—and from these He created the world.

B'reishith Rabbah 10

The New York *Times* of September 8, 1954, telling of a meeting of the British Association for the Advancement of Science, mentions a paper presented by a group of Cambridge astro-physicists which "asserts in essence that the basic elements of the universe were not created in one colossal cosmic explosion . . . but that the elements are still being created in the voids left by the eternally outward moving stars."

∾ "Each day The Almighty with His goodness renews [revitalizes, recreates] the works of Creation."

Siddur (based on Psalm CXXXVI)

This thought, part of the daily prayers, answers the scientific dispute as to whether the universe is an expanding or contracting one, and whether its resources are exhaustible.

∾ Can the number of stars be counted? The Almighty created twelve constellations [signs of the Zodiac], and for each He created thirty armies; for each army, He created thirty legions; for each legion, thirty cohorts; for each cohort, thirty divisions; for each division, thirty corps; and in each corps He suspended 365,000 myriads of stars (a myriad is 10,000) to correspond to the days in the solar year.

Berachoth 32b

The total number of stars, therefore, would be $12 \times 30 \times 30 \times 30 \times 30 \times 30 \times 365,000 \times 10,000 = 1,064,340,000,000,000,000$.

∾ The sphere of the sun has a sheath and a vast lake of fluid before it. When it starts on its daily journey, the Almighty diminishes its strength in the fluid, so that it may not ignite the earth with its intense heat.

B'reishith Rabbah 6

∾ Three creations preceded the world itself: water, wind, fire. The water gave birth to darkness; fire gave birth to light; the wind gave birth to wisdom.

Sh'moth Rabbah 15

◄§ The world is like a globe [ball] floating on water.

>   *Bamidbar Rabbah* 13
>   Talmud Jerushalmi *Avodah Zarah* III, 1

◄§ When Alexander the Great asked the elders of the south which is a greater distance—from heaven to earth or from east to west, they replied, "From east to west." To prove this, they showed that when the sun is in the east or west, one may gaze at it, but this is not possible [without being blinded] when it is directly overhead. But the sages said that there is no difference in the distances—the reason for not being able to look at the sun directly overhead is that there is nothing in between to act as a shield or curtain.

>   *Tamid* 31, 32

◄§ The stars give off intense, consuming heat—evident only when one is near them.

>   *Baba Bathra* 73a

◄§ It takes twenty-four hours for the earth to revolve around the sun.

>   *Baba Bathra* 74a

◄§ Four hours after sunrise there is heat only where the sun's rays penetrate.

>   *B'reishith Rabbah* 34

◄§ Sultry heat, produced by the passage of the sun's rays through cloudy atmosphere, is more intense than that of direct sunlight.

>   *Yoma* 28b

◄§ There is a certain comet [star] which appears only once every seventy years [Halley's Comet].

>   *Horayoth* 10a

◄§ The planet Saturn completes its circuit in thirty years.

>   *B'reishith Rabbah* 10

The *Zohar,* a mystical work attributed to Rabbi Simeon ben Yochai of the second century, speaks of the revolution of the earth as the cause of day and night, the antipodal habitation of the globe, and the existence of an unknown world.

◆§ The Deluge was caused by the removal of two stars from one of the constellations.

Yalkut Shimoni B'reishith 56

◆§ During the twelve months of the Deluge, the functions of the planets were suspended.

B'reishith Rabbah 33

◆§ Rabban Gamaliel had a chart on the wall of his upper chamber, showing the phases of the moon.

Rosh Hashanah II, 8

◆§ Samuel stated that the paths of the heavens [the courses of the heavenly bodies] were as clear to him as the streets of Nehardea [where his academy was located].

Berachoth 58b

◆§ The sages knew that the heavenly bodies were in constant motion. A Roman emperor once asked Rabban Gamaliel why the Psalmist considered the Almighty so great because He knew the number of stars in the sky . . . "Who counts the number of stars, Who calls them all by name." (Psalm CXLVII, 4). The Rabbi asked him if he could count grains of wheat in a revolving sieve [according to other authorities, "small quinces"]. "Yes," replied Caesar, "if you let the sieve come to a stop." "True," Rabban Gamaliel answered, "but the stars revolve without stopping!"

Sanhedrin 39a

◆§ The sages of Israel declare that the Zodiac is in an established position and the planets revolve around this "wheel," whereas the wise men of the other nations contend that the wheel turns while the planets are stationary. To prove the truth of the former theory, Rabbi Judah pointed out that

Taurus is never in the south, nor Scorpio in the north. [Thus the position of the constellations does not change.] Rabbi Acha ben Jacob suggested that perhaps the wheel is situated like the socket in the lower millstone or a swinging door on its pivot.

Pesachim 94b

&⸱ The sages were not stubborn in their theories. When they expressed the opinion that during the day the sun moves underneath the sky and at night it recedes above it, and the scholars of the other nations declared that its course was just the opposite, Rabbi Judah found the latter theory more acceptable and reasonable, because during the day the springs are cold, while at night they are warm. Rabbi Nathan taught that in the summer the sun is in the zenith of the sky and that is why the entire earth is warm but the springs are cold; and in winter, the sun moves in the nether part of the sky; hence the entire earth is cold but the springs are warm.

Pesachim 94b

&⸱ The constellation of Taurus is in the north and Scorpio in the south, and the entire civilized world is situated between them. It occupies no more space than it takes the sun to travel in one hour. In the fifth hour of the day the sun is toward the east and in the seventh hour it is toward the west. For a half hour after the sixth hour and a half hour before the seventh, it is directly over every human being's head.

Pesachim 94a

&⸱ There are planets which are many times larger than the earth. The earth is about forty times larger than the moon, and the sun about one hundred and seventy times larger than the earth.

Maimonides, *Yad ha'Chazakah, Y'sodei* Torah, III

&⸱ There is no cause for superstitious fear of such celestial events as eclipses of the sun or moon.

Succah 29a

◅§ Celestial fire [electricity?] gives birth to lightning, which brightens the world with its flash of light.

Va'yikrah Rabbah 31

◅§ No human being could possibly stand the terrific noise of thunder if it reached the earth in its full, original strength.

B'reishith Rabbah 12

◅§ Rabbi Joshua ben Levi declared that thunder was created solely for the purpose of "leveling the protuberances of the heart," i.e., breaking man's pride.

Berachoth 59a

◅§ There was never a universal wind [*cosmikon*] extending throughout the world since Creation, except that mentioned in connection with Elijah (I Kings XIX, 11).

B'reishith Rabbah 24

◅§ Sometimes a globe-shaped cloudlet may be mistaken for the moon.

Rosh Hashanah 24a

◅§ The clouds are not entirely filled with water.

Berachoth 59a

◅§ The salt water of the ocean becomes sweet in the clouds.

B'reishith Rabbah 13

◅§ When the clouds are bright, they contain little water.

Taanith 10a

◅§ The moisture in clouds is constantly in motion.

Eirubin 46a

◅§ When the clouds are heavily laden with water, they receive a dark color from the waters, and afterward drop them as through a sieve.

Midrash Tehillim to Psalm XVII, 12

The Earth and Its Inhabitants

> *"How many are Thy works, O Lord! In wisdom hast Thou made them all—the earth is full of Thy creations. There is the sea, great and broad, where are reptiles innumerable, creatures small and great. . ."*
>
> Psalm CIV

When man was created, the Almighty said to him: "Subdue the earth, and have dominion" over its creatures. (Genesis I, 28). This is a keynote in Jewish scientific thinking —subjection of and dominion over the earth mean learning everything possible about all possible things.

People often ridicule what they call the "quibbling" or "hairsplitting" of Bible and Talmud. Yet on analysis it is found that these statements and discussions are an integral part of dialectics (defined by Webster as "the science or art of discriminating truth from error . . . systematic analysis of conceptions for the purpose of developing what is implied in them").

An excellent example is the biblical prohibition against eating toads, and the talmudic amplification that the touch of a toad causes ritual defilement. While frogs are equally prohibited as food, their touch is not contaminating. In 1910, Professors David I. Macht and John J. Abel (in the *Journal of Pharmacology and Experimental Therapeutics*) proved that the secretions of the skin glands of the toad contain a powerful poison— but that no such poisonous substances (epinophrin and bufagin) have been isolated or found in the skin or glands of the frog. This is further proved by the fact that if an animal bites a toad, it is poisoned and salivates at its mouth, whereas biting a frog produces no such effect. They therefore concluded that in the literal pharmacological or toxicological sense of the term, the very touch of the toad is actually contaminating and dangerous, while that of the frog is not. Hence the distinction drawn by Jewish Law between the toad and the frog is quite comprehensible.

The acquisition of knowledge and its consequent contribution to wisdom has always been a cardinal precept in Judaism, exemplified by the aphorism (*Pirkei Ahvoth* II, 6): "An ignorant person cannot be pious."

Hence Jewish thinkers have always thirstily sought for information about everything in creation, in order that they might (as expressed in the Daily Prayers) "understand and discern, mark, learn and teach, heed, do, and fulfill in love all the words of instruction in the Torah."

The curiosities in this chapter, "The Earth and Its Inhabitants," are quoted from the following sources:

APPROXIMATE DATE	SOURCE
1st-5th Century, C.E.	*Mishnah* and *Talmud* (*Horayoth, Rosh Hashanah, Sanhedrin, Shabbath, Avodah Zarah, Taanith, Yoma, Baba Bathra, Chullin, Eirubin, Menachoth, Megillah, Killaim, Berachoth*)
1st Century, C.E.	Wisdom of Solomon
1st and 2nd Centuries, C.E.	*Pirkei d'Rabbi Eliezer*
1st-3rd Centuries, C.E.	*Midrashim* (*Midrash Rabbah, Temurah, Mechilta, Avkir, Tanchuma, Pesikta*)
2nd Century, C.E.	Wisdom of Sirach (Ben Sira)
2nd and 3rd Centuries, C.E.	*Tosefta*
12th Century, C.E.	Maimonides (Moses ben Maimon)
12th-13th Centuries, C.E.	*Tosfoth*
13th Century, C.E.	*Zohar* (authorship attributed to Simeon ben Yochai of the 2nd century)

❧ It is possible for all elements to be changed in their order, and form different combinations—just as on a harp the notes vary the character of the tune, yet keep their pitch; land animals may be changed into water creatures, and swimming things changed to those of the land; fire may retain its power in water, and water forget its quenching property; it is possible for flames not to wither the flesh of perishable animals.

Wisdom of Solomon XIX, 18-21

&§ There are strange and wonderful things in the sea . . . all kinds of living things.

Wisdom of Sirach, XLIII, 25

&§ Rabbi Elazar ben Chismah and Rabbi Jochanan ben Gudgadah could calculate the number of drops of water in the ocean.

Horayoth 10a

&§ The world will last 6,000 years and lie waste for 1,000.

Rosh Hashanah 31a

&§ The creation of the elements of water, air, and fire preceded the creation of the world.

Sh'moth Rabbah 15

&§ The world is composed of one-third water, one-third desert, one-third land.

Tosfoth Pesachim 94

&§ The Almighty left the most extremely northern portion of the earth uncompleted, so that anyone claiming to be His equal might attempt to prove that contention by finishing it.

Midrash Temurah 5

&§ Adam was the final act of Creation, so that heretics might not say that he was the Lord's partner or associate in creating the world.

Sanhedrin VIII, 7

&§ The Bible calls the "gathering of the waters" (Genesis I, 10) "seas," although they are all one body of water, because their waters differ: fish from Accho taste different from those from Tyre; those from Tyre do not taste like those from Spain.

B'reishith Rabbah 8

ఆక్ All matter—animal, vegetable, and mineral—is composed of the same elements, which are intermingled and altered in each. All are subject to ultimate decomposition, but the original elements are never lost.

Maimonides, *Yad ha'Chazakah Y'sodei* Torah III, IV

ఆక్ No one ever drowned in the Dead Sea [because of its buoyancy].

Shabbath 108

ఆక్ The land at the bottom of the Red Sea is flat and hard, without any abysses.

Mechilta B'shallach 5

ఆక్ New land is formed by rivers casting out and depositing alluvial soil.

B'reishith Rabbah 13

ఆక్ Along the coast from Tyre to Accho there are bays formed by protruding rocks, and shallow waters caused by melting snows.

Avodah Zarah 34b

ఆక్ Evidence of prehistoric erosion is indicated by the name *Pi-hachiroth,* mentioned in Exodus XVI, 2, as this refers to cavernous rocks resembling human figures.

Mechilta B'shallach 1

ఆక్ For every drop of rain which falls to the earth, two drops of moisture rise from it.

Taanith 6b

ఆక్ If rain from the atmosphere above Sodom [site of the Dead Sea] falls on a garden, the seeds will not sprout.

B'reishith Rabbah 49

ఆక్ Rabbi Jochanan stated that clouds are formed from moisture in the air, while Rabbi Simeon ben Lakish declared they are formed from moisture from the earth.

B'reishith Rabbah 13

In this connection, the words of Isaiah (LV, 6) are quite pertinent, corroborating the latter theory: "For as the rain and the snow descend from the Heavens, and will not return there until the earth has been watered . . ."

◆§ Wind after rainfall is as beneficial as rain; clouds after rain are like rain; sunshine after rain is as beneficial as two successive rainfalls. Snow on the mountains is as beneficial as five rainfalls to the soil. Snow on the mountains is as good as excessive rain for the trees. A soft rain is good for budding fruits. Drizzling rain is beneficial even to seeds under a hard clod of soil.

Taanith III, IV

◆§ If the Festival of *Shevuoth* is clear and bright, it is a sign of a pleasant year. If the first day of *Rosh Hashanah* is warm it will be a warm year; if cold, the year will be a cold one.

Baba Bathra 147a

◆§ At the conclusion of the last day of *Succoth* (Eighth Day of Solemn Assembly, *Sh'mini Atzereth*) everyone gazed at the column of smoke arising from the altar. If it wafted toward the north, the poor rejoiced and the wealthy were downhearted, for it indicated that there would be plentiful rain and the fruit would rot [thus preventing speculation]; but when it wafted to the south, the poor were downhearted and the rich rejoiced, for this indicated that there would be little rain and the fruit would remain intact [for speculation]; when it wafted eastward, all rejoiced; and when westward, all were downhearted. The phenomenon of this sacred smoke was that it bent in a straight line, and did not scatter.

Yoma 21b

◆§ A human being's voice is not as audible during the day as during the night because of the revolution of the sun which cuts through the atmosphere [and causes din] like a carpenter sawing through a cedar.

Yoma 20b

∽§ There are three sounds which penetrate from one end of the earth to the other: that of the revolution of the sun; that of the tumult of Rome; the cry of the soul when it leaves the body.

Yoma 20b

∽§ To these, other sages add the cry of a woman in labor, and that of *Ridiah*. The latter is interpreted as "the angel of rain." But it is indeed curious to note that in the talmudic text, this "voice heard 'round the world" is spelled exactly the same as our English word, "radio."

Yoma 21a

∽§ There are six kinds of fire: ordinary [earthly] fire which "eats" but does not "drink" [consumes dry but not wet matter]; that which "drinks" but does not "eat" [fever]; that which "eats and drinks" [the fire invoked by Elijah the Prophet, I Kings XVIII, 38]; that which consumes moist things like dry ones [the fire on the altar]; that which repels [resists] fire [of Gabriel the Angel who delivered Chananyah, Mishael, and Azaryah from the furnace]; fire which burns fire [that of the *Shechinah*, Divine Presence, the "Finger" of The Lord which burned the fiery angels].

Yoma 21b

∽§ The fire in the burning bush seen by Moses (Exodus III, 2) was of celestial incandescence. It "sprouts branches of flame," burns within itself but does not consume, and it is "black"; earthly fire has no "branches," is red, and it consumes but does not burn of itself.

Sh'moth Rabbah 2

∽§ Adam was made of dust collected from all parts of the world.

Sanhedrin 38a

∽§ A human being makes one die and from it he stamps many coins, all exactly alike. But the Almighty has stamped every human being from one die [Adam] and none is like his fellow-man.

Sanhedrin IV, 5

&s§ Birds were created out of alluvial mud.

Chullin 27b

&s§ The skin on the feet of chickens resembles the scale-covered skin of fish.

Bamidbar Rabbah 19

&s§ The nails on the fingers and toes are the only vestiges of the nail-like skin which completely covered Adam and Eve before their expulsion from the Garden of Eden.

Pirkei d'Rabbi Eliezer 14

&s§ Man was created with a tail like an animal, but it was removed for the sake of his honor.

Eirubin 18a

&s§ Up to the time of Noah, man's fingers were all joined; thereafter they were separated.

Midrash Avkir

&s§ The faces of human beings were like those of monkeys up to the generation of Enosh.

B'reishith Rabbah 23, 9

&s§ The age-old riddle as to which came first—the chicken or the egg—is solved simply by the talmudic statement: "All the works of Creation were brought into being in full-grown stature, in complete understanding, in their designated shape and form."

Rosh Hashanah 11a

&s§ Thorns were produced by the earth while it was still in its incipiency.

B'reishith Rabbah 2

&s§ One hundred and twenty years before the Deluge, Noah planted the trees from which he later constructed the Ark.

B'reishith Rabbah 30

❧ Common leek, garlic, onion, and allium porrum are all species of the leek plant.

Tosefta Terumah IX, 3

❧ A young shoot may be grafted on either a young or old tree.

Menachoth 69b

❧ The palm tree has only one "heart" [the sap-cells are only in the stem, but not in the branches].

Megillah 14a

❧ The chrysanthemum is called *M'uyan*—a word meaning "having many eyes."

Talmud Jerushalmi *Killaim* I, 27

❧ The seeds of a pomegranate may be seen shining through its skin.

Tanchuma Va'eira 14

❧ There is a species of cedar called *sasmagur* because it is subject to decay by the inroads of a certain kind of worm named *sas*. *Magur* means "sawed by."

Yoma 9b

❧ It is only due to the limitation of our minds that we cannot grasp the purpose of many of the Lord's creations—as, for instance, why some ants are winged and others wingless.

Maimonides, Introduction to *Seder Zeraim*

❧ There is a parasitic worm called the mud-eater [*achlah* or *ochlah*] which lives in certain fish.

Baba Bathra 73b

❧ The shellfish, *chalazon*, was the source of the purple dye used in biblical times, and this species vanished from the world.

Targum Jerushalmi to Deuteronomy XXXIII, 19

❧ As the snail grows, its shell grows with it.

Pesikta B'shallach 92

  No fly lives a whole year.

Chullin 58b

  The locust is called *chasol* because it peels off and bares [*chaseil*] everything.

Talmud Jerushalmi *Taanith* III, 66

  When the proboscis of a locust breaks off, it becomes blind.

Shabbath 77b

  There is a species of locusts born without legs.

Tosefta Chullin III, 25

  The skeleton of a fish changes into [or resembles] a centipede.

Talmud Jerushalmi *Shabbath* I, 3

  The fitness of its body and its ways of life make the ant convincing testimony to the wisdom of the Creator.

Chullin 63a

  The serpent sheds its skin once in seven years.

Pirkei d'Rabbi Eliezer 20

  A serpent's venom grows weaker with old age.

Avodah Zarah 30b

  King David would sing the Almighty's praises half the night, from midnight on; and when he therefore called himself *chassid* [pious, righteous], a little frog told him that it was an even greater *chassid* than he, because it praised its Creator all night long.

Zohar IV, 222b

  The cormorant [a bird of prey] is so called [*shalach*] because it catches [draws out] fish from the sea.

Chullin 63a

  A homing pigeon always returns to its base no matter in which direction it has been sent forth.

Shir HaShirim Rabbah IV, 1

ৼ§ The dove, when flying and tired, flaps one wing and flies with the other.

B'reishith Rabbah 39

ৼ§ A bird which buries its eggs at the seashore is named the grave-digger.

Esther Rabbah III, 6

ৼ§ There is a bird called *k'rum* whose plumage changes color in the sun.

Berachoth 6b

ৼ§ The chameleon [which changes colors to blend with its background] apparently lives on air.

Sanhedrin 108b

ৼ§ A camel has canine teeth.

Chullin 59a

ৼ§ The deer sleeps with one eye open and the other closed.

Shir HaShirim Rabbah VIII, 14

ৼ§ The hedgehog was believed to suck and injure the udders of cattle.

Shabbath 54b

ৼ§ The *sh'suah* is a creature with two backs and two spinal columns.

Chullin 60b

The fabulous phoenix is called *chol* in Hebrew, and *avrashnah* in Aramaic, and is mentioned several times in the Talmud (*Sanhedrin*) and *Midrashim* (*B'reishith Rabbah, Yalkut Shimoni*).

ৼ§ The ox which Adam brought as an offering had only one horn in its forehead [unicorn?].

Avodah Zarah 8a

◆§ The *r'eim* [wild ox] was so colossal that King David once found one asleep in the desert and thought it was a mountain.
Midrash Tehillim XXXII

◆§ Rabbi Zeira once asked Rabbi Judah some questions concerning the secrets of nature. Why do she-goats lead the flock? Because that is in accordance with Creation—at first darkness, then light. Why are she-goats not provided with tails like sheep? Because those who cover us are themselves covered; those that do not cover us are not covered. Why has the camel a short tail? Because it feeds among thorns. Why has the ox a long tail? Because it grazes in plains and must protect itself against gnats. Why are the feelers of the locust flexible? Because the locust swarms in fields—were the feelers inflexible, the locust would be blinded by losing them in knocking against trees, because "all that is necessary to blind the locust is to tear its feelers." Why do the eyelids of the chicken close upward? Because it ascends at night upon elevated roosts, and if the eyelids would close downward, the least smoke coming from below would blind its eyes.
Shabbath 77b

2

DISCOVERIES AND INVENTIONS

While the following remarks could well serve as a preface to the chapter on medicine, they apply to these discoveries and inventions as well.

In the introduction to his commentary on the *Mishnah*, Moses Maimonides of the twelfth century states that all things on earth exist only for the sake of man. There are certain species of animals, for instance, which we utilize for food, and others for work and transportation—and still others whose utility for man is not yet understood or discovered. This is also true, he declares, of trees and plants.

"Wherever you find animals or plants which are unsuitable for food and are useless according to your thinking, know that this is due to the weakness of our intellect . . . it is impossible for any herb or fruit or living creature, from elephant to worm, to be void of all utility for man. The proof of this is that in every generation there are discovered by us important uses for herbs and various kinds of fruits which were unknown to our predecessors . . . through experimentation by successive generations that which is unknown becomes known."

Maimonides further points out that deadly poisons like bella-donna and the blood-flower (*Haemanthus*), which are fatal to man, serve as curative aids when applied externally; and when we consider the great benefit which we derive through such creatures as vipers and snakes, how much more beneficial must be those things which are less injurious.

Necessity is described as the mother of invention. For example, the inhabitants of Tiberias showed their ingenuity in keeping water warm (*Mishnah Shabbath* III, 4) by passing a tube of cold water through hot springs. In general use was a *miliarum*, or *antikhi* (water-heating vessels with fuel compartments), the latter retaining its heat for many hours—predecessors to today's thermos bottle!

Many surprising curiosities were discovered and invented centuries ago through man's eternal quest for knowledge and improvement. And often we discover that the words of King Solomon (*Kohelleth*, Ecclesiastes I, 9) are undeniably true: "There is absolutely nothing new under the sun!"

The following sources have been used for the material in this chapter:

APPROXIMATE DATE	SOURCE
15th Century, B.C.E.	Genesis
9th Century, B.C.E.	Psalms
8th Century, B.C.E.	Ecclesiastes
8th Century, B.C.E.	Proverbs
8th Century, B.C.E.	Kings
1st-5th Century, C.E.	*Mishnah* and *Talmud* (*Shabbath, Baba Bathra, Mikvaoth, Beitzah, Chullin, Eirubin, Baba Metziah, Mo'ed Katan, Kelim, Sanhedrin, Kiddushin, Sotah, Chagigah, Avodah Zarah, Shekalim, Taanith, Yoma, Killaim, Pesachim, Succah, Niddah, Sheviith, Berachoth, Peah, Orlah, Makkoth, Kesuboth, Maaseroth, Terumah, Ohaloth,*

APPROXIMATE DATE	SOURCE
	Gittin, Bechoroth, Baba Kama, Yebamoth, Kerisoth, Nedarim)
1st and 2nd Centuries, C.E.	*Pirkei d'Rabbi Eliezer*
1st-3rd Centuries, C.E.	*Midrashim (Midrash Rabbah, Pesikta, Tanchuma, Sifre, Yalkut Shimoni*—13th century collection of ancient *Midrashim)*
2nd and 3rd Centuries, C.E.	*Tosefta*
1st-3rd Century, C.E.	*Targum*
11th Century, C.E.	Rashi (Solomon ben Isaac)
12th Century, C.E.	Abraham ibn Ezra
12th Century, C.E.	Maimonides (Moses ben Maimon)
13th Century, C.E.	Gershon ben Solomon (*Shaar Ha' Shamayim*)
13th Century, C.E.	*Zohar* (authorship attributed to Simeon ben Yochai of the 2nd century)
14th Century, C.E.	*Sefer Ha'Brith*

MOST DISCOVERIES and inventions have taken place during the past hundred years or so. This is forecast in the *Zohar* (*Vayeirah*). In commenting on Genesis VII, 11: "In the 600th year of the life of Noah . . . the wells of the great deep were opened," the *Zohar* states: "In the 600th year of the 6,000th [the year 5600 in Hebrew—1840] will all the doors of the wells of wisdom be opened."

⋘ A hint of future discoveries of nuclear fission and fusion for atomic power is evident from the following quotation: Each drop of rain is a complete entity; for if two raindrops emanated from the same "frame," the force would be so terrific that it would muddy the entire earth and make it unfruitful. There are many thunderbolts in the clouds, and each has its individual path toward the earth; for if two went forth in one path, their force would destroy the world.

Baba Bathra 16a

With all the current modern talk about protein, carbohydrates, and other food elements essential for health, it is indeed interesting to note that Verse 16 of Psalm LXXXI is literally translatable as follows:

> *"And he would be fed with wheat from fat . . . and I would satisfy you with honey from rock."*

Here we have a direct allusion to chemical and biochemical transformations. And with regard to synthetic foods, and the concentration of a complete meal into pill or capsule form, we find the following incident concerning the Prophet Elijah (I Kings XIX, 6-8):

> *"And when he looked, behold! there was at his head a cake baked on hot stones, and a cruse of water. So he ate and drank and lay down again. But the Angel of the Lord returned a second time and touched him and said: 'Arise, eat, for the journey is too great for you.' So he arose and ate and drank . . . and went in the strength of that food forty days and forty nights to Horeb."*

וש Benjamin Franklin's experiment with the kite and key (1706) is credited with discovering electricity. Yet we find this statement in the Talmud: "If one places an iron bar among fowl to ward off bad luck, that is forbidden superstition ['the practices of the Emorites']; but if it is done because of electrical storms [to attract lightning], it is permitted."

Tosefta Shabbath VII

The calendar ordained by Moses is a lunar one, consisting of twelve months totaling 354 days, 11 less than in the solar calendar. Rabbis Samuel and Adah had a controversy concerning the length of the solar year. Adah claimed it consists of 365

days, 5 hours, 55 minutes, and 25-25/47th seconds, and that
the difference between the equinoxes is 91 days, 7 hours,
28-15/18th minutes. Samuel said this difference is 91 days and
7½ hours (a difference in their theories of 1-3/8 minutes).

The amazing thing about Adah's calculation, made some sixteen hundred years ago, is that it is almost identical with the
one made by Professor William Harkness, former astronomical
director of the U.S. Naval Observatory at Washington, who,
with modern scientific instruments, calculated the length of the
solar year as 365 days, 5 hours, 55 minutes, and 25.439 seconds.

*   *   *

The telephone was invented by Alexander Graham Bell in
1878. Yet in the year 1722, Rabbi David Oppenheim of Prague
asked his brother-in-law, Rabbi Jacob Risher, if it is permitted
on the Sabbath, according to Jewish Law, to use an instrument
capable of transmitting the human voice miles distant.

*   *   *

Dr. Halley, in 1720, invented the diving-bell, taking his idea
from Professor Scott's discovery in 1664 based on a book by
John Thessnier in 1538. Yet in the treatise, *Mikvaoth,* in the
Mishnah, we are told that a utensil immersed with its mouth
(opening) toward the water is not considered immersed properly for religious purification. And Obadiah ben Abraham Ber-
tinoro (1430–1500) comments that the reason for its invalidity
is that the air remaining in the utensil prevents the water from
entering fully.

⋖§ The bathysphere is not a modern invention, either. The
Midrashim tell how the Emperor Hadrian constructed arks of
glass into which he put some men, then lowering the arks into
the Mediterranean, so that he might learn how the seas praise
the Almighty. When the arks were raised, the men reported
that the ocean kept on murmuring, "More than the noise of

the great waters, than the mighty billows of the sea, is the Lord mighty on high." (Psalm 93).

Yalkut Shimoni 93

The invention of the bicycle is credited to Joseph Nieppes of France, in 1808. In treatise *Beitzah,* mention is made of *agalah shel katan* (vehicle for children), which the *Tosafists* describe as a sort of carriage used to teach youngsters how to walk, which stands on three wheels. The child holds on to it with his hands, and the carriage revolves forward.

*   *   *

In 1900, Count Ferdinand Zeppelin invented the airship known by his name, which was a continuation of the principle of the balloon invented by Blanchard of France in 1782. The Talmud mentions traveling a distance of 300 flights (literally, teaching 300 rules) in a tower flying through the air, and also says that Alexander the Great had such a "tower" from which he looked down at the world beneath him.

◦§ Experiments with and observation of ant life by Rabbi Simeon ben Chalafta proved the truth of King Solomon's assertion in the Book of Proverbs (VI, 6-8) that the ant "has no guide, overseer, or ruler."

Chullin 57b

◦§ The ant has three sexes—male, female, and neuter. The first two acquire wings upon reaching maturity. The neuters perform all the labor and also hatch the eggs. A single female will lay no less than eight thousand eggs.

Sefer Habrith

◦§ The ant gathers its wheat in the harvest, biting off the germs of the grains so as to prevent them from sprouting, thus preserving them from rotting. [This fact has been verified scientifically.] The ant is proportionately the strongest of all crea-

tures, able to carry from two to four times its own weight, and
can move both ways, forward and backward.

Shaar Ha' Shamayim, of Gershon ben Solomon
(13th century)

⊷§ Rabban Gamaliel had a tube through which he could look
and distinguish objects two thousand cubits away on land and
sea. Whoever wanted to find out the exact depth of a valley
looked through this tube and ascertained its exact depth. Whoever wanted to know the height of a palm tree, looked through
this tube and measured the shadow in comparison with the
shadow cast by a man, whose height is known.

Eirubin 43b

The supposedly modern method of constructing a tunnel by
digging from both ends was utilized in the digging of the Siloam
conduit at Jerusalem in biblical times, as described in the
Siloam inscription, which is the earliest lengthy inscription ever
discovered in the Holy Land. It reads in part: "And when
there were only three cubits more to cut through, the men were
heard calling from one side to the other . . . and on the day
of piercing, the workmen struck each to meet the other, pickax
against pickax; and there flowed the waters from the spring to
the pool."

⊷§ There was a "Lost & Found Department" in Jerusalem—
a place called "The Stone of Claiming." Whoever lost or found
an article went there. The finder announced what he had
found, and the claimant recovered it after proper identification.

Baba Metziah 28a

⊷§ Probably the lengthiest shipbuilding operation on record
was the construction of Noah's Ark; it took 120 years to complete.

Rashi to *B'reishith* VI, 14

⊷§ Chain-stitching [in sewing] is described as a "ladderlike"
[stairs] series of stitches.

Mo'ed Katan 26a

◄§ Sunlit spots [in a painting] appear to be sunken [deeper], while the shaded spots appear raised.

Sifra Taazriah 1

◄§ Canvas sheets [of linen] were used for painting.

Tosefta Baba Metziah I, 14

◄§ Cement that does not contain sand will not endure.

Bamidbar Rabbah 2

◄§ Honey is a good liniment for a scab on an animal's back caused by friction.

Baba Metziah 38b

◄§ A scale known as a *charistion* was used for exceedingly minute weights.

Kohelleth Rabbah I, 5

◄§ Locks and keys were made of wood or metal; a wooden lock could have metal clutches and vice versa, and likewise the teeth of a key. Sometimes a nail was fashioned to open a lock.

Kelim XII, 5; XIII, 6; XIV, 8

◄§ Stibium was used to blacken the eyelids, applied with a kohlstick whose other end was shaped for cleaning out the ears.

Kelim XII, 2

◄§ A paste-dye for nails, hair, etc., was made from the leaves of henna. Henna was also the name of a tree in Cyprus from which a chip was taken and placed in the nostrils of an ailing ewe, so that it might sneeze and thereby dislodge the worms in its head.

Shabbath 54b

◄§ Iron plates were used for paving to prevent water from seeping up; loose wickerwork was used for making beehives, screens, strainers for wine presses.

Sanhedrin 107b, 108a

◄§ Leather that is split can be so mended as to regain its original strength.

Chullin 123b

◄§ Identification beads used in hospitals on newborn infants are no novelty: "If the child is found with the beads [placed by the mother] it is not considered a foundling."

Kiddushin 73b

◄§ Certain athletes had their milt [spleen] cut out, and the flesh cut off the soles of their feet, so as to make them speedier runners.

Sanhedrin 21b

◄§ Carbonate of soda was known as *nitron* [nitrum] or *nesser*.
Talmud Jerushalmi *Shabbath* IX, 12; *Shabbath* IX, 5

◄§ White naphtha must not be used for lighting purposes, as it is explosive.

Shabbath 26a

◄§ Naphtha was used by besieging armies for the tips of arrows, and also as a propelled explosive.
Talmud Jerushalmi *Sotah* VII, 22; *Pesikta Rabbati* 17

◄§ A chalked cord was used for marking purposes.
Targum Isaiah XLIV, 13

◄§ Chalk was utilized for cleaning silverware.

Shabbath 50a

◄§ There are places where it is customary to line the inside of shoes with wool.
Talmud Jerushalmi *Killaim* IX, 32

◄§ A sun-dial was known as *Eben-ha'sha'oth*—"stone depicting the hours."

Sanhedrin 107b

◄§ A substance [*illitha*] was used for fireproofing or as a fire-extinguisher.

Sanhedrin 108b

And in Talmud Jerushalmi *Shabbath* VII, we read of *amiant* —a variety of asbestos from which linen was spun and which was cleansed by being thrown into the fire. In *Chagigah* 27a, it is said that one who anoints himself with the blood of a salamander becomes fireproof.

◈§ Hadrian distributed to his soldiers pieces of earthenware soaked in wine, to be immersed in water for drinking. [A precursor to concentrated and dehydrated foods.]

Avodah Zarah 32a

Open-toed shoes (*calceoli*) are mentioned in Talmud Jerushalmi *Beitzah* V, 63. That the sages were style-conscious is evident from the use of the word *gelima* in *Shabbath* 77b to denote a certain kind of cloak, because in it the wearer was a shapeless lump (*golem*). And in Esther *Rabbah* I, 16, we read of *kurdikan*, low and loosely-fitting slippers; in *VaYikrah Rabbah* 16, of high-soled shoes to give a taller appearance; in *Tosefta Mo'ed Katan* II, 16, of gilt slippers.

◈§ Nechuniah was a mineralogist who knew which rocks gave forth water, and in which there was dry heat [radioactivity?].

Talmud Jerushalmi *Shekalim* V, 48

◈§ Hezekiah showed his "guests" iron consuming iron—the manufacture of hardened, tempered steel.

Sanhedrin 104a

Modern packaging is no innovation. The Talmud frequently mentions vessels of glass; in the *Targum* to Jeremiah XXXII, 11 and 14, we read of wrapping and sealing in tinfoil; Targum II to Esther I, 3, speaks of a tube containing eye-paint. They did not know of vacuum-packing, but in *Kelim* X, 5 and *Tosefta Baba Kama* VII, 7, they tell of a vessel sealed by connecting the paste with the rim, leaving air-space between the cover and the vessel.

◈§ Instantaneous, simultaneous translation is no novelty. "The voice [of Revelation at Mount Sinai] went forth and was di-

vided into seventy voices corresponding to the seventy languages of the nations of the world."

Sh'moth Rabbah 5

꿀 One of the reasons for Babylonia's wealth was the utiliza-
tion of canals which made its crops independent of rainfall.

Taanith 10a

꿀 As long as the hind [deer] grows, its antlers form additional
branches every year.

Yoma 29a

꿀 Luther Burbank had his predecessor: a man grafted the
shoot of a nut tree on to a peach tree, and produced "Persian
Walnuts."

Talmud Jerushalmi *Killaim* I, 27

꿀 White flour cannot be produced without moistening the
wheat.

Pesachim 40a

꿀 The fruit best adapted for cooking is the quince.

Talmud Jerushalmi *Succah* I, 27

꿀 When breaking ground, if flint is found it is sure to be
virgin soil.

Niddah 8b

꿀 A grafting which does not take root within three days will
never do so.

Sheviith II, 6

꿀 No matter how old a cinnamon-tree is, if manuring and
hoeing are done around it, it will grow fruit.

B'reishith Rabbah 46

꿀 The flower of the caper bush is no longer in existence
when the fruit is developed.

Berachoth 36b

◆§ Plants were smeared with rancid oil to keep worms off.
Talmud Jerushalmi *Shabbath* VII, 10

◆§ Soil that has been inundated will yield more produce the following year.
Talmud Jerushalmi *Peah* VII, 20

◆§ If the stones of the ground are of clayish nature, the fruits are lean.
Bamidbar Rabbah 16

◆§ Strong rain is good for the trees.
Taanith 3b

◆§ The best eye-paint is made from garden crocus.
Baba Bathrah 16b

◆§ There is a desert shrub called *rothem* which, when lighted, burns within even after it is extinguished on the surface. Some men once lighted one of these broom shrubs, and it burned for twelve months.
B'reishith Rabbah 98

◆§ The pits of pressed olives slip out effortlessly.
Avodah Zarah 40b

◆§ Pepper and spices do not lose their pungency even when in a mass a thousand times their quantity.
Chullin 97b

◆§ But elsewhere it is said that spices have no seasoning effect in a mixture larger than two hundred times their quantity.
Talmud Jerushalmi *Orlah* I, 61

◆§ King Solomon imported pepper-plants from India.
Kohelleth Rabbah II, 5

◆§ When the fig tree is plucked at the proper time, it is good for both the tree and the figs.
Shir HaShirim Rabbah VI, 2

◄§ The almond tree takes twenty-one days from the time it blossoms to mature its fruit.

Kohelleth Rabbah XII, 7

◄§ All other trees produce leaves first, then fruit [buds]; but the apple tree produces its buds first, then its leaves.

Shir HaShirim Rabbah II, 3

◄§ In its first stage of fermentation, fresh wine bubbles for three days.

Avodah Zarah 30b

◄§ A razor destroys the hair-roots when shaving.

Makkoth 21a

◄§ The more flax is beaten, the better it grows.

B'reishith Rabbah 34

◄§ The root of crowfoot [Ranunculus] was used as a spice, but it is poisonous to beasts.

Chullin 58b

◄§ Resin smeared over the root of a bulbous plant advances its ripening by softening it.

Tosefta Shabbath I, 8

◄§ Fine, drizzling rain is beneficial even for seeds under a hard clod.

Taanith 4a

◄§ The bark of a young palm-shoot is as smooth as fine woolen garments.

Shabbath 30b

◄§ The wood of the trunk of the sycamore tree can endure in the ground for six hundred years.

Pesikta Rabbati 1

&§ The trunks of the palm and cedar trees have neither cavities [curves] nor excrescences.

B'reishith Rabbah 41

&§ Cutting mushrooms advances their growth.

Talmud Jerushalmi *Shabbath* VII, 10

&§ Thinning a field strengthens the remaining plants and they produce more fruit the following year.

Talmud Jerushalmi *Peah* VII, 20

&§ There is an interval of fifty days from the sprouting of leaves to the coming forth of buds of fruit.

Talmud Jerushalmi *Sheviith* V, 35

&§ Rain beautifies and enlarges growing fruit.

Kesuboth 10b

&§ The method of fertilization of plants is to put the male flower [pollen] over the female tree.

Pesachim 56a

&§ The lily shrinks and withers when the heat strikes it, but is rejuvenated and blossoms again with the dew.

Shir HaShirim Rabbah II, 2

&§ Plants grown on a manured part of a field mature earlier than those grown elsewhere.

Talmud Jerushalmi *Peah* III, 17

&§ If someone says there is nothing quadrangular in nature, consider mint, which has a quadrangular stem.

Talmud Jerushalmi *Maaseroth* V

&§ The first wine was that which Eve gave to Adam, pressing the juice out of the grapes, which she induced him to drink.

B'reishith Rabbah 19

&§ One of the delights reserved for scholars in the future world is wine preserved in its grapes from the six days of Creation.

Sanhedrin 99a

◦§ The cherubs above the Ark in Solomon's Temple were suspended in mid-air without support.

Yoma 21a

◦§ The show-bread at the altar was as fresh and warm when removed as when it had been placed there [a miracle the secret of which modern bakers would give much to learn].

Yoma 21a

◦§ There are three stories in the house of the ant.

D'vahrim Rabbah 5

◦§ The venom of the serpent when released into liquids does not dissolve, but remains as a netlike film on top.

Talmud Jerushalmi *Terumoth* VIII, 45

◦§ A cave can be formed by salt-corrosion.

Ohaloth III, 7

◦§ Salt may be obtained by putting sea-water in a cavity and permitting it to evaporate.

Shabbath 66b

◦§ Cooking was developed into such an art in talmudic times that one individual boasted of knowing a hundred different ways of preparing eggs.

Eichah Rabbah III, 16

◦§ The kernels of the fruit of *kurame,* a water plant, can be made edible by cooking.

Eirubin 22a

◦§ Oil derived from olives, cotton-seeds, sesame, nuts, radish seeds, fish, colocynth, as well as tar, naphtha, liquid wax, pitch, tallow, and animal fat was utilized for illuminating purposes. Some of these were prohibited for the Sabbath lamp for various reasons. Wicks made of cedar-bast, uncombed flax, floss-silk, willow-fibre, nettle-fibre, or water weeds were not permitted for the Sabbath lamp as they formed imperfect ones.

Shabbath II

◂§ Among space-saving devices was a table used for meals, which had a ring on the edge so that it might be hung up when not in use.

Baba Bathra 57b

◂§ All gums are good for ink, but that of the balsam tree is best. Resin of the plum tree is ideal for making ink. All soot is good for making ink, but that produced by burning olive oil is best.

Shabbath 23a

◂§ In northern Palestine, there was a district called Chumton, whose sandy soil contained salty substances used for wheat preservation.

Shabbath 31a

◂§ A shawl made of extra-fine linen could be compressed to the size of a nut.

Gittin 59a

◂§ The linen garments made in Bethshan were so fine and delicate that the slightest stain would ruin them.

B'reishith Rabbah 19

◂§ Not only writing paper, but also "linen" garments were made of papyrus.

B'reishith Rabbah 37

◂§ Casks were filled with the smoke of fragrant spices on the day before a Holy Day, so that they might be opened and disperse their aromatic pleasantness when desired.

Talmud Jerushalmi *Beitzah* II, 61

◂§ Adam was the first cross-breeder. He mated two different animals and their offspring was the mule.

Pesachim 54a

◂§ Olives were packed in barrels made of loosely joined splices lined with pitch.

Beitzah 33b

∾ The juice of the wild strawberry was used for adulterating honey.

Kohelleth Rabbah VI, 1

∾ An animal does not give birth prematurely.

Bechoroth 21a

The "Alfonsine Tables" are a series of astronomical data furnishing the exact hours for the rising of the planets and fixed stars. They were compiled at Toledo in 1251 or 1252. Abraham Zacuto, whose revisions of them enabled Columbus to reach the New World, declared that they were composed by Isaac ibn Sid, a *Chazzan* (Cantor) of Toledo.

∾ At the time Abel was killed by Cain, man had no knowledge of burial. Abel's body was being watched by his dog, so that no animal might touch it. Two birds flew past, and one died. The other dug a hollow place in the sand and buried it. Then Adam did likewise—the first interment.

Pirkei d'Rabbi Eliezer XXI, *Tanchuma B'reishith* 10

∾ Artificial light was known even before the Deluge: jewels and precious stones were the means of illuminating Noah's ark, giving light as bright as the midday sun.

Sanhedrin 108b

Artificial arms are mentioned in *Shabbath* VI, 8; artificial legs are spoken of in *Yebamoth* 102b.

∾ Toothpicks were made of wood or stone.

Tosefta Beitzah III, 18

∾ Soap may remove dye, but not restore the original color.

Baba Kama 101a

∾ Whistling with a finger in the mouth produces a shrill sound.

Talmud Jerushalmi *Yoma* I, 39

◆§ Cain inflicted many wounds on Abel until he succeeded in killing him, as he did not know how death would come.

Sanhedrin 37b

◆§ Cimolian earth is alkaline, and is used for cleaning clothes and in medicine.

Niddah IX, 6; *Shabbath* 89b

◆§ Jabal was the first shepherd and tent-dweller; Jubal was the inventor of musical instruments; Tubal-Cain was the first metal-worker.

Genesis IV, 20, 21, 22

◆§ Natron [carbonate of soda] uproots weakly-rooted hair.

Niddah 66b

◆§ The "balm of Gilead" [*tsori*] is actually sap dripping from resinous trees.

Kerisoth 6a

◆§ There were special cups which had a number of tubes extending therefrom, enabling several persons to drink at the same time.

Baba Kama 38b

◆§ Waxing the interior of a barrel will prevent absorption.

Baba Metziah 40a

◆§ Barley put into wine will turn it into vinegar.

Talmud Jerushalmi *Pesachim* II, 29

◆§ When Alexander of Macedon attempted to ascend to heaven, he rose higher and higher until he saw the earth like a ball below him.

Talmud Jerushalmi *Avodah Zarah* III, 42

◆§ Water was piped to and distributed in cities from reservoirs.

Tosefta Mikvaoth IV, 6

◦§ Certain dyes cannot be removed with soap.

Baba Kama 93b

◦§ The ear is to the body what the fumigating vessel is to garments. Just as many garments are put on one *cancellus* [perforated vessel] and all are fumigated, so are all 248 limbs of man made to relive by what he hears through his ear.

D'vahrim Rabbah 10

◦§ Stencils were used in cases where witnesses to a document did not know how to sign their names. The names were cut out of blank paper and placed on the document, and the witnesses filled the cut places with ink.

Talmud Jerushalmi *Gittin* II, 44

◦§ Cedar should be used for roofing, and cypress for rafters.

Shir HaShirim Rabbah I, 17

◦§ A hair-removing instrument utilized in talmudic times was undoubtedly the first safety-razor, as its name was the same as that given to a wood-planing tool.

Makkoth III, 5

◦§ A brazen mortar will not rust.

Niddah 36b

◦§ Eggs may develop chicks with no wing formations.

Talmud Jerushalmi *Beitzah* I, 60

◦§ Mankind's first fire was produced by Adam, who struck two flints against each other.

Talmud Jerushalmi *Berachoth* VIII, 12

◦§ Certain species of cucumber are made edible by baking in hot ashes.

Nedarim 51a

◦§ Another variety, which is bitter, is made sweet by rolling in ashes.

Talmud Jerushalmi *Killaim* I, 27

ᴥᶫ The woolly leaves of mullein were used for lamp wicks.

Shabbath 20b

ᴥᶫ Dill is used for seasoning foods.

Uktzin III, 4

ᴥᶫ The well was the progenitor of the refrigerator; vessels containing food or drink were kept there for cooling.

Shabbath XXII, 4

ᴥᶫ Some poisons float, others sink.

Talmud Jerushalmi *Shabbath* I, 3

ᴥᶫ The scorpion casts sixty young at a time.

VaYikrah Rabbah 13

ᴥᶫ Dipping a live coal into a mustard mixture will season the mixture sweetly.

Tosefta Beitzah III, 15

ᴥᶫ A depilatory made of the sap of the plant *nashah* was so powerful that no hair grew again where it was smeared.

Baba Kama 86a

ᴥᶫ One method of capturing deer involved plaited nets; horse-hair was utilized for snaring birds.

Baba Metziah 85b; *Shabbath* 90b

ᴥᶫ Rope was woven out of the bast of coconut-palm.

Eirubin 58a

ᴥᶫ Faded writing on a document could be made legible by the application of a violet-colored liquid made from the bark of the pomegranate tree.

Gittin 19b

ᴥᶫ *Yaranah* is an alkaline plant which was used as soap.

Tosefta Sheviith V, 6

ᴥᶫ Baskets were fumigated with sulphur, and sulphur was also used for bleaching wool.

Berachoth 27b, *Baba Kama* 93b

Silverplated copper is mentioned in *Pesikta Eichah* 122.

◄§ Drinking straws, made out of hollow reeds, were utilized for sucking juice.

Yoma 82a

◄§ Solomon's throne was operated by machinery.

VaYikrah Rabbah 20

Magnifying and diminishing mirrors are mentioned in *B'reishith Rabbah* 4, and in *Kelim* XIV, 6, a mirror made by polishing part of a metal cover.

*   *   *

The compass, or a similar instrument for surveying, is mentioned in *Sifre* to Deuteronomy VII, *Yalkut* Deuteronomy 801, and *Targum Jerushalmi* to Deuteronomy I, 8.

◄§ Relay stations, like the famous "Pony Express," were known in ancient times. "He increased for them the speed [of the mail bearers] and the number of mail stations."

Yalkut Shimoni 16

◄§ The Two Tablets were of sapphire [diamond?] yet were like a light object in the hands of Moses. Another miraculous feature was that they could be rolled up.

Tanchuma Ki Thissah 26; *Shir HaShirim Rabbah* V, 14

◄§ The Talmud speaks of a "revolving door."

Baba Kama 112a

Lightweight substitutes for metal were known in talmudic times. In *Sanhedrin* 110a and *Pesachim* 119a, we are told of locks and keys made of leather; and in the *Targum* to I Samuel XVII, 5, of armor made of the skin of fish.

◄§ A powder-room [for toilette] was known as "the room of mirrors."

Talmud Jerushalmi *Berachoth* VIII, 13

✒ Diocletian had an artificial bay made, and it was called the Lake of Emesa [Hums], a city of Syria on the banks of the Orontes.

Talmud Jerushalmi *Killaim* IX, 32

✒ Some people had the faculty of knowing whether certain soil was suitable for agricultural purposes by its taste.

Shabbath 85a

✒ The mucilaginous juice of mallows was used for the preservation of gourd seed.

Killaim I, 8

✒ The streets of Jerusalem were swept daily.

Pesachim 7a

Silk culture was introduced in Spain by Baruch, ancestor of the Albalia family, who had been transported from the land of Israel to Spain by Titus in the year 70–71, at the request of the local proconsul.

*   *   *

Ancient Babylon was rediscovered in 1854 by Jules Oppert, who also unraveled the mysteries of the long-forgotten Sumerian languages, thus making possible the translation of many records.

*   *   *

Eldad ben Machli Ha-Dani was a Jewish traveler and scholar of the ninth century, who claimed to be a descendant of the Tribe of Dan and to have been born in one of the Red Sea lands. In the account of his travels, he describes the life and laws of the Ten Lost Tribes of Israel, reporting that Asher, Gad, and Naphthali lived in the southern and western region of Ethiopia; adjacent to them lived the Sons of Moses; Issachar lived in Central Asia; Reuben and Zebulun on Mount Paran; Ephraim and half of the Tribe of Menasseh dwelt on the hills around Mecca; and Simeon and the other part of Menasseh lived in the Kingdom of the Chazars, in the Crimea. His cita-

tion of their laws and customs, which he claims originated with
Joshua, shows a number of variations from those of rabbinical
tradition.

*   *   *

Another great traveler, Benjamin of Tudela of the twelfth
century, visited most of the then-known world—Europe, Asia,
and North Africa—covering some three hundred cities. He describes the various Jewish settlements he encountered and their
religious, political, and social life, his book representing one
of the most important commercial geographies of the Middle
Ages as well as a deep insight into Jewish cultural history.

*   *   *

The first Jewish account of the discovery of America was
written by Abraham ben Mordecai Farissol, in his *Iggeret
Orchoth Olam,* composed toward the end of the fifteenth century. He was a scribe, geographer, and polemist, and had met
Columbus at the court of the Duke Ercole d'Este at Ferrara.

*   *   *

The first white man to set foot on Western soil was Louis de
Torres, a Marrano, who had accompanied Columbus on his
voyage of discovery. He introduced tobacco to Europe, and
the bird we now know as the turkey was called *tukki* by him,
as he mistook it for a peacock (mentioned by that name in
I Kings X, 22).

*   *   *

According to Rabbi Abraham ibn Ezra, Arabic numerals
were first brought from India by an ancient Jewish traveler.

*   *   *

"Jacob's Staff," an instrument used by all mariners during
the Middle Ages for ascertaining their position at sea, was invented by Levi ben Gershom in the thirteenth century. He
also invented the camera obscura, a device for throwing an
image on a screen which is the basis of the modern camera.

3

PEOPLE

This chapter contains a miscellany of little-known facts concerning people throughout history, for the most part Jewish, though some of the material deals with non-Jews in some aspect of relevance to Judaism.

Interesting items are revealed in talmudic and midrashic literature concerning the lives of the sages. It is indeed worthy of note to mention that these men, whose intellectual contributions have been preserved in the Talmud and *Midrash,* combined physical work with scholarship. To cite a few examples, Akiba was a shepherd, Joshua a charcoal-burner, Meir a scribe, Jose ben Chalafta a leather-worker, Jochanan a sandal-maker, Judah a baker, Abba Saul a grave-digger, Shesheth a logger, Joseph a miller, Abba Joseph worked for a builder, Chiyya bar Abin a carpenter, Abba ben Abba a silk-dealer, Yitzchak Nafcha a smith.

Also we can trace how temperament and outlook on life caused divergence of opinion and influenced the thoughts and words of the sages. For example, while Rabbi Eliezer (*Mishnah Shabbath* VI, 4) commented that such weapons as a sword, bow, shield, club, and spear are man's "adornments," his colleagues emphatically declared that they are definitely "a reproach," citing as their authority the words of Isaiah (II, 4): "And they shall beat their swords into plowshares and their spears into pruning-hooks; nation shall not lift up sword against nation, neither shall they learn war any more."

The sources of the curiosities about people in this chapter (aside from the later historical ones) are as follows:

APPROXIMATE DATE	SOURCE
15th Century, B.C.E.	Genesis
8th Century, B.C.E.	Kings
1st-5th Century, C.E.	Mishnah and Talmud (Shabbath, Succah, Yoma, Chullin, Baba Bathra, Sanhedrin, Sotah, Taanith, Derech Eretz, Niddah, Berachoth, Eirubin, Avodah Zarah, Megillah)
2nd and 3rd Centuries, C.E.	Tosefta
1st-3rd Century, C.E.	Midrashim (Midrash Rabbah, Tanchuma, Pesikta, Yalkut Shimoni— 13th century collection of ancient Midrashim)
2nd Century, C.E.	Ahvoth d'Rab Nathan
1st-3rd Centuries, C.E.	Targum

⊷§ Rabban Simeon ben Gamaliel was a talented acrobat; he could juggle eight flaming torches simultaneously. He also performed something which it was said no man could do. He would press his toes against the floor, bend forward and touch his lips to the ground and then regain an upright position without the use of his hands. Levi tried to perform the same thing in the presence of Rabbi Judah, and became lame, but he was able to juggle eight knives simultaneously. Rabban

Simeon juggled eight glasses filled with wine, without spilling a drop, and Abaye, eight eggs, but according to some onlookers, only four.

Succah 53a

◄§ Ben Kamtzar could write the four-letter Holy Name with one stroke, by holding four quill pens between his fingers.

Yoma 38b

◄§ Rabbi Jonah ben Tachlifah was so adept and accurate with darts that he could slaughter a bird in flight in full compliance with the laws of *Shechitah* [ritual slaughter].

Chullin 30b

◄§ Four individuals said things for which others, had they uttered them, would have been mocked: Moses, Nebuchadnezzar, Jethro, and Solomon.

Tanchuma Yithro 7

◄§ Mimics were included among actors who performed in public.

Eichah Rabbah III, 13

◄§ Both professionals and amateurs would compete in the Roman arenas.

Sh'moth Rabbah 30

◄§ The Prophet Amos was so called because he was a stammerer [*Amos* means "hard-pressed in speech"].

VaYikrah Rabbah 10

◄§ The name of Abraham's grandmother was *Carn'vo* ["lamb of Nebo"].

Baba Bathra 91a

◄§ Ishmael's wife's name was Adishah [*Khadija* in the Koran].
Targum Jerushalmi B'reishith XXI, 21

◄§ Serach, daughter of Asher, was the only one of the original seventy emigrants to Goshen who survived until the Exodus.

B'reishith Rabbah 94

◆§ Balaam introduced rooms for licentiousness, dice, gladiatorial games, and divinations.

Tanchuma Noach 20

◆§ Abraham was the first man mentioned in the Bible for old age, for a wayfarer's inn, and for disposing of property during his lifetime.

Tanchuma Noach 14

◆§ The generation submerged by the Deluge is not subject to resurrection, as they were scalded to death and their destruction was final and complete.

VaYikrah Rabbah 7

◆§ Because Methusaleh was so pious, the Deluge did not submerge the world during his life; and when he passed away, it did not start until seven days thereafter, as this was the period of mourning.

Ahvoth d'Rabbi Nathan 32

◆§ When the earth engulfed Korach, it became like a funnel. All of his possessions—even linen at the launderer's and needles borrowed by others a distance away—rolled into this chasm and were swallowed up.

Talmud Jerushalmi *Sanhedrin* X, 1

◆§When King Solomon built the Temple, he planted all sorts of precious delicacies of gold which bore fruit and which fell when ripe and shaken by the wind.

Yoma 21b

◆§ Certain conjurers were proficient in the art of ventriloquism.

Tosefta Sanhedrin X, 6

◆§ Five individuals were gifted with certain physical perfections which Adam had possessed, but because they abused this privilege, each was afflicted in these attributes. Samson had superhuman strength, but it was taken from him; Saul towered above his fellow-men, but perished by falling on his sword; Absalom's beautiful hair was the means whereby he was caught in the branches of an oak; Zedekiah's eyes were put out by his captors; Asa suffered from gout, because he forced even those biblically exempt from service to march to war.

Sotah 10a

৺ Asahel, son of Zeruiah, King David's sister, was so fleet that he could overtake deer; and when he ran over a field of ripening corn, the ears of grain did not even bend but remained as erect as if untouched.

Kohelleth Rabbah IX, 11

৺ The incidents in the Book of Daniel are not in chronological order, to indicate that they were told by divine inspiration, and are not merely historical annals.

B'reishith Rabbah 85

৺ Gesticulating with the hands while talking was looked upon with disfavor and disdain.

Derech Eretz II

৺ Og, King of Bashan, was a tremendous giant, the only one spared by the Deluge because, according to legend, he sat astride Noah's Ark. Abba Saul [and according to some sages, Rabbi Jochanan] related that he once chased a roe for three parasangs [Persian miles], but could not overtake it, as it had entered the thighbone of a man and ran too fast, nor could he reach the end of the bone. When he returned, he was informed that it was a bone of Og's.

Niddah 24b

৺ The only passengers on Noah's Ark who were guilty of incontinence were Ham [Noah's son], the dog, and the raven.

Talmud Jerushalmi *Taanith* I, 64

৺ King Solomon used 24 expressions for "prayer."

I Kings VIII, 23-53 (*Berachoth* 29a)

✑§ Ben Yehozedek prided himself on his gymnastic ability [leaping performances].

Talmud Jerushalmi Succah V, 55

✑§ Great distances were traversed by miraculous flight or leaps.

Eirubin 43a

✑§ For three persons the earth shrank [they were transferred from one place to a distant point suddenly]: Eliezer, Abraham's servant; Jacob the Patriarch; Abishai ben Zeruiah.

Sanhedrin 95a

✑§ One boaster claimed he could run for three parasangs in front of horses.

Sanhedrin 96a

✑§ Samson's eyes were put out because he succumbed to the temptation seen by them.

Sotah I, 8

✑§ The Amazons live behind the Dark Mountains [Mountes Amazonici].

Sh'moth Rabbah XVIII, 14

✑§ At their banquets, the Persians had a huge goblet called *puska* which each guest must drain.

Yalkut Esther 1048

✑§ King Saul's leniency towards Agag, King of the Amalekites, in disregard of the command to "blot out the memory of Amalek," made it possible for Agag to have a descendant, Haman, who in later generations tried to exterminate the Jewish people. It was only through another descendant of Kish [Saul's father], Mordecai, that the plot was foiled.

Pesikta Rabbah 13

✑§ Rabbi Ishmael, in order to illustrate a point of Jewish Law, related an incident about Cleopatra, Queen of Egypt, and her handmaidens.

Niddah 30b

🔊 On Sigillaria, the Image Feast, the last day of the Roman Saturnalia, little images were given and received as presents.

Talmud Jerushalmi Avodah Zarah I, 40

🔊 The way the Romans worshipped Mercury [and the Greeks, Hermes] was to cast stones at a waymark consisting of two stones with a third across them.

Sanhedrin VII, 6; *Avodah Zarah* IV, 1

🔊 Worship of the idol Baal-Peor by the Canaanite heathens included a rite of uncovering one's nakedness.

Talmud Jerushalmi Avodah Zarah III, 42; *Sanhedrin* VII, 6

🔊 Adrammelech, the chief idol of the *Sepharva'im,* to whom its followers sacrificed their children by fire, was in the shape of either a mule or a horse, as they worshipped the same animal which carried their burdens. *Adar* means "to carry," and *melech* means "king." Another opinion was that this idol was in the shape of a peacock, as *adar* also means "magnificent."

Sanhedrin 63b; *Talmud Jerushalmi Avodah Zarah* III, 42

Sacrificial mice were raised by the Edomites, as discovered by the Palestine Exploration Fund, reported in its *Quarterly Statement* of 1893. In Genesis XXXVI, we are told of the descendants of Esau who ruled in the land of Edom, and a hint of this rodent-worship is evident from verses 38 and 39, mentioning *Baal-Chanan ben Achbor* (Baal being one of the chief pagan gods, and *achbor* a mouse). *Baal-Chanan,* incidentally, is identical in meaning with *Hannibal—*"Baal is favorable."

🔊 While most of the sages criticized the Romans for their theaters and circuses, one remarked that one redeeming feature was that people amused themselves there, thus avoiding the opportunity to talk with each other and come to vain quarrels. [Apparently he never saw rabid rooters in action!]

B'reishith Rabbah 67, 80

🔊 The Roman legions carried scalps with them, which they considered charms against their enemies.

Chullin 123a

ا⋛ The Romans do not allow the son of a king to succeed his father on the throne.

Avodah Zarah 10a

ا⋛ Ahasuerus started his own dynasty [was an upstart].

Megillah 11a

ا⋛ Nebuchadnezzar was called "the Babylonian dwarf."

Yalkut Daniel 1062

ا⋛ Shimshai, a scribe at the court of Ahasuerus, and supposedly a son of Haman, erased the royal record telling of Mordecai's deed which saved the king's life, but the Angel Gabriel rewrote it.

Megillah 16a

ا⋛ Sennacherib covered a ten days' march in one day.

Sanhedrin 95a

ا⋛ Herod put a garland made out of hedgehog skins on the head of Baba ben Buta, and it pricked out his eyes.

Baba Bathra 3b

ا⋛ It is said in the Talmud that Job never existed, but was merely an allegory or parable, but this has been explained to mean that he was born to serve as an example. There are diverse opinions as to when he lived: in the time of Moses; in the days of the Babylonian exile; in the days of the Judges; in the days of Mordecai and Esther; in the time of King David; in the days of King Solomon; in the time of the Chaldeans; in the days of Jacob and his sons; in the days of Abraham—and some of the sages claimed that he was a non-Jew, and was one of Pharaoh's advisers during the days of the Israelite bondage.

Baba Bathra 14, 15, 16; *B'reishith Rabbah*

Pope Anacletus II (Pietro Pierleoni)—1130-1138—was called "the Jewish Pope" by Voltaire and others because of his Jewish ancestry.

*   *   *

The use of tobacco was introduced into Europe by Louis de Torres, a Jewish member of Columbus' crew on the voyage to America in 1492. Having settled in Cuba, he became acquainted with tobacco and exported it to Spain, whence its use became widespread throughout Europe and the rest of the world.

*   *   *

Girush Spania (the exile from Spain) started on August 2, 1492 (the day before Columbus sailed) when 300,000 Jews left that land to find new homes. By queer coincidence this was the anniversary of the destruction of both the First and Second Temples—the 9th of Ab.

*   *   *

According to historical legend, Queen Isabella of Spain pawned her jewels to raise funds for Columbus' expedition. Actually Louis de Santangel, a Jew who was quite influential at the Court of Spain and who had been saved from the flames of the Inquisition by King Ferdinand, advanced a loan of 17,000 florins (close to 5,000,000 maravedis) to finance the project. The account books showing the transfer of this sum from Santangel to Columbus are preserved in the *Archive de India* at Seville, Spain.

*   *   *

Information given by Gaspar da Gama of the fifteenth century was one of the factors leading to Amerigo Vespucci's discovery of Brazil. This famous Jewish mariner of Portugal was also a friend of Vasco da Gama (no relative), Pedro Alvarez Cabral, and the Jews of Cochin, and his name is mentioned by many fifteenth-century chroniclers.

*   *   *

As an example of the melting-pot that is America, Leonard Lyons reports in his column of December 6th, 1954, in the New York *Post* that "the American-Irish Historical Society in New York is giving a dinner next Monday in honor of Rabbi

Theodore Lewis of Newport's Touro Synagogue. Rabbi Lewis, a native of Dublin, delivers speeches in Gaelic."

As further evidence of the diversity of American-Jewish origins, the first Jews to settle in Newport (1656) came from Curaçao, followed by fifteen Dutch families two years later, emigrants from other islands of the West Indies in 1694; and settlers from Portugal, Germany, and Poland in the years preceding the Revolutionary War. Isaac Touro, of Portuguese descent, came to Newport from Jamaica in 1760 to serve as the rabbi of the synagogue, now known as the Touro Synagogue because its maintenance was assured by bequests made by the Rev. Touro's sons, Abraham and Judah. In 1947, the National Park Service of the U.S. Department of the Interior designated this synagogue as a national historic shrine. Its cemetery, purchased in 1677, has been immortalized in verse by Henry Wadsworth Longfellow and Emma Lazarus.

It was after George Washington's visit to this synagogue in 1790 that he wrote his famous statement on religious freedom: "The citizens of the United States of America have a right to applaud themselves for having given to mankind examples of an enlarged and liberal policy; a policy worthy of imitation. All possess alike liberty of conscience and immunities of citizenship. It is now no more that toleration is spoken of, as if it was by the indulgence of one class of people, that another enjoyed the exercise of their inherent natural rights. For happily the Government of the United States, which gives to bigotry no sanction, to persecution no assistance, requires only that they who live under its protection should demean themselves as good citizens, in giving it on all occasions, their effectual support."

*   *   *

Abolition of the barbarous practice of corporal punishment in the United States Navy was brought about by the efforts of Uriah Phillips Levy (1792–1862), cabin-boy who rose to the rank of commodore despite many difficulties and six courts-martial (in which he was vindicated).

*   *   *

One of Abraham Lincoln's staunch and influential supporters in his 1860 campaign was Abraham Kohn, city clerk of Chicago. After Lincoln's election, Kohn presented to him an American flag with a Hebrew quotation on it—the words of encouragement uttered by Moses to Joshua: "Be strong and of good courage; be not afraid nor dismayed; for the Lord thy God is with thee wherever thou goest."

*   *   *

In 1849, during the Gold Rush days, more than one hundred congregants held *Yom Kippur* (Day of Atonement) services in a tent-synagogue in San Francisco, improvised by Hyam Joseph, and led by Joel Noah, brother of Mordecai Manuel Noah.

*   *   *

Mordecai Manuel Noah, incidentally, was an American journalist, lawyer, editor, playwright, and politician, who served as U.S. Consul to Tunis, and was the most distinguished American Jew of his time. In 1825, because of the reactionary policy of many European governments leading to considerable Jewish emigration, he planned the establishment of an autonomous Jewish settlement at Grand Island, in the Niagara River, near Buffalo, N.Y. He appropriately named it Ararat, because that was where the original (biblical) Noah and his ark of refuge had landed.

Impressive ceremonies were held on September 2, 1825, in an Episcopal church at Buffalo, attended by state and federal officials, Christian clergymen, and many American Indians whom Noah identified with the Ten Lost Tribes of Israel. As "Judge and Governor," he announced the restoration of the Jewish State at Grand Island as a preliminary to the revival of a Jewish state in Palestine, for which he had also made grandiose plans.

He also ordered a Jewish census throughout the world, and the levy of an annual poll-tax of three silver shekels; ordained various religious reforms; provided for elections of a "Judge of Israel" every four years with deputies in each country; commanded the Jews of the world to cooperate; appointed a number of distinguished European Jews as commissioners; directed Jewish soldiers in European armies to remain there until further orders were issued; permitted those Jews who wished to remain in their adopted lands to stay there.

His schemes, however, met with ridicule and ultimate failure. The proposed city was never built. The only memento of the entire plan, aside from some letters and newspaper accounts, is the foundation stone of the contemplated city of Ararat, which is on display at the Buffalo Historical Society.

*   *   *

Elijah of Wilna (known as "The Wilna Gaon"), 1720–1797, was a Lithuanian Talmudist, who had mastered the entire range of rabbinical literature, as well as a skilled mathematician and a student of other sciences. He is mentioned in Ripley's *Believe It Or Not* as having had a photographic mind.

*   *   *

On February 8, 1807, Napoleon convened the Paris *Sanhedrin* consisting of 71 members, two-thirds of whom were rabbis, and whose aim was to reconcile political views and decisions with Jewish religious law.

*   *   *

Jehuda Cresques, son of Abraham Cresques of Palma, and a renowned Jewish scholar and philosopher, was known as "the Map Jew" in the early part of the fifteenth century. He was appointed director of a navigation school by Prince Henry of Portugal, and a map prepared by him for King Juan the First of Aragon, which was presented to the King of France, is among the archives of the National Library of Paris.

*   *   *

Joseph Faquin, a Jew of Barcelona, had the reputation of having navigated the entire world in 1334. His knowledge of trade routes was attested to by Jaime the Third, King of Mallorca.

*   *   *

Among the famous edicts of Rabbi Gershom ben Judah ("Rabbenu Gershom, Light of the Exile"), who lived in Mayence in the latter part of the tenth and the early part of the eleventh centuries, were the prohibition of polygamy among Jews living in European lands, necessity for a husband to obtain his wife's consent before securing a divorce, prohibition against opening correspondence not addressed to the recipient.

*   *   *

A seventeenth-century Sephardic rabbi in Holland, Jacob Judah de Leon, was nicknamed "Templo" because of the exact and intricate blueprints and plans he drew of the Tabernacle and the Temple, accompanied by learned monographs on both subjects, which were translated into several languages.

*   *   *

The Falashas, a tribe of black Jews living in Ethiopia, claim descent from the tribe of Levi. They celebrate the major Jewish holidays, but do not know of *Purim* (Feast of Lots) and *Chanukah* (Feast of Dedication, or Lights), both of which are post-biblical. They apparently settled in the land at an extremely early period, since they mourn the destruction of the First Temple but have no knowledge of that of the Second.

*   *   *

The royal house of Ethiopia claims descent from King Solomon who, according to their tradition, had a son, Menelik, by the Queen of Sheba. The same legend also relates that King Solomon sent warriors from all of the tribes of Israel and priests under the leadership of Ebiatar, to live in her land.

*   *   *

Psalm XCII, "A Song for the Sabbath Day," is attributed by some authorities to Moses. The initial letters of its opening words in Hebrew, incidentally, form the words, "To [by] Moses."

*   *   *

Johann Andreas Eisenmenger, a German anti-Jewish writer and agitator, devoted nineteen years of his life to the study of rabbinical literature, collecting all passages which he thought could be utilized for attacking Judaism. In 1700 he published his *Entdecktes Judenthum (Judaism Unmasked)* which, despite its scholarly appearance, became the mainstay of anti-Semitism, and which is replete with distortions, half-quotations, and statements taken out of context.

*   *   *

The victory over Israel of King Mesha of Moab, as mentioned in II Kings, III, was recorded on a stone stele discovered in the year 1868 by a German missionary at Diban, capital of the Moabite kingdom. Although the stele was destroyed by the local Arabs, a paper-squeeze had been taken, and from this a cast was made and some of its wording deciphered. The fragments of the original stele are preserved in the Louvre in Paris.

*   *   *

Michelangelo Buonnarroti, Renaissance artist whose marble statues of Moses and David are among the world's greatest treasures in sculpture, executed the frescoes on the ceiling of the Sistine Chapel in Rome, a rectangle about 120′ long by 39′ wide. In the corners are portrayed "David Slaying Goliath," "Judith and Holofernes," "The Brazen Serpent," and "The Death of Haman." The prophets Jeremiah, Ezekiel, Joel, Zachariah, Isaiah, Daniel, and Jonah, and biblical personalities are depicted near the ceiling, which consists of biblical scenes such as "The Fall of Man," "Cain and Abel," "The Deluge," and "The Drunkenness of Noah." According to most authorities, the concept, despite its biblical nature, is pagan, being neither Jewish nor Christian.

*   *   *

Although Charlemagne (742–814) imposed many prohibitions on the Jewish inhabitants of the Holy Roman Empire, he gave them the right to own farmland, and protected Jewish merchants in their business transactions.

*   *   *

There was a Chinese Jewish mandarin named Chao Yng-Cheng, who was appointed in 1652 to restore the city of Kai-Fung-Foo, which had been destroyed. He induced the Jewish population to return and rebuild its temple. A stele was erected to record his achievements.

*   *   *

Antonío Jose da Silva, an eighteenth-century Portuguese Marrano playwright, was burned at the stake by the Inquisition for practicing Judaism in secret. The same night, one of his comedies was played at the principal theatre in the same city, Lisbon.

*   *   *

Michel de Nostradamus (1503–1566) was a French doctor of the Jewish faith. After devoting many years to combating the severe plagues which were the scourge of France and Europe, he turned to astrology and wrote a series of prophecies in cryptic verse which thousands of people still believe foretell world events for generations to come. Because many of his predictions were fulfilled during his lifetime, King Charles IX appointed him his personal physician.

*   *   *

The Durrani and Jusufsani of Afghanistan claimed to be descendants of the Ten Lost Tribes of Israel, and their progenitor, Afghana, was supposed to have been a son or grandson of King Saul or a contemporary of King Solomon. In Kabul, there are ruins of a synagogue which it is claimed was built in the time of Nebuchadnezzar.

*   *   *

Rabbi David Jaffe of Dorhiczyn is reputed to have created a *golem* (living automaton or robot) for doing such work on the Sabbath as is prohibited by religious law.

*   *   *

There have been a number of false Messiahs, claiming to be either the Messiah himself (son of David) or his forerunner, son of Joseph. Among them were Theudas of the first century of the current era; Menachem ben Judah of Galilee shortly thereafter; Bar Cochba of the second century; Moses of Crete in the fifth century; Isaac ben Jacob Abu Isa in the seventh century; David Alroy in the twelfth; Moses Botarel, Jacob Carcassoni, and Asher Laemmlein in the fourteenth century; David Reubeni and Solomon Malcho in the sixteenth, and also Isaac ben Solomon Ashkenazi Luria and his disciple Chaim Vital; Shabbethai Zevi in the seventeenth century, followed by Jacob Querido and the latter's son, Berechiah, and his contemporaries Miguel or Abraham Cardoso, Mordecai Mochiach, Loebele Prossnitz, and Isaiah Chasid; Jacob Frank in the eighteenth century; and Joseph Abdallah the Yemenite in the nineteenth. Some of these individuals, notably David Reubeni, Solomon Molcho, and Isaac Luria, never personally claimed "Messiahship," the title being imposed upon them by their followers.

*   *   *

4

PLACES

It is only natural that most of the places mentioned and described in talmudic and midrashic literature are in *Eretz Israel,* the land of Israel.

For Israel has always been considered the Holy Land, and as such it occupied the forefront of discussion and activity. In fact, the sages declared (*Kedoshim* 10, *Midrash Tanchuma*) that the Land of Israel is in the center of the world; Jerusalem is the center of the Land of Israel; the Temple is the center of Jerusalem; the Holy of Holies is the center of the Temple, whose center is the Holy Ark in front of which is the Foundation Stone of the world. And in *Derech Eretz Zuta* IX, this world is compared to the human eye. The white is the ocean girding the earth; the iris is the earth upon which we dwell; the pupil is Jerusalem, and the image therein is the Temple. A Latin psaltery of the thirteenth century contains a map of the world, as does a Latin book of the sixteenth century on Sacred Scripture, and both show as the center of the world Jerusalem in the land of Israel.

To Israel was given, it is mentioned in *Kiddushin* 49, ninetenths of the wisdom meted out to the world; and in *Baba*

Bathra 158 it is stated that "the very air of the land of Israel induces wisdom."

Yet many other geographical designations are encountered in ancient Hebrew literature. For instance we learn (*Mishnah Shabbath* VI, 6) that the women of Arabia (long before the days of Mohammed—seventh century) went veiled; and those of Media looped their cloaks over their shoulders, a habit apparently native to that land.

We also come across the fact that the Jews of Valencia in the year 1262 were granted various privileges by King James I of Aragon, one permitting Jews who had been imprisoned for non-payment of taxes to be released from jail at sundown on Fridays for their full freedom on the Sabbath, conditional upon their giving formal assurance that they would return for detention after the Sabbath.

"All over the world" is often given a nationalistic tinge. For example, when Macauley used the expression, "as every schoolboy knows," he naturally meant every British schoolboy, but his term would imply the inclusion of schoolboys all over the world. Just so, when various biblical writers wanted a phrase to imply something taking place universally, they used the words, "From Dan to Beersheba" (Judges, Samuel, Chronicles), as Dan was the most northern and Beersheba the most southern city in the Holy Land.

The quotations which are in this chapter have been taken from the following sources:

APPROXIMATE DATE	SOURCE
1st-5th Centuries, C.E.	*Mishnah* and *Talmud* (*Taanith, Shabbath, Gittin, Rosh Hashanah, Avodah Zarah, Middoth, Succah, Makkoth, Eirubin*)
2nd and 3rd Centuries, C.E.	*Tosefta*
1st-3rd Centuries, C.E.	*Midrashim* (*Midrash Rabbah, Mechilta, Tanchuma*)

THE *Sambatyon* (also called *Sambation* or *Sabbation*) is a legendary river which is one of nature's proofs of the divine origin of the Sabbath. It was placed variously in Media, India, Ethiopia, or near the Caspian Sea. According to one school of thought, it runs rapidly during the six days of the week with a torrent of stones and sand, but is completely inactive on the Sabbath. Others claim it contains no water, but only rocks which move turbulently all week, except on the Sabbath, when it resembles a placid lake of sand. One of its peculiarities is that even its sand, when placed in a glass, is agitated on weekdays but quiet on the Sabbath. The Sambatyon is purported to surround the yet undiscovered region where the Ten Lost Tribes of Israel and the Sons of Moses dwell.

When the Emperor Hadrian mocked the truth of the biblical phrase describing the Holy Land as one "wherein thou shalt not lack anything" (Deuteronomy VIII, 9), and asked Rabbi Joshua ben Chananyah to bring him pepper, pheasants, and silk originating there, the sage was not dismayed. He brought the Emperor pepper from Nizchamah, pheasants from Sidon [or Akbeir], and silk from Giscala.

Kohelleth Rabbah

When the mother of Remus and Romulus died, a she-wolf suckled them; and they built two large huts, founding the city of Rome.

Midrash Tehillim X, XVII

In the chief synagogue of Alexandria, the *Zeradel*, there are many ancient treasures, including a Bible written by hand. Each column or page is surrounded with elaborate ornamentation consisting of the entire *Masorah* (critical notes on the external form of the biblical text), both the "Great" and the "Small," written in such microscopic letters that they are legible only through a magnifying glass.

The only part of the Holy Temple in Jerusalem which still stands today is the Western Wall [known as the "Wailing

Wall"]. This corroborates the talmudic prophecy: "The Western Wall shall never be in ruins."

Bamidbar Rabbah XI, 2

❦ Every prophet whose home is not mentioned is from Jerusalem.

Bamidbar Rabbah 10

❦ The Holy Land was not submerged during the Deluge.

B'reishith Rabbah 33

❦ In the town of Tur Simon, 300 *garabs* [measures] of wafers were distributed to the needy every Sabbath eve.

Talmud Jerushalmi *Taanith* IV, 69

❦ Wells which supplied only enough water for seventy date palms furnished drinking water for the 600,000 Israelites who encamped around them, and for a second and a third time as well.

Mechilta B'shallach 1

❦ Land may be made arable by burning off the reed-thicket covering it.

Talmud Jerushalmi *Shabbath* VII, 10

❦ Towns were often named after the characteristics or habits of their inhabitants. For example, *K'far Shichlayim* was so-called because the people's support came from traffic in cress [*shichlayim*], or because they reared their children as carefully as cress is cultivated, or because they reared their children on cress-dishes.

Gittin 57a; Talmud Jerushalmi *Taanith* IV, 69;
Eichah Rabbah II, 2

❦ The city of Sebaste was built by Herod on the site of old Samaria.

Bamidbar Rabbah 10

The Romans built a city on the site of Jerusalem, which they had destroyed, and called it *Aelia Capitolina,* formed from the

name of the Emperor Aelius Hadrianus and Jupiter Capitolinus.

✌§ All kinds of statuary existed in Jerusalem except sculptures
of human faces.

                              Talmud Jerushalmi *Avodah Zarah* III, 42

✌§ During the time the pilgrims were in Jerusalem for the
three Festivals, no troubles took place in their homes.

                                        Shir HaShirim Rabbah VII, 2

✌§ A picture of the Castle of Shushan was sculptured on the
eastern gate of the Temple Mount.

                                                   Middoth I, 3

✌§ When the cymbal was struck in the Temple in Jerusalem,
its sound was audible in Jericho.

                                    Talmud Jerushalmi *Succah* V, 55

✌§ The din of the city of Rome was so great it was once heard
in Puteoli, 170 miles away.

                                                  Makkoth 24a

✌§ Rome seized the Eastern Empire twice—once in the days
of Queen Cleopatra, and once in the days of the Greeks.

                                                Avodah Zarah 8b

✌§ Rabbi Mattnah claimed that he had slept on the flower
[capital] of one of the columns of the palace of Ahasuerus
[Esther I, 6], and there was room there for a body at full length
with outstretched hands and legs.

                                              Esther Rabbah I, 6

✌§ The city of Neapolis was built on the site of the ancient
town of Shechem mentioned in Genesis.

                              Talmud Jerushalmi *Avodah Zarah* V, 44

✌§ Twin cities were also known in talmudic times. The Jordan
River ran between the twin-towns of N'mire-Hashulami.

                                         Tosefta Bechoroth VII, 3

The Valley of Hinnom, outside of Jerusalem, is the site, according to legend, of Gehenna (*Ge-Hinnom*) because of the perpetual fires which burned there. (It was also, in pre-Jewish times, the furnace of Moloch, where human sacrifices were cast into the fire.) According to Rabbi David Kimchi, twelfth-century scholar, the perpetual fires which burned there in the days of the Jewish Commonwealth were used to consume the city's refuse for health purposes, thus making it the first municipal incinerator or garbage-disposal plant.

⊷ The pasture ground of each Levitic township was one-fourth of its area.

Eirubin 56b

⊷ The serpents in the Desert of Kub were so enormous that one once swallowed a carriage of King Shabur.

Tanchuma B'shallach 18

It is a custom among Jews not to pass under the Arch of Titus in Rome. On its southern side there is a relief of the Jordan and the sacrificial procession. Within the Arch, the right wall shows Titus on his chariot of victory, and the left depicts the Jewish captives in the triumphal procession carrying the Temple utensils, the Shew-bread table, the *Menorah* (candelabrum), and the *Shofroth* (trumpets).

*   *   *

There is an ancient ossuary near the ravine of Hinnom, on the southern extremity of Jerusalem, which is called Aceldama ("field of blood"), because of the rich red clay deposits it originally contained, used by potters for their products.

*   *   *

A venerable and famous tree, "Abraham's Oak," grows at Mamre, west of Hebron. It is surrounded by a wall over which it projects. It was opposite this oak, according to tradition, that Abraham pitched his tent before the three angels visited him.

In 1852, lightning struck a large branch, and eight camel-loads of wood were removed. In former years, a terebinth grew to the north of Abraham's Oak, which the historian Josephus claimed had existed since the beginning of the world. In Hadrian's time, it was under this tree that the great sales of Jewish slaves took place, numbering over 135,000.

*   *   *

The first settlement of Jews in China took place in the first century of the current era, and these people were known to the Chinese as "the pluckers-out of the sinew," because of their adherence to the Jewish law based on the biblical story in Genesis XXXII, 33, when the Angel with whom Jacob wrestled struck him on the leg and caused a sinew to shrink. This sinew (the sciatic nerve) has to be removed from slaughtered cattle before the meat may be eaten.

5

ANALOGIES

This chapter presents a diversity of selected comments, for many of which analogies are evident in other fields of literature, including mythology. For example, the familiar saying, "Familiarity breeds contempt" is expressed by Moses Maimonides of the twelfth century in his *Guide for the Perplexed* (III, 47): "When we continually see an object, however sublime it may be, our regard for it will be lessened, and the impression we have received of it will be weakened." Shakespeare's famous line, "A rose by any other name would smell as sweet," had its predecessor in the early centuries of the Common Era: "A myrtle even in the desert remains a myrtle."

"Empty barrels make the most noise" appears in the Talmud (*Baba Bathra* 85) as, "A small coin in a large jar makes a loud sound." *Shabbath* 31 states the converse of the Golden Rule: "What is hateful to thee, do not do to thy fellow-man." "Where there's a will, there's a way" has its talmudic equivalent: "Nothing can withstand the will to do." "Every man for himself" expresses the mishnaic thought, "If I am not for myself, who will be?" The *Mishnah* says, "Look not at the flask but at what it contains," which is identical in meaning with "Don't judge a book by its cover."

"Speech is silver, silence is golden" has its counterpart in the talmudic expressions, "Silence is a fence to wisdom" and "If speech is worth one coin, silence is worth two." "Grasp all, lose all" has its equivalent in "If you have grasped too much, you have grasped nothing." "Heaven helps those who help themselves" is expressed as "When man learns a trade, the Almighty will give him sustenance [provide him with a livelihood]."

The talmudic statement, "Whoever is bigger [or stronger] than his fellows, swallows them," clearly expresses the theory of "survival of the fittest." The moral of the fable about the tortoise and the hare, wherein the plodding turtle persevered over the fleet but flighty rabbit, is expressed in Ecclesiastes X, 11 by King Solomon: "The race is not to the swift."

The following sources are quoted:

APPROXIMATE DATE	SOURCE
1st-5th Centuries, C.E.	*Mishnah* and *Talmud* (*Pirkei Ahvoth, Sanhedrin, Berachoth, Shabbath, Menachoth, Chullin, Baba Kama, Pesachim, Yebamoth, Baba Bathra, Taanith, Killaim, Kiddushin, Avodah Zarah, Shebuoth, Nazir*)
1st-3rd Centuries, C.E.	*Midrashim* (*Midrash Rabbah, Mechilta, Sifre, Yalkut Shimoni*— 13th century collection of ancient *Midrashim*)
1st-3rd Century, C.E.	*Targum*
1st Century, C.E.	Josephus
1st-2nd Century, C.E.	Tacitus

◄§ The saying of Archimedes: "If I had a fulcrum, I could move the world," is paralleled by the statement of Abner, captain of King Saul's army: "If I could only catch hold of the earth, I would be able to shake it."

Yalkut Jeremiah 285

⚬§ The poem, "For want of a nail, the kingdom was lost," has its counterpart in talmudic dissertation: Had Jonathan provided David with but two loaves of bread, the priests of Nob would not have been slain, Doeg the Edomite would not have been lost, and Saul and his three sons would not have been killed.

Sanhedrin 104a

⚬§ When we see orators or other public speakers with a pitcher of water and a glass at hand, we are reminded of the rabbinical saying: "He who talks gets thirsty."

B'reishith Rabbah 98

⚬§ While there's life, there's hope.

Talmud Jerushalmi *Berachoth* IX, 13

⚬§ The traditional Saturday night bath might have originated from the statement: Warm water after the departure of the Sabbath is soothing.

Shabbath 119b

⚬§ The expression, "Carrying coals to Newcastle," has its talmudical forerunner: "Would you carry straw to Afarayim?"

Menachoth 85a

⚬§ The inhabitants of Narash (Narse) in Babylonia were such notorious thieves that there was a saying, "If a Narashean kissed thee, count thy teeth!"

Chullin 127a

⚬§ The proverb, "A burned child dreads the fire," has its equivalent in "Whom a snake has once bitten, a rope will frighten!"

Kohelleth Rabbah VII, 1

◄§ The rule of *"Caveat Emptor!"* ["Let the buyer beware!"], is stated thus: It is the buyer's fault if he was satisfied to purchase a pouch sealed with knots.

Baba Kama 9a

◄§ Two equivalents of the modern saying, "The bigger they are, the harder they fall," are: "According to the size of the ax is the feast"; and "As you call Rome great, so will its punishment be great."

Targum Mishlei VII, 22

◄§ The proverb about retribution, "Hoist by his own petard," has its talmudic predecessor: "The arrow-maker killed by his own arrow."

Pesachim 28a

◄§ Throughout literature concerning seamen, we find that the captain's ambition is to have a farm in his old age. This tradition may well be based on Ezekiel's statement (XXVII, 29): "And all that handle the oar, the mariners, and all the pilots of the sea will come down from their ships and stand upon the land." In explanation of this, Rabbi Elazar said: "In the future, all skilled workers will become farmers." In addition, he deduced that farming is the poorest of occupations, because the biblical text reads, "will come down." And once when he noticed a field being ploughed widthwise, he remarked, "Even if you would plough it again lengthwise, trading in business would yield you more profit!"

Yebamoth 63a

Oscar Wilde's epigram, "We live in the age of the overworked and the uneducated; the age in which people are so industrious that they become absolutely stupid," is expressed in five terse words in *Pirkei Ahvoth* II, 6 (translation): "Not all of those who devote themselves excessively to business grow wise."

⋙ The proverb, "A bird in hand is worth two in the bush," is expressed in midrashic language as, "Better one bird tied than a hundred flying."

Kohelleth Rabbah IV, 6

⋙ When the early American pioneers exclaimed that "the only good Indian is a dead one," they were re-echoing the comment made about the Egyptians who pursued their erstwhile slaves: "The best of the Egyptians, kill; the best among the serpents, crush its brains."

Mechilta B'shallach

⋙ The adage that "birds of a feather flock together" is indicated by the experience of Rabbi Chiyyah bar Abba. A flock of starlings had migrated to the land of Israel, and the rabbi was asked if this species was edible, i.e., if this bird came within the category of permissible fowl. Rabbi Chiyyah told his questioners to see with what birds the starlings associated. When it was discovered that they followed the Egyptian raven, the Rabbi declared they were forbidden, because they belonged to the same species as the raven, which is unclean.

B'reishith Rabbah 65

The histories of Abraham and Job are interwoven in many Jewish legends. In one of them, it is told that Abraham was miraculously nourished by milk and honey in the cave in which he had been concealed. The name of Abraham's mother is said in the Talmud (*Baba Bathra* 91a) to have been Amiltai, daughter of Karnebo, and some etymologists claim that this is a corrupt reproduction of Amaltai-Keren-Happuch, the name of one of Job's daughters. According to Greek mythology, Zeus was nursed by a goat whose horn overflowed with nature's riches. This incidentally, is the origin of the cornucopia as a symbol of the "horn of plenty." And in Hebrew, *keren-happuch* means "inverted horn."

*   *   *

One of the non-Jews immortalized in Jewish legend is Aristotle, the renowned Greek philosopher, whose writings were claimed to be derived from Jewish teachings.

◆§ The Talmud has its "Rip Van Winkle." While traveling one day, Choni Ha'm'agel noticed a man planting a carob-tree. When he asked the planter how long it would take for the tree to bear fruit, the man answered, "Seventy years." Choni laughed, exclaiming that the man could not be certain he would live long enough to enjoy its fruit. But the planter replied that he had found carob-treees in existence when he came into the world, and since his ancestors had provided them for him, he was planting one for his descendants. Choni became tired, and fell asleep alongside of the newly planted tree. A grotto formed around him, in which he slept for seventy years, unnoticed. When he awoke, he observed a man gathering fruit from the carob-tree. He asked the man who had planted it, and the answer came, "My grandfather." Other tales are related concerning Choni's subsequent adventures . . . no one would believe he was actually Choni . . . he was a man whom life had left behind.

Taanith 23a

The "apple of Sodom" or "Dead Sea Apple," mentioned by Josephus in *The Jewish War* and by Tacitus in his *History,* is described as a fruit growing near Sodom, beautiful in appearance, but turning to ashes and smoke when plucked.

*   *   *

The proverb, "Sufficient unto the day is the evil thereof," is mentioned in two different variations, practically in the same language, in *Berachoth* 9b and *Yebamoth* 61b.

*   *   *

◆§ The solution of the riddle of the Gordian Knot, which had to be cut and not unravelled, is given in the statement: "A permanent knot requires cutting through."

Talmud Jerushalmi *Killaim* VI, 30

The Hebrew name of Esther, heroine of the Book of Esther ("*Megillath Esther*"), is *Hadassah*, meaning "myrtle." "Esther" comes from either the name of the Babylonian goddess, Ishtar, or the Persian word for "star," *stara*. In the Talmud, incidentally, the star thus referred to is Venus.

*   *   *

Issachar, ninth son of Jacob, is pronounced *Yisachar* in Hebrew, and not *Yisas'char*, as written. One reason advanced is that he had a child named "Jove" (*Yov*), as mentioned in Genesis XLVI, 13. In later generations, this was the name of the father of the Roman gods, Jove, or Jupiter. The second "s" was therefore taken from Issachar's name and given to his son, making it "Yashuv" (I Chronicles VII, 1), so as to avoid confusion with a heathen god.

*   *   *

Literary sleuths attribute about forty-five stories (one-ninth of the total) in *The Arabian Nights* (*One Thousand-and-One Nights*) recited by Queen Scheherazade in order to avert execution, to Wahb ibn Munabbuh, a Jewish convert to Islam who edited the Cairene edition in the seventh or eighth century. Others, primarily because in the Persian tradition Scheherazade was the mother-in-law of Ahasuerus, claim that the framework story of the collection is identical with the Book of Esther, as Ahasuerus beguiled his nights by having tales told to him.

⋘ The riddle of the Cretan Labyrinth [where the Minotaur was imprisoned] has its solution in midrashic literature: There was a great palace in which everyone would get lost as in a maze, until a clever man came along with a coil of rope. He tied one end to the entrance, unwound the rope as he walked through, and was able to retrace his steps by rewinding it.

B'reishith Rabbah 12

⋘ Centaurs [legendary creatures, half-man, half-horse] were the result of mankind's degeneration in the days of Enosh.

B'reishith Rabbah 23

◆§ The legend of the Hydra, monster of the Lernean marshes slain by Hercules, has its parallel in talmudic literature, which speaks of a serpent with seven heads.

Kiddushin 29b

◆§ The modern custom of choosing by placing fist over fist on a baseball bat was originally a pagan practice used as a method of divination.

Sifre D'vahrim 17

◆§ Shades of the Borgias! The *Midrash* speaks of a ring containing poison, which caused death when sucked.

D'vahrim Rabbah 2

The *"Chad Gadyah,"* the poem sung at the conclusion of the *Seder* service on the first two nights of Passover, is constructed along the lines of the famous children's verse, "The House That Jack Built." Although ascribed by some scholars to the Middle Ages, its origin is traceable back to talmudic times, and it affords a bird's-eye view of Jewish history from Mount Sinai through various persecutions and conquests, with the ultimate promise of redemption from all oppression.

*   *   *

The word "alchemy" is probably derived from the Greek *chymeia* ("mingling"), or "chymos" ("juice"), because chemistry was originally the art of extracting medicinal juices from plants. However, there is another theory that the word is derived from *Cham* (Ham), son of Noah and ancestor of the Egyptians, who, according to medieval alchemists, was one of the first skilled members of the profession. They also claim that Adam and Tubal-Cain were the fathers of their art, and that it was transmitted to later generations by Me-Zahab and Mehetabel (Genesis XXXVI, 39), the three Patriarchs, Moses, Aaron, David, and Solomon.

*   *   *

A pagan ritual similar to the Aztec rite of offering to an idol the heart cut from a living body is mentioned in *Avodah Zarah* II, 3.

*   *   *

Amraphel, King of Shinar (Genesis XIV, 1), is identical with Nimrod according to talmudic authorities; and with Hammurabi, the Babylonian king and lawgiver, by modern biblical scholars and Assyriologists.

⋅⋅§ The word for *Gesundheit!* after sneezing is *Zat,* an abbreviation of the two words meaning, "May your sneezing be for good!"

Talmud Jerushalmi *Berachoth* VI, 10

⋅⋅§ The exclamation, "Amen!"—meaning "true" or "So may it be!" implies an oath, a promise, and a prayer for fulfillment.

Shebuoth 36a

The fairy tale of Jack and the beanstalk and the giant's daughter has its prototype in an ancient midrashic account of the daughter of Anak (there are various giants or titans mentioned in the Bible: Anakim, Rephaim, Nefilim, Gibborim, Zamzummim, and Emim):

> *"The daughter of Anak had gone into her father's garden and taken a pomegranate, which she ate after having peeled off the skin and cast it aside. Then the twelve spies came, and seeing her father, were struck with fear and hid themselves under the pomegranate-skin, thinking it a cave. In the meantime, Anak's daughter returned, and seeing the skin lying there, was afraid her father would scold her for lack of neatness. She therefore picked it up with the twelve spies still hidden there, and cast it out of the garden, noticing the weight added by the men no more than if the skin had been an eggshell."*

*   *   *

La Fontaine's fable of the ant and the wasp (seventeenth century) is almost identical with that of Berechia ha'Nakdan in his *Mishlei Shu'alim* (twelfth century).

* * *

Five-sided buildings, actually called "pentagons," are mentioned in *Nazir* 8b, *Baba Bathra* 164b, and elsewhere in the Talmud.

* * *

My father, of blessed memory, a learned scholar of Baltimore, was of the opinion that *Me-Zehab*, mentioned in Genesis XXXVI, 39, was the King Midas of Greek mythology. *Me-Zehab* means "waters (or fluid) of gold," and according to the Greek legend, everything Midas touched turned to gold. Medieval alchemists, as recorded in a previous item, claimed "Me-Zehab" as one of the early proponents of their art.

EDUCATION

"The world is sustained by the breath from the mouths of school children." (*Shabbath* 119b) One of the prophetic ideals of the future is expressed by Isaiah (XI, 9), hoping for the time when "the entire earth shall be full of the knowledge of the Lord as the waters cover the sea."

One of the main objectives in Jewish life has always been moral and religious training, which naturally includes a well-rounded education.

In biblical times instruction was given to the people at large in public; assemblies were held at specific intervals for teaching and learning the Law. The original instructors were the priests and Levites, and in later years members of the tribe of Issachar and descendants of Jethro the Kenite were distinguished as pedagogues. In the royal palace tutors were employed, whereas in ordinary homes in the days of the kingdom, professional teachers continued instruction after the primary education given by the parents.

The *Beth Ha'Midrash* (house of learning, or schoolhouse) is first mentioned by Ben Sira (Wisdom of Sirach, LI, 23) in the second century of the Common Era. In *Baba Bathra* 21a, mention is made of state-employed teachers in Jerusalem who took care of youngsters from the provinces who lacked the advantage of home instruction.

There were various types of schools in talmudic times, ranging from the primary or elementary school (*Beth Ha'Sefer*) to the *Beth Ha'Midrash* (high school) and to the talmudic academies of advanced learning. In this connection, it is interesting to cite a statement (in *B'reishith Rabbah* 63) to the effect that "Esau and Jacob went together to the *Beth Ha'Sefer* until they finished their thirteenth year, when they parted; the former entering the houses of idols, and the latter the *Beth Ha'Midrash*."

While it was recognized that teachers must have a means of livelihood, it was also stressed that instruction should not be denied because of lack of funds on the scholar's part: "As I have taught you without pay, says the Lord, so must you do likewise." (*Nedarim* 36a) And the teacher must not rely on his memory or ingenuity. "Instruct thy son with the assistance of a good text," states *Pesachim* 112a. As for the student, "The advantage of reviewing is unlimited; to review 101 times is better than to review 100 times." (*Chagigah* IX, 6)

In *Pesikta d'Rab Kahana Eichah* 15 (1st to 3rd century, C.E.) the destruction of schools by Vespasian is bemoaned: "There were 480 synagogues in Jerusalem, each having its own elementary and its own advanced school of learning, all destroyed by Vespasian."

One final point is worthy of inclusion in this introduction. The habit of swaying back and forth while learning is attributed by some authorities to the lack of sufficient textbooks—forcing the pupil to lean forward to read from the text, and then to lean back when finished to permit his neighbor to read.

The quotations used in this chapter are from the following sources:

Approximate Date	Source
1st-5th Centuries, C.E.	*Mishnah* and *Talmud* (*Ahvoth, Kiddushin, Baba Bathra, Chullin,*

APPROXIMATE DATE

◈§ An ignorant person cannot be pious; one who is bashful cannot learn [he is afraid or ashamed to ask questions]; he who is irritable and impatient cannot teach.

Pirkei Ahvoth II, 6

◈§ A father is required to have his son taught to swim.

Kiddushin 30b

◈§ One should not train his son to be a muleteer, camel-driver, barber, sailor, herdsman, or tavern-keeper.

Kiddushin IV, 14

◈§ One who does not teach his child an occupation is as if he is instructing him in burglary.

Kiddushin 30b

◈§ Intensive education should begin at the age of six.

Baba Bathra 21a

◈§ Joshua ben Gamla established a public school system, instituting primary schools in all the provinces and small towns to be attended by children starting at the age of six or seven.

Baba Bathra 21a

◈§ Opinions varied as to educational practices. One authority declared that if in a school there were two teachers—one well-

versed but inexact, and the other exact but not well-versed—
the former should be retained, as the errors would correct themselves. Another authority, however, maintained that the one
who is exact should be retained, as an error impressed on a
child's mind is not eradicated.

Baba Bathra 21a

◄§ Short-cuts in teaching are advantageous.

Chullin 63b

◄§ Instruction is best when the teacher has a good text to
which to refer.

Pesachim 112a

◄§ The advantage of reviewing is unlimited—to review 101
times is better than to review 100 times.

Chagigah IX, 6

◄§ School sessions should be curtailed during the summer,
because of the heat.

Bamidbar Rabbah 12

◄§ A primary school teacher should not have a class of more
than twenty-five pupils.

Baba Bathra 21a

◄§ Idleness leads to dullness or idiocy.

Kesuboth V, 5

◄§ One should not differentiate among children.

Shabbath 10b

◄§ One who studies by himself does not learn as much as one
who studies under a teacher.

Kesuboth 111a

◄§ If one studies too many subjects simultaneously, his learning will decrease.

Eirubin 54b

◄§ One should study a subject carefully and not rely on one's ingenuity.

Eirubin 90a

◄§ The sages believed that audible study was the only kind which would endure in the student's mind, that uttering the words of the lesson cause them to be remembered. Samuel said to Rabbi Judah that a scholar should open his mouth when he reads and studies so that the lessons would endure. And Rabbi Eliezer ben Jacob had a disciple who studied in silence, but who forgot after three years all that he had learned.

Eirubin 54a

◄§ Rabbi Meier used to divide his teaching time into three parts: he would devote one-third of the lesson to legal subjects, one-third to homiletic preaching, and one-third to parables.

Sanhedrin 38b

◄§ One who combines verses from various books of the Bible for homiletical purposes is termed "a stringer of pearls."

Shir HaShirim Rabbah I, 10

◄§ If there is a fitting or appropriate word in your own language, do not resort to a foreign phrase.

Sanhedrin 14a

◄§ The blessings and curses mentioned in the Book of Deuteronomy were transcribed [translated] into the seventy languages of the world on the stones by Moses.

Tosefta Sotah VIII, 6

◄§ The entire Torah was inscribed on stone in the seventy languages in the days of Joshua.

Sotah 36a

◄§ Members of the *Sanhedrin* were required to know all languages, because they were not permitted to hear evidence through interpreters.

Makkoth I, 9

◄§ He who understands the science of cycles and planets and does not practice it, is considered a sinner.

Shabbath 75a

◄§ Learning while young is like ink written on clean paper; learning when old is like ink written on used [or blotted] paper. Learning from the young is like eating unripe grapes or drinking wine from the vat; learning from the old is like eating ripe grapes or drinking old wine.

Pirkei Ahvoth IV, 25, 26

◄§ Technical laws like those concerning the sacrifices of birds and the purification of women who are unclean are ordinances of moment [essential, even though superficially they may seem minor]; astronomy and mathematics [geometry] are the after-courses [desserts, or "on the periphery"] of wisdom.

Pirkei Ahvoth III, 23

◄§ Students may be compared in types to four objects: (1) A sponge, which soaks up everything; (2) a funnel, which takes in at one end and lets out at the other; (3) a strainer, which forfeits the wine and retains the dregs; (4) a sieve, which gives up the bran and retains the fine flour.

Pirkei Ahvoth V, 18

◄§ A successful teacher must know his subject thoroughly; he must conduct his life along the lines of the principles he wishes to impart; he must not demand remuneration for his teaching; he must treat his pupils as though they were his own children; he must train them to live an ethical life; he must not lose patience, and he must have a happy demeanor; he must teach his pupils in accordance with their intellectual abilities. A recommended curriculum consists of the following, in this order: the Torah, *Mishnah,* grammar, poetry, Talmud, religious philosophy, logic, arithmetic, geometry, optics, astronomy, music, mechanics, medicine, metaphysics.

As far as students are concerned, they are to keep their bodies and souls pure; they are not to be ashamed to ask for instruc-

tion in matters of which they are ignorant; they are not to
think of future gain from study or that their study has an
ulterior object; they should begin their studies of sciences by
learning the elements and principles first; no moment is to be
passed in idleness; they should travel to places renowned for
learning if their home towns are inferior in this respect; they
should show their teachers even greater honor than they show
their parents (which latter naturally is of primary importance).

Cure of Souls

◄§ A chest of furniture with an arched top-piece is measured
by drawing an equilateral [or isosceles] triangle circumscribing
the curve. [The apex is the highest point in the arch, and the
volume contained inside the triangle is added to the chest's
bulk.]

Kelim XVIII, 2

◄§ The size of a bean can be calculated by circumscribing a
quadrilateral around it.

Talmud Jerushalmi *Maasroth* V, 52

◄§ People say that what a child speaks outdoors it has heard
from either its father or mother.

Succah 56b

◄§ Rabbi Jeremiah, a fourth-century sage, was once expelled
from the talmudic academy because of his habit of asking cap-
tious questions. He was later readmitted, however, and eventually became the chief Palestinian authority on talmudic
matters.

Niddah 23a, *Baba Bathra* 23b, 165b

The father of traditional sermons was Isaac ben Moses Arama
(1420–1494) whose sermons in his *Akedath Yitzchak* (Offering
of Isaac) served as a model for future generations of preachers.

*   *   *

Aramaic, a Semitic language closely akin to Hebrew, and in
which most of the Talmud is written, was the vernacular of the

Jewish people starting about 300 years before the current era and for about 800 years thereafter. It was supplanted by Arabic, and later by Yiddish.

*   *   *

❧ King Solomon understood the language of animals.
Shir HaShirim Rabbah I, 1

❧ King Solomon, wisest of mortals, was outwitted by the ants.
Maase Ha'Nemalah 22

❧ The first public vote was conducted by Moses, who took 22,000 ballots and instructed the voters to draw them.
Talmud Jerushalmi *Sanhedrin* I, 19

❧ Sherlock Holmes or other great detectives of fiction and history might have taken lessons in deduction from two Jews captured on Mount Carmel, as related in the name of Rabbi Jochanan: They were walking along the road one day, and their captor overheard them conversing. One said to the other, "There is a camel ahead of us—I assume, because I have not seen it. It is blind in one eye, and bears two bags, one containing wine and the other oil. Two drivers accompany it, one of whom is an Israelite, the other a heathen." The captor rebuked them for their apparent fabrication. But they answered, "The grass is cropped on only one side of the road—hence the camel cannot see on the other side; wine has dripped down and soaked into the earth, whereas the oil has dripped, and floats on top; one of the drivers turned aside from the road to ease himself, while the other did not leave the road for that purpose." The captor then hurried on ahead of them, and found that the captives' deduction was correct in every detail. As a reward, he gave them their freedom.
Sanhedrin 104b

7

PHYSICS

Webster defines physics as "that branch of knowledge treating of the material world and the phenomena of inanimate matter involving no change in chemical composition . . . more specifically, the science of matter and motion—including mechanics, heat, electricity, light, sound, radiation, and atomic structure."

Actually the items included in this chapter could have been grouped in other categories, because as the *Encyclopedia Britannica* states, "it is difficult to give a good and impossible to give a perfect definition of physics. One of the approaches consists in separating off the other provinces of natural science. Biology is set apart because it deals with life. Geology and astronomy are set apart because they are, at least to some extent, descriptive sciences pertaining to the earth and the heavenly bodies. Really serious trouble is met when one tries to distinguish chemistry from physics, for it is impossible to find a chemical phenomenon in which a physicist can take no interest. One is then forced back onto the semijocular definitions, as for instance the one which states that physics is the subject

84

cultivated by physicists. This is not so frivolous as it sounds, for physicists not infrequently invade the terrain of other sciences and sometimes with so much success that they acquire at least a sort of condominium over it. Examples of this practice of invasion are the fields of biophysics, geophysics, astrophysics, physical chemistry, and chemical physics. The boundaries of physics are in fact constantly changing."

For example, the following item could have been included in the chapter, "The Earth and Its Inhabitants," or "Discoveries and Inventions," or "People": The specific gravity of metal was changed by Elisha the Prophet (II Kings VI, 5, 6). As one woodcutter was felling a beam, the axehead fell into the water, and Elisha cut down a stick, cast it into the water at the spot where the iron had sunk, and it floated up so that he was able to grasp it.

By the same token, the reader will undoubtedly encounter other items in other chapters which could well have been included here. The quotations appearing in this section are from the following sources:

Approximate Date	Source
1st-5th Centuries, C.E.	*Mishnah* and *Talmud* (*Sotah, Pesachim, Terumoth, Baba Metziah, Gittin, Avodah Zarah, Chullin, Eirubin, Menachoth, Baba Kama, Shabbath, Yoma, Rosh Hashanah, Baba Bathra, Ahvoth, Yebamoth, Taanith*)
1st-3rd Centuries, C.E.	*Midrashim* (*Sifre, Pesikta, Mechilta, Midrash Rabbah, Tanchuma*)
1st-3rd Century, C.E.	*Targum*
12th Century, C.E.	*Sefer Shaashu'im* (Joseph ben Meir ibn Zabara)

❧ A load which a man can lift up and put on his shoulders is one-third of the weight he can carry.

Sotah 34a

◄ঙ When there is contact between cold and warm substances, the lower one prevails, cooling or heating the one poured into it.

Pesachim 76a

◄ঙ Heat causes all things to expand. When cold is opposed by heat, it manifests its power more rapidly.

Sefer Shaashu'im IX

◄ঙ Scalding with hot water or soaking in vinegar causes contraction.

Targum II Samuel XIII

◄ঙ The heat of a loaf of fresh-baked bread placed on top of an open wine casket delays the wine's evaporation.

Talmud Jerushalmi *Terumoth* X

◄ঙ An increase in the size of a load is as difficult for an animal to carry as an increase of the weight.

Baba Metziah VI, 5

◄ঙ Deerskin that has been flayed will shrink and no longer fit on the original frame.

Gittin 57a

◄ঙ All the wine in the barrel moves towards the siphon.

Avodah Zarah 72b

◄ঙ Iron will make no impression on a diamond, but lead will break it into pieces.

Sefer Shaashu'im IX

◄ঙ The Ark of the Covenant had many miraculous properties, among which was its power to transcend the limitation of space [according to which two objects cannot occupy the same space]. It and the Cherubim above it did not in any way diminish the space in the Holy of Holies.

Baba Bathra 99a

⋞§ In connection with calculating proportions of substances which make a mixture prohibited, it was stated that none gave a stronger taste than onion, and that the pungency of pepper and certain other spices is not neutralized in a mass of a thousand times their quantity.

Chullin 97b

⋞§ The handle of an axe, wedged in horizontally between two buildings whose walls are leaning toward each other, can support both.

Talmud Jerushalmi *Eirubin* V, 22

⋞§ Smelting metal causes considerable loss of its weight.

Menachoth 29a

⋞§ No matter how small an iron weapon may be, it can cause death.

Sifre Bamidbar 160

⋞§ Slapping a barrel of fermenting wine may check fermentation.

Avodah Zarah IV, 10

⋞§ The anterior edge of a notch in a blade will cut smoothly, whereas the posterior edge will rip and tear.

Chullin 17b

⋞§ A certain sapphire was so adamant that the hammer used on it broke in two, and the anvil split.

Pesikta Aniya 135

⋞§ A rooster may shatter a glass vessel by crowing into it.

Baba Kama 18a

⋞§ A kiln does not raise smoke until the fire has seized the larger portion of the fuel.

Menachoth 26b

⋞§ Hot water penetrates the skin of the hands, but does not wash away the fatty substance thereon.

Chullin 105a

◄§ A wick that is extinguished ignites faster when relighted.

Shabbath II, 5

◄§ An unglazed earthen vessel is porous, lets moisture ooze through.

Yoma 78a

◄§ That which is in the light can be seen by the one who is in the darkness.

Mechilta B'shallach

◄§ Oil may be poured soundlessly from one vessel to another.

VaYikrah Rabbah 3

◄§ The confusion of sounds during the day prevents a voice from being heard at a distance.

Eichah Rabbah I, 2

◄§ Two different sounds produced simultaneously by the same person are not distinctly perceived, but they are if produced by two different persons.

Rosh Hashanah 27a

◄§ Vibration from traffic may cause columns to sink and bend.

Talmud Jerushalmi *Baba Bathra* II, 13

◄§ Lead absorbs [deadens] sound.

Yoma 69b

◄§ A tree with many roots and few branches will withstand any wind which will uproot a many-branched tree with few roots.

Ahvoth III, 17

◄§ Marble columns were covered with carpets in the winter, so that they might not contract and thereby crack.

B'reishith Rabbah 33

◄§ Because water is heavier, fruit will float on its surface.

Chullin 26b

✑ The blood of flesh sinks, but that of the liver floats.

Chullin 111b

✑ Identification of a drowned man was made long after his death, as the cold water had preserved his features perfectly.

Talmud Jerushalmi *Yebamoth* XVI, 15

✑ A live body is lighter than a dead one.

Gittin 56a

✑ It was the letters of the Two Tablets which made them light; when the letters flew off, the Tablets became too heavy for Moses to carry.

Talmud Jerushalmi *Taanith* IV, 68

✑ When Aaron's staff swallowed the staffs of the Egyptian magicians (Exodus VII, 12), it was no thicker than before.

Tanchuma Va'eirah 3

8

BUSINESS

There are thirty-nine main classes of work (all prohibited on the Sabbath). These categories are derived from the description of the labor involved in constructing the Tabernacle in the Wilderness in the days of Moses.

Jewish workers have always been engaged in all phases of labor—agricultural, industrial, professional, and educational.

The items included in this chapter deal with various aspects of business. In passing, it is interesting to note that Jews have been merchants for many centuries, and the following quotation from the *Book of Ways* by Ibn Khordadhbeh, around the year 817, describes their routes in his day:

"They speak Persian, Roman [Greek], Arabic, the language of the Franks, Spanish, and Slav. They journey from west to east, from east to west, partly on land, partly by sea. They transport from the west, among other items, silk, castor, marten and other furs, and swords. They take ship in the land of the Franks, on the Western Sea, and steer for Farama [Pelusium]. There they load their goods on the backs of camels and go by land to Kolzum [Suez] in five

days' journey over a distance of twenty-five parasangs [Per-
sian miles]. They embark in the East Sea [Red Sea] and
sail from Kolzum to El-Tar [Port of Medina] and Jeddah
[Port of Mecca]; then they go to Sind, India, and China.
On their return they carry back musk, aloes, camphor,
cinnamon, and other products of the Eastern countries to
Kolzum, and bring them to Farama, where they again em-
bark on the Western Sea. Some make sail for Constanti-
nople to sell their goods to the Romans; others go to the
palace of the king of the Franks to place their goods."

The Jewish merchants practically monopolized the spice and
condiment trade in the eighth and ninth centuries, and led
to a complaint by the French prelate and reformer, Agobard
(at the beginning of the ninth century) that the market-day in
Lyons had been changed from Saturday to another day in the
week in deference to their religious convictions.

It is also interesting to note that mutual insurance was known
even in talmudic times, as in the case of a ship owned by a
group of investors, spoken of in *Baba Kama* 116b.

The quotations in this chapter are taken from the following
sources:

Approximate Date	Source
1st-5th Century, C.E.	*Mishnah* and *Talmud (Baba Met-ziah, Mo'ed Katan, Gittin, Yeba-moth, Kiddushin, Taanith, Demai, Baba Kama, Niddah, Beitzah, Rosh Hashanah, Sotah)*
2nd and 3rd Centuries, C.E.	*Tosefta*
1st-3rd Century, C.E.	*Midrashim (Tanchuma, Midrash Rabbah, Sifre, Sifra, Peskita)*

◆§ Sharp business practices are forbidden by Jewish Law, and
unfair methods frowned upon. When Rabbi Judah, however,

stated that a storekeeper should not offer sweets to attract youthful customers, his colleagues replied that this is permitted, as competitors have the right to do likewise. When he further declared that a merchant should not cut prices, they responded that the public would be grateful as this would prevent exorbitant food prices and militate against others withholding merchandise from sale in order to await higher prices.

Mishnah Baba Metziah IV, 12

◂§ A good division of capital is to invest one-third in real estate, one-third in commerce, and to retain one-third in ready money.

Baba Metziah 42a

◂§ Agreements were made between parties to submit to arbitration.

Talmud Jerushalmi *Mo'ed Katan* III, 82

◂§ Purchases or sales of movable property by minors are valid.

Gittin VII, 1

◂§ Masons and other artisans belonged to guilds.

Talmud Jerushalmi *Yebamoth* XII, 13

◂§ The residents of a town have the right to stipulate measures, food prices, and laborers' wages.

Baba Bathra 8b

◂§ Market prices fluctuate with the hour of the day.

Baba Bathra 90b

◂§ Fear of impending scarcity of commodities will cause a sudden rise in market prices.

Taanith II, 9

◂§ By giving a dealer a deposit in advance, a buyer received all he purchased from him at the lowest prices of the entire year.

Talmud Jerushalmi *Baba Metziah* V, 10

&§ One of the sins of Sodom was the abolition of free trade.

Tanchuma B'shallach 12

&§ Bakers were permitted to form a combination to set the weight and the price of bread.

Tosefta Baba Metziah XI, 25

&§ A deaf-mute may transact business by sign language.

Gittin V, 7

&§ The coinage of Mordecai, like that of the king, was legal tender throughout the realm.

Esther Rabbah 5

&§ Each baker bakes his own individual style or shape, whereas the dealer handles the merchandise of many bakers.

Talmud Jerushalmi *Demai* V, 24

&§ During a Hebrew leap year [when there is an additional month in the calendar], a tenant does not pay an extra month's rent, unless the tenancy is on a monthly basis.

Baba Metziah VIII, 7; 102b

&§ It is deceitfully dishonest to brush up the hair of an animal offered for sale in order to give it the appearance of fatness.

Baba Metziah 60b

&§ Overtime is not compulsory on the laborer if the custom of the place where he works is not to start work earlier or finish later.

Baba Metziah VII, 1

&§ The hired laborer must neither starve himself nor undergo privations, because he thereby lessens his usefulness to his employer.

Talmud Jerushalmi *Demai* VII, 26

&§ In the case of an injury for which one is responsible or must indemnify, he is bound to pay for the medical expenses as well as for the loss of time. Where permanent incapacitation is involved, the larger indemnity is for the value of the earning capacity, and the smaller for loss of time in sickness.

Baba Kama 85a, 86a

⊷§ When labor is dear, the workers strike; when cheap, the employers refuse to bargain.

Baba Metziah 77a

⊷§ Nodding is an indication of consent.

Niddah 42a

⊷§ Those practices which are forbidden for appearance's sake are also forbidden in strictest privacy.

Beitzah 9a

⊷§ Business transactions were sometimes conducted on a credit basis.

Kiddushin 40a

⊷§ Barter and exchange were practiced by the tribe of Asher, which supplied oil and mullets, among other things, in return for grain.

Sifre Deuteronomy 355

⊷§ Certain tradesmen [traveling salesmen] were licensed to go with goods throughout an entire territory.

Rosh Hashanah 9b

⊷§ Market prices of certain kinds of merchandise were regulated.

Baba Bathra 89a

⊷§ A portion which has been weighed should not be used as a weight for other portions.

Sifra Kedoshim 3, VIII

⊷§ A man's money can act as his broker [dealers come directly to the capitalist]; business transactions often involve middlemen, speculators, and accountants.

Baba Metziah 42b

❧ Monopolies controlled production and prices where the number of bakers was limited.

Demai V, 4

❧ Whoever makes building his business will eventually grow poor.

Sotah 11a

❧ There was an exchange outside of Jerusalem called the Arch of Accounts, where debits and credits were settled.

Pesikta Rabbathi 41

9

LAW

The *Mishnah,* and basically the Talmud as well, are books of law. The quotations which follow are not concerned with religious regulations, however, but rather with those concerning civil and criminal jurisprudence—also incorporated into the religion itself.

Although there is no record of any attempt on the part of the ancient sages to abolish capital punishment, there is clear evidence that many of the prominent religious leaders were opposed to it. In the *Mishnah (Makkoth* I, 10), Rabbis Tarfon and Akiba, outstanding *Tannaim* of the second century, declared that had they belonged to the *Sanhedrin* ("supreme court") during Judea's independence, no man would ever have been executed, as they would have found some legal technicality releasing the culprit from the death sentence.

In this connection, it is noteworthy that circumstantial evidence was not accepted. A minimum of two reputable witnesses was required to establish guilt. We are told of a hypothetical instance (*Tosefta Sanhedrin* VIII, 3) wherein the accused was seen to run after a man, with a sword in his hand; the man who was pursued entered a shop, followed by the accused; the slain man was seen there, together with the accused holding the sword dripping with blood. Yet the charge of murder and its sentence of capital punishment could not be sustained, as the actual commission of the crime had not been seen by two capable witnesses.

A court which condemned more than one human being to death during a period of seven years was stigmatized as "murderous," and Rabbi Eleazar ben Azaryah (of the second century) utilized this expression in referring to a court which executed more than one man in every seventy years.

The criminal, of course, did not get off scot-free. Sentences of imprisonment for life or shorter terms were imposed when guilt was established but technicalities prevented the imposition of the death penalty.

Quotations which follow have been taken from the following sources:

Approximate Date	Source
1st-5th Centuries, C.E.	*Mishnah* and *Talmud* (*Yoma, Baba Metziah, Mo'ed Katan, Kethuboth, Nedarim, Sanhedrin, Shebuoth, Yebamoth, Baba Kama, Ahvoth, Makkoth, Berachoth, Baba Bathra, Gittin, Chullin, Kiddushin, Niddah, Chagigah*)
1st-3rd Centuries, C.E.	*Midrashim* (*Midrash Rabbah, Sifre, Yelamdenu, Pesikta*)
2nd and 3rd Centuries, C.E.	*Tosefta*

&§ The New York State Baumes Laws, which include life imprisonment for a fourth conviction, have a talmudic precedent. A man may be forgiven after a third identical transgression, but he is not pardoned if he repeats the same offense a fourth time.

Yoma 86b

⋙ The origin of the Fifth Amendment to the Constitution of the United States may very well lie in the rule: "One is not supposed to offer evidence against himself."

Baba Metziah 28b

⋙ Contempt of court was punishable by imprisonment.

Mo'ed Katan 16a

⋙ Although Jewish Law did not provide for payment of alimony to a divorcee, she was protected by her marriage contract or settlement [*Kethubah*], which had to be in writing. The *Kethubah* provides that a certain sum of money is secured to the wife by her husband, and this is to be paid out of his estate upon her divorce or widowhood. It is a lien on his estate, having priority over other debts, and it may even be collected out of property which has been transferred to a third party, in the event the husband left no estate sufficiently large to pay it.

Kethuboth 82b

⋙ Just as a vow cannot be confirmed before it is made, so it cannot be invalidated in advance.

Nedarim X, 7

⋙ Those engaged in the administration of justice must abstain from strong drink.

Sanhedrin 42a

⋙ A judge must declare himself ineligible in a case involving someone he either loves or hates.

Kethuboth 105b

⋙ Judgment should never be given in a hesitant manner.

D'vahrim Rabbah 5

⋙ A rule of evidence to aid the judge in arriving at a correct decision when there are conflicting statements from litigants permits him to accept as true a statement which, if the deponent had intended to tell a lie, might have been one more advantageous to his case, if in such circumstances the "stronger" statement would also have been uncontradictable. This is termed "Miggo," "from the content of" or "from the inner-most meaning thereof."

Kethuboth 16a; *Shebuoth* 45b

⋞§ A judge is not permitted to favor either party with his speech.

Shebuoth 30b

⋞§ If a judge notices that witnesses are testifying falsely, he must denounce them publicly, and not decide the case on the basis of their evidence.

Shebuoth 30b

⋞§ Both litigants must be present to submit their testimony—otherwise the judge shall not render a decision.

Shebuoth 31a

⋞§ Voice vote in court was taken by the sheriff or crier call-ing out each judge's name and asking him to respond.

Tosefta Sanhedrin IX, 1

⋞§ At a trial, one litigant is not permitted to speak freely if the other's testimony is cut short.

Shebuoth 30a

⋞§ Collusion is a crime.

Shebuoth 31a

⋞§ Identification of a corpse can be established only on seeing the face with the nose on.

Yebamoth XVI, 3

⋞§ In certain instances, workers were indemnified for loss of time incurred in going to and returning from the fields in which they labored.

Talmud Jerushalmi *Baba Metziah* VI, 10

◄§ In cases involving capital punishment, the verdict may be reconsidered in favor of the defendant, but it may never be reversed from acquittal to conviction.

Sanhedrin IV, 1

◄§ Even after conviction, and after sentence has been pronounced, the defendant may be brought back for retrial repeatedly even on his own evidence before execution is carried out [in cases of capital punishment].

Sanhedrin VI, 1

◄§ In the courts of justice they used a *Clepsydra* [water clock] for measuring the time given for argument.

B'reishith Rabbah 49

◄§ An advocate [defense attorney] engaged by a party to a suit or claim speaks from the platform in the court.

Sifre Deuteronomy 343

◄§ An individual who fans or blows the wood aflame after someone brought the wood and another the fire, is culpable.

Baba Kama VI, 4

◄§ A guilty criminal about to have the sentence of capital punishment carried out was given a grain of frankincense in a cup of wine to benumb his senses before execution.

Sanhedrin 43a

◄§ Intricate cross-examination may lead a witness to lie.

Ahvoth I, 9

◄§ Evil spoken in the presence of the vilified person is not classified as evil gossip [slander].

Arakhin 15b

◄§ Even though in ordinary cases a woman is not considered a qualified witness, a midwife's evidence as to which of a pair of twins was first-born is admissible, but only as long as she is seated by the obstetric chair, and not after she has left the mother.

Tosefta Baba Bathra VII, 2;
Talmud Jerushalmi Baba Bathra III, 13

◆§ The legal assumption is that no man will sue his neighbor unless he has a just claim.

Shebuoth 40b

◆§ False evidence may sometimes be inadvertent. If a man saw a huge bird and called it "a camel," and then swore he saw a "camel flying through the air," he was swearing according to the judgment of his senses.

Shebuoth 29a

◆§ Before a culprit is lashed, he must be examined by a medical expert to ascertain if he can stand the punishment.

Tosefta Makkoth V, 14

◆§ He who is unjustly suspected shall offer proof of his innocence.

Berachoth 31b

◆§ The reason one need not incriminate himself by testifying is that he is considered a relative to himself [and relatives need not incriminate each other].

Sanhedrin 9b

◆§ There is no need for a gladiator to make a will [he has no property to leave].

Yelamdenu B'reishith XLIX, 1

◆§ The verbal will and testament of a woman, a slave, or a minor is valid—and the trustee may append his commentary as to their motives if for some reason he distrusts the statement.

Baba Bathra 52a

◆§ The best attestation to the authenticity of a document is through its signers.

B'reishith Rabbah 78

&§ If two offenses are committed simultaneously, the culprit is held answerable only for the severer one.

Gittin 52b, 53a; *Chullin* 81b

&§ Witnesses in capital punishment cases were closely cross-examined to prove their testimony as to seven points of evidence: "In what week, year, month, date, day, hour, place."

Sanhedrin V, 1

&§ The estate of a fugitive is similar legally to that of a captive.

Baba Metziah 38b

&§ A trust received from a minor must be invested safely, as it is returnable when he becomes of age.

Baba Bathra 52a

&§ It is not proper to leave an estate to strangers while bequeathing nothing to one's own children.

Baba Bathra 133b

&§ When faithless judges are numerous, false witnesses are also frequent.

Introduction to *Esther Rabbah*

&§ Both parties to a lawsuit must be represented at court when evidence is presented.

Sanhedrin 7b

&§ Sometimes when justice is rendered, there is no peace [there is dissatisfaction], and if there is peace, there is no justice. In such cases, arbitration is meritorious, and the case should be submitted to arbitration before trial.

Sanhedrin 6b

&§ A divorce decree written on a ready-made blank [prepared form] is invalid.

Talmud Jerushalmi *Gittin* II, 44

✑§ A divorce decree [*Get*] may be written with ink, caustic, red dye, gum, copperas, or anything that is permanent; but not with liquids or fruit juices which are not lasting . . . it may not be written on papyrus from which previous writing has been erased, or on unprepared skin, as such can easily be forged [by erasing again and writing over].

Gittin II, 3, 4

✑§ Writing cannot be forged [erased or written over] on material treated with gall-nut.

Gittin 19b

✑§ A husband may compel his wife to move from a worse to a better dwelling.

Kesuboth XIII, 9

✑§ Suicide is equivalent to murder.

Pesikta Rabbah 24

✑§ Identification of a body by the forehead without the face or vice versa is inconclusive and illegal.

Yebamoth 120a

✑§ Proper signature was required for certain legal documents. For example, trust money could not be delivered if the power of attorney was signed with a mere figure or mark.

Baba Kama 104b

✑§ Confession of an act with which a fine is connected exempts the confessor from paying it.

Baba Kama 38b

✑§ One is guilty of practicing sorcery if a real effect is produced, but not merely for an optical illusion or delusion.

Sanhedrin VII, 11

✑§ An executed criminal was not buried in the regular cemetery, but after the flesh had wasted away, the bones could be interred in a family burial plot.

Sanhedrin VI, 5, 6

◄§ A girl's consent is required before marriage; a man may not betroth a woman to himself before he has seen her.

Kiddushin 41a

◄§ A deaf-mute may marry and divorce by gesture.

Yebamoth XIV, 1

◄§ There is no specific law prohibiting women of legitimate birth from marrying men of illegitimate birth.

Yebamoth 84b

◄§ A wall may not be built within four cubits of a neighbor's water-spout [roof-gutter], as he must have room for a ladder in case repairs are necessary.

Baba Bathra II, 5

◄§ A carob or sycamore tree may not be planted within fifty cubits of a neighbor's well.

Baba Bathra II, 11

◄§ Legally, resin tapped from trees is in the same category as the fruit of that tree.

Niddah 8b

◄§ As long as a fruit tree continues to bear an appreciable amount of fruit, it may not be felled.

Baba Kama 91b

◄§ In order to be assessed for a town tax, one must have been a resident for at least twelve months.

Tosefta Peah IV, 9

◄§ In times of emergency, even the planning of a breach of law is punishable.

Talmud Jerushalmi *Chagigah* II, 78

◄§ Conspiracy to defraud is immoral and illegal.

Baba Bathra 173b

10

PSYCHOLOGY AND PHILOSOPHY

While it may not be customary to group remarks on psychology with those on philosophy, this after all is a volume of oddities, and the groupings are flexible.

To turn again to Maimonides, the following quotation is given from his *Eight Chapters:* "Reason is that faculty peculiar to man which enables him to understand, reflect, acquire knowledge of the sciences, and to discriminate between proper and improper actions. Its functions are partly practical and partly speculative—the practical being, in turn, either mechanical or intellectual. By means of the speculative power, man knows things as they really are and which, by their nature, are not subject to change. These are called the sciences in general. The mechanical power is that by which the arts such as architecture, agriculture, medicine, and navigation are acquired. The intellectual power is that by which one, when he intends to do an act, reflects upon what he has premeditated, considers the possibility of performing it, and if he thinks it possible decides how it should be done."

The psychology of the donor and the recipient of charity is

also taken into consideration in Jewish thought (and is another instance of psychology and philosophy interrelated). Maimonides, in chapter 10 of *Mattenoth Aniyyim* (gifts to the poor) in his *Mishneh Torah* enumerates eight degrees of alms-giving, one higher than the other: "Supreme above all is he who aids the poor in supporting himself by advancing money, going into partnership, or helping him to a lucrative occupation; one degree below that is he who gives charity without knowing the recipient, and without the recipient knowing the giver; then is he who gives in secret, casting his money into the houses of the poor who remain ignorant of their benefactor; then is he who gives without knowing the recipient, although the recipient knows the giver; then is he who gives before he is asked; then he who gives after he is asked; then he who gives inadequately but with good grace; and finally, he who gives but grudgingly."

This philosophical and psychological ladder of charity is indubitably based on the talmudic statement (*Shabbath* 63a): "Greater is he who loans money than he who gives it as charity, and greatest of all is he who provides the funds in advance [before poverty sets in]."

A maxim much stressed (*Chagigah* 5a) is that the poor should never be put to shame when receiving charity.

As can be seen from the foregoing, the psychological effect on all parties is taken into consideration. And the philosophical viewpoint is based on the statement in Deuteronomy XV, 11: "For the poor shall never cease out of the land—therefore I command thee, saying: Thou shalt surely open thy hand unto thy poor and needy brother in thy land."

Incidentally, it is interesting to note that the Hebrew term for "charity" is *Tzedakah*, which actually means "righteousness," as acts of charity are ordained duties. The Talmud (*Baba Bathra* 11a) tells of the charitable act of King Monobaz II (although Josephus, first century, for political reasons credits the deed to Queen Helena of Adiabene, wife of Monobaz I and mother of Monobaz II, who was noted for her generosity), who during a famine at Jerusalem dispatched shiploads of food from Alexandria and Cyprus for distribution among the starving populace—the first Jewish account of organized public relief.

The sources of the quotations in this chapter are as follows:

APPROXIMATE DATE	SOURCE
1st-5th Centuries, C.E.	*Mishnah* and *Talmud* (*Gittin, Kesuboth, Pesachim, Shabbath, Ahvoth, Avodah Zarah, Beitzah, Yoma, Baba Metziah, Derech Eretz, Nedarim, Kiddushin, Niddah, Berachoth, Horayoth, Shekalim, Baba Bathra, Sanhedrin*)
1st-3rd Centuries, C.E.	*Midrashim* (*Midrash Rabbah, Shochar Tov, Tanchuma, Pesikta, Sifra, Yalkut Shimoni*—13th century collection of ancient *Midrashim*), *Temurah*
2nd and 3rd Centuries, C.E.	*Tosefta*
12th Century, C.E.	Maimonides (Moses ben Maimon)
12th Century, C.E.	*Sefer Shaashu'im* (Joseph ben Meir ibn Zabara)

⤙§ When man enters the world, his hands are clenched, as if to say: "The whole world is mine and I shall possess it." But when he leaves the world, his hands are open, as if to say: "I possess nothing from this world."

Kohelleth Rabbah 5

⤙§ If a human being is deprived of his intellectual faculties and possesses only vitality, he becomes like a beast and is soon lost.

Maimonides, *Guide for the Perplexed*, I, 72

⤙§ A king was angry at his son and swore to cast a huge stone at him. Upon calmer reflection, he realized that he would undoubtedly kill the child if he did so. However, he could not retract his oath. He cleverly solved the problem by ordering the rock broken up into tiny pieces, with which he pelted him gently one at a time.

Shochar Tov 6

&⸂ Whatever is in nature, man is able to know and reflect upon.

Responsa of Maimonides, II, 23b

&⸂ An example of sanity tests: "Shall we ascertain his sanity [according to the season of the year] by asking him whether he desires light or heavy covers?"

Gittin 70b

&⸂ Some persons are gifted with an almost prophetic sense, because of the extremely high development of their intuitive faculties, whereby their intellect draws inferences quickly, and sometimes almost instantaneously.

Maimonides, *Guide for the Perplexed,* II, 38

&⸂ Just as weakness of vision causes invalids to see unreal images, especially when they have gazed long at dazzling or very minute objects, so does confusion rule the mind whose mental perceptions have been overstrained or exhausted.

Ibid, I, 32

&⸂ Man is his own worst enemy. This is reminiscent of the parable told about the creation of iron, which caused the trees to tremble and complain. But the iron remarked: "Why tremble? If none of you gives me a handle, none of you will be harmed!"

B'reishith Rabbah V

&⸂ The imagination can combine various impressions which the senses of man have received into fresh ideas which he could not have perceived, such as an iron ship floating in the air, a man whose head reaches the heavens and whose feet rest on the earth, or an animal with a thousand eyes.

Maimonides, *Eight Chapters,* I

◄§ That disaster comes if one does not follow the qualified leader is illustrated by the fable of the snake whose tail insisted on assuming leadership over the head. Successively the tail [because of its blindness] led the snake into a pit of water, a fire, and a thicket of thorns.

D'vahrim Rabbah I

◄§ Instruction should be gradual; one should not attempt to master matters beyond his comprehension, just as an infant fed with wheat bread, meat, and wine will undoubtedly die, not because the food is unfit for the human body, but because of the child's weakness and inability to digest the food so as to benefit from it.

Maimonides, *Guide for the Perplexed,* I, 33

◄§ The sufferings of homelessness are more severe on man than on woman.

Kesuboth 28a

◄§ The brain consists of three lobes, each of which is the seat of a different function. The anterior lobe, in front of the head, holds the imagination; the posterior lobe, in back of the head, holds memory; the middle lobe holds the intellect. That is why a man lowers his head when thinking of things he has never known, since the intellect acts upon the imagination and evolves new ideas; he raises his head with thinking of what he once knew but has forgotten, because then the intellect comes in contact with the memory and revives forgotten ideas.

Sefer Sha'ashu'im IX, 7

The evil principle (Ahriman) as opposed to goodness (Ormuzd) in the *Zend-Avesta* (the sacred books of the Parsees, a fire-worship faith) is mentioned in *Sanhedrin* 39a.

◄§ The drunkard's eye turns to his glass, but the bartender's to his pocket.

Tanchuma Sh'mini to *Mishlei* XXIII, 31

ʘ Men are prevented from discovering the exact truth by four causes: arrogance or vainglory; the subtlety, depth, and difficulty of the subject; ignorance and want of capacity to comprehend; habit and training which act as a deterrent or preventative.

> Maimonides, *Guide for the Perplexed*, I, 31

ʘ Man does not know on what day relief from his troubles will come.

> *Pesachim* 54b

ʘ If one believes in omens, what he fears will eventually befall him.

> Talmud Jerushalmi *Shabbath* VI, 8

ʘ It is absolutely untrue that a man must do or refrain from doing a certain thing; the constellation at the time of his birth does not determine his line of conduct. No compulsion or external influence is exerted, unless it is his own nature to be weak.

> Maimonides, *Eight Chapters*, VIII

ʘ This same thought is expressed in four Hebrew words by Rabbi Akiba—"*Ha'kol tzafui, v'ha'r'shuth n'thunah*"—"Everything is foreseen by the Almighty, yet free-will is given to man."

> *Ahvoth* III, 19

ʘ Originally it was thought that a signet ring on the hand of a statue was merely an ornament. But later it was found that it was symbolic of the wearer's "sealing" himself for death as a vicarious sacrifice for the entire world.

> *Avodah Zarah* 41a

ʘ If one gives even a piece of bread to a child, its mother must be informed.

> *Beitzah* 16a

๛ A man should not start eating garlic or onions (scallions) from the root, but rather from the leaves, for if he does, he is a glutton; likewise he should not empty his goblet at one draught; if he does, he is a drunkard.

Beitzah 25b

๛ The Almighty does not conduct His affairs the way mortal man does. When man provokes his fellow-man, the offended one tries to embitter his life. But though the serpent was cursed by the Lord, it finds its food wherever it climbs or descends; He cursed Canaan [making him a slave] yet he eats and drinks what his master eats and drinks; He cursed woman—yet all run after her; He cursed the earth, yet all are sustained by it.

Yoma 75a

๛ A thousand people will stand looking at a portrait, and each one will think its eyes are gazing at him.

Pesikta Rabbathi 21

๛ Even a sneak-thief may be tempted to commit murder.

Avodah Zarah 15b

๛ An epidemic causes panic.

Sifra B'chukothei 2, IV

๛ A person traveling with money usually feels for his purse from time to time.

Baba Metziah 21b

๛ If a man's relative is rich, he claims kinship; if poor, he disowns him.

D'vahrim Rabbah 2

๛ One should not weep among those who laugh, or laugh among those who weep.

Derech Eretz Zuta V

๛ An angry man forgets his learning and becomes a fool.

Nedarim 22a

◄§ The grape is silent when you cut it and tread it; but in the end it stirs up its horns which cause man to reel and thrust him down.

Yalkut Tehillim 829

◄§ The only thing a hot-tempered man accomplishes is the harmful effect of his excitement on himself.

Kiddushin 40b

◄§ He who tears his garments in his wrath, or breaks his vessels in his wrath, or throws away his money in his wrath, shall be considered in your eyes as an idolator; for that is the treacherous habit of the evil inclination—today it says, "Do thusly," and tomorrow it says, "Do thusly," until it tells one to go and worship idols, and man obeys and worships. The biblical passage proving this is (Psalm LXXXI, 10): "There shall not be within thee a foreign god; nor shalt thou bow thyself down to any strange god." The "foreign god" within a man's body is the evil inclination. However, if one does the aforementioned things to inspire fear and discipline in his household [merely pretending to be infuriated], he is permitted to do so. For example, when Rabbi Judah wanted to show disapproval of his family's actions, he once pulled out the thrums of his garment; Rabbi Acha bar Jacob took broken vessels and shattered them; Rabbi Abba broke the cover of a pitcher.

Shabbath 105b

◄§ Man easily accepts conciliatory words, but woman does not; because he follows the nature of the material of which he was created [earth is easily crushed, bone is not].

Niddah 31b

◄§ One who does not use common sense deserves no pity.

Berachoth 33a

◄§ Even in talmudic times, certain individuals would wait to see how much the entire assembly subscribed before they donated an amount equal to the total.

Talmud Jerushalmi *Horayoth* III, 48;
D'vahrim Rabbah 4

◄§ Rulership buries its holders—there was not one Prophet who did not outlive four kings.

Pesachim 87b

◄§ Curly-headed people should not be cashiers, as they may be suspected of concealing coins in their hair.

Talmud Jerushalmi *Shekalim* III, 47

◄§ Before marrying a woman, a man should investigate the character of her brothers.

Baba Bathra 110a

◄§ Part of a dream may come true, but not the entire dream.

Berachoth 55a

◄§ Since man dreams only of what passes through his mind when he is awake, he is never shown in his dreams a gold palm tree or an elephant walking through a needle's eye.

Berachoth 55b

◄§ An animal emerging from the water on to land is timid; emerging from the forest, it is not.

Va'Yikrah Rabbah 13

◄§ Courage was implanted in his son by a king who made the boy attack a lion [which had been tamed].

Tanchuma Sh'moth 14

◄§ No wild beast has power over man unless he appears to it to resemble a brute creature.

Sanhedrin 38b

◄§ One who attends the arena [where the gladiators performed] as a spectator is like a murderer [countenancing shedding blood].

Tosefta Avodah Zarah II, 7

ᵉᵍ Do not reproach your neighbor for a fault that is also your own.

Baba Metziah 59b

ᵉᵍ He who equivocates in his speech is like an idolator.

Sanhedrin 92a

ᵉᵍ The academy of Rabbi Ishmael explained that the Torah teaches good manners—that the garments worn while cooking for a master should not be worn when serving him with a cup of wine at his table. This is based on the statement in Leviticus VI, 4: "And he shall take off his garments, and put on other garments."

Shabbath 114a

ᵉᵍ Behold how all of the Almighty's creations borrow from each other: The day borrows [hours] from the night, and the night from the day. The moon borrows [light] from the stars, and the stars from the moon. Light borrows from the sun, and the sun borrows from the light. The heavens borrow from the earth, and the earth from the heavens. Wisdom borrows from understanding, and understanding borrows from wisdom. Mercy borrows from righteousness, and righteousness borrows from mercy. The Torah borrows from the Commandments [*mitzvoth*], and the Commandments borrow from the Torah. All of the Almighty's creations borrow and repay each other— except man, who borrows from his neighbor and seeks to swallow him up with usury and theft.

The usurer says to the Almighty: Why do you not take remuneration from the earth which You water, from the plants which You cause to grow, from the constellations to which You give light, from the soul You breathe with life, from the body You guard? And the Holy One, blessed is He, answers: See how much I lend, and take no interest . . . how much the earth lends and takes no interest . . . but I take merely the principal which I have loaned, as does the earth, as it is written (Ecclesiastes XII, 7): "And the dust shall return to the earth as it was, and the spirit shall return to God Who gave it."

Tanchuma Mishpatim, Sh'moth Rabbah 31

◄§ The Almighty created everything in pairs and opposites, without which nature could not exist. Without death there could be no life, without life no death. Without peace there could be no evil, without evil no peace. If all men were fools, they would not realize they were fools; if all were wise, they would not realize they were wise. If all were poor, they would not recognize wealth; if all were wealthy, they would not recognize poverty. He created loveliness and repulsiveness, male and female, fire and water, iron and wood, light and darkness, heat and cold, food and famine, drink and thirst, water and land, deeds and inaction, anxiety and satisfaction, laughter and weeping, cure and sickness. If there is no cleanliness, there is no uncleanness; if no uncleanness—no cleanliness. If there is no pious man, there is no evil man; if no evil, no piety. All to make known the greatness of the Holy One, blessed is He, for He created everything in pairs and partnership, and everything has its opposite, except the Holy One, blessed is He, Himself —for He is One, and there is no other!

Midrash Temurah

11

MEDICINE

Medicine has been an integral part of Judaism, but as is the case with so many other sciences, medical subjects in the Talmud are treated of or alluded to only where they elucidate a point of Jewish Law. Mention is made of a medical book called *Sefer Ha'Refuoth* (*Book of Remedies*) attributed to King Solomon, and a treatise on pharmacology, *Megillath Sammanim* (*Scroll of Medicines*), neither of which has come down to our day.

The physician is an important member of the community and has divine permission to heal, because it is stated in the Bible, "And he shall cause him to be completely healed" (Exodus XXI, 19), and this is interpreted (*Baba Kama* 85a, b) to mean, "And he shall pay the physician's fee." In this same tractate of the Talmud appears the viewpoint highly popular today: "A physician who charges nothing is worth nothing!"

Detailed descriptions of various parts of the body are given in the Talmud, particularly in the tractate *Chullin* (which deals with the fitness of animals for food and similar subjects), with emphasis in certain instances on the types of muscles (which, it was noted, change their form when in motion), tendons, glands, cartilage, intestines. Here it is indeed interesting to note (*Chullin* 59a) the comment of Rabbi Chisdai that the *psoas* (internal muscle in the loin) in all permissible (Kosher) animals (those that chew their cud and have cloven hoofs) has two accessory muscles whose respective fibers run longitudinally and transversely, while that of prohibited (non-Kosher) animals does not have these extra muscles.

The structure of the esophagus, larynx, and trachea is traced, as is the course of the alimentary canal and the gastro-intestinal tract. Among the organs described are the liver and diaphragm, spleen and kidneys, lungs, pleura, heart, spinal cord, and brain. A radical opinion for his time was expressed by Rab (Abba Areka of the third century of the Common Era) when he declared that the aorta contains blood, not air (*Chullin* 45b). And in the *Zohar* (on Leviticus XXVI), attributed to Simeon ben Yochai of the second century, the skull is described as containing three cavities in which the brain is lodged; and from the brain thirty-two paths extend to various parts of the body.

Ancient Hebrew literature is replete with remarks concerning all phases of medical knowledge, as, for instance, the mention in *Mishnah Shabbath* VI, 8, of wooden stumps for legless cripples, some having cavities in the concave top where pads were placed to protect the amputated limb.

In the preface to the chapter, "Discoveries and Inventions," a statement by Moses Maimonides is quoted . . . "it is impossible for any herb or fruit . . . to be void of all utility for man . . . in every generation there are discovered by us important uses . . . unknown to our predecessors." A case in point is a report in the New York *Times* of May 18, 1955, of a statement made by Dr. Frank Ayd, Jr., a Baltimore neuropsychiatrist, to the Senate Appropriations Subcommittee on Health regarding treatment of mental cases with drugs, among them "reserpine." This drug, derived "from the root of the rauwolfia plant, was used in India for centuries for snakebites and in pregnancy cases. It was 'looked down on' by scientists until it was recently found to be effective in the treatment of high blood pressure."

The tremendous diversity of thought and subjects under "Medicine" is evident from the following quotations, whose sources are given herewith:

Approximate Date	Source
850 B.C.E.	Kings
550 B.C.E.	Daniel
1st-5th Centuries, C.E.	*Mishnah* and *Talmud* (*Sanhedrin, Chullin, Berachoth, Kiddushin, Baba Bathra, Nazir, Shabbath, Yoma, Gittin, Niddah, Terumoth, Baba Kama, Oholoth, Yebamoth, Menachoth, Taanith, Me'ilah, Shekalim, Derech Eretz, Nedarim, Baba Metziah, Pesachim, Horayoth, Negaim, Bechoroth, Sotah, Semachoth, Avodah Zarah, Rosh Hashanah, Killaim, Eirubin, Kesuboth, Chagigah, Maasroth*)
2nd and 3rd Century, C.E.	*Tosefta*
2nd Century, C.E.	Ben Sira (Wisdom of Sirach)
2nd Century, C.E.	*Ahvoth d'Rab Nathan*
1st-3rd Century, C.E.	*Midrashim* (*Sh'muel, Midrash Rabbah, Yalkut Shimoni*—13th century collection of ancient *Midrashim*) *Tanchuma, Lekach Tov, Agadah B'reishith, Kohelleth, Tehillim, Eichah Rabbah, Shir Ha'Shirim Rabbah, Shochar Tov, Sifra, Mechilta, Pesikta Rabbatthi, Tanna d'bei Eliayahu Rabbah*)
1st-3rd Century, C.E.	*Targum*
1st-2nd Century, C.E.	*Pirkei d'Rabbi Eliezer*
2nd Century, C.E.	*Pirkei Rabbeinu Ha'Kodesh*
12th Century, C.E.	*Sefer Shaashu'im* (Joseph ben Meir ibn Zabara)
12th Century, C.E.	Maimonides (Moses ben Maimon)

Approximate Date	Source
12th/13th Century, C.E.	*Tosfoth*
13th Century, C.E.	*Zohar* (authorship attributed to Simeon ben Yochai of 2nd Century)

❧ He who is instrumental in saving one person's life is like one who saves the entire world.

Sanhedrin IV, 5

❧ Regulations concerning health and life are made more stringent than laws of ritual.

Chullin 10a

❧ Healing by a physician is not interference with divine dispensation.

Berachoth 60a

❧ No scholar should live in a town that does not possess a physician and a surgeon.

Sanhedrin 17b

❧ In the interpretation of a law, where there is doubt about a prohibition based on danger to health, the stricter practice is preferred.

Chullin 9b

❧ A man once told Rabbi Ishmael and Rabbi Akiba of his sickness, and when they prescribed certain remedies, he reproached them for interfering with the Almighty's ways, as He had smitten him with his ailments. When they discovered that he was a farmer, they pointed out that the Lord had also created the earth and its produce but that if he did not till the soil and care for the plants, they could not grow. The human body, they reminded him, is just like a tree; it has to be cared for properly and treated with medicines in order to remain healthy.

Midrash Sh'muel 4

⋖⧧ Modern medicine's discovery of therapeutic drugs from animals [such as cortisone, adrenalin, insulin, antitoxins, bacterial serums, vitamin B complex, hormones, glandular extractions] is predicted: "Animals and beasts, reptiles and insects, were created for human therapy."

Tanna d'bei Eliayahu Rabbah 1

⋖⧧ Take precautions before you become sick [an ounce of prevention is worth a pound of cure].

Ben Sira 18

⋖⧧ Pay heed to the physician while you are still healthy.

Talmud Jerushalmi Taanith III, 6

⋖⧧ People die prematurely because of self-neglect.

Ahvoth d'Rab Nathan 9

⋖⧧ It is forbidden to dwell in a city that does not possess a physician.

Talmud Jerushalmi Kiddushin (end)

⋖⧧ The apprentice [interne] should accompany the physician making his rounds.

Devahrim Rabbah 10

⋖⧧ The part-owner of a house may not rent his part of the dwelling to a physician, without the partner's consent, because of the noise and disturbance caused by the visiting patients.

Baba Bathra 21a

⋖⧧ Theodos, a well-known physician, was an expert osteologist.

Nazir 52a

⋖⧧ The surgeon wounds with the knife, and heals with the plaster.

Sh'moth Rabbah 26

⋖⧧ With regard to superstitious use of charms, talismans, and incantations, the sages had one general rule: If it is used as a *practical* cure or remedy, it is permissible; but if that is not the intention, it is forbidden.

Shabbath 67a

◄§ The physician should not be discharged until the patient is cured.

Ben Sira 38

◄§ The physician should examine the patient's pulse.

Yalkut Shimoni *Tehillim* 73

◄§ Every sickness has its remedy, provided the physician makes the proper diagnosis and thereby prescribes the proper medicines.

Tanchuma Yithro 8

◄§ The third day of a sickness (or operation) is the most difficult.

Lekach Tov B'reishith XXXIV, 25

◄§ An invalid requires constant care.

Berachoth 54a

◄§ It is permissible to heat water on the Sabbath for a patient's drink or cure.

Yoma 84a

◄§ Man has five senses: sight, sound, smell, taste, touch.

Bamidbar Rabbah 14

◄§ When sight is lost, the other senses become keener.

Gittin 23

◄§ A question thoroughly discussed is whether one who hastens the death of a person afflicted with a fatal organic disease is guilty of murder.

Sanhedrin 78a

◄§ Abba Saul, who was also an embryologist, mentions that an embryo should not be examined in water—but in oil—and only by sunlight. His description of an embryo at the end of the sixth week, when it is completely formed, is that it is the size of a locust; its eyes are like two specks at some distance from each other, as are its nostrils; its feet are like two silken cords, and its mouth like a hair.

Niddah 25b

◄§ That physical well-being is dependent upon mental health is evident from the wording of the ancient prayer still current to this day, in which the Almighty is asked to bless the invalid with "healing of the spirit and healing of the body."

Siddur

◄§ When one is in a stupor, he feels neither hunger nor pain.

Yoma 83a, *Niddah* 37b

◄§ Tearing one's clothing may be a symptom of melancholia, but not necessarily of insanity.

Talmud Jerushalmi *Terumoth* I, 40

◄§ An individual is not responsible for things said in delirium; he need not retract them when he is rational again.

Gittin 70b

◄§ Insanity need not be incurable; in certain cases it is only temporary.

Talmud Jerushalmi *Gittin* VII, 48

◄§ It is possible for a madman to regain his sanity.

Baba Kama IV, 4

◄§ Abnormalities may affect speech: a man may have a thin, feminine voice and a woman a deep, masculine one.

Tosefta Yebamoth X, 6, 7

◄§ A person suffered from delirium tremens after drinking new wine.

Gittin 67b

◄§ Expired air cannot sustain life.

Sanhedrin 77a

◆§ Although all of the glands derive their material from the same source, each gland secretes a fluid peculiar to itself.

Bamidbar Rabbah 15

◆§ The structure of the teeth differs in herbivorous and carnivorous animals.

Chullin 59

◆§ Birds digest their food rapidly, dogs slowly.

Shabbath 82a, *Oholoth* XI, 7

◆§ The reasoning faculties are lodged in the brain.

Yebamoth 9a

◆§ The salivary glands situated in the mouth and under the tongue are referred to as "fountains."

Niddah 55b

◆§ The heart is composed of two ventricles, the right one being larger than the left, and is situated to the left of the median line. Each lung has five lobes. The aorta contains blood, not air [as was commonly believed].

Chullin 45b, 47a, *Menachoth* 37b

◆§ A small bone at the base of the spine called *luz* [*os coccygis*—the coccyx] is the only part of the human body which is indestructible, and is the one from which Resurrection will start. Rabbi Joshua ben Chananyah proved its immortality to the Emperor Hadrian. He immersed one in water, but it would not soften; he placed it in fire, but it was not consumed; he put it in a mill, but it could not be ground; he pounded it with a hammer, but the hammer broke, the anvil split, and the bone remained unharmed.

Midrash Kohelleth 114, 3

◆§ The condition of the heart changes from hour to hour.

Agadah B'reishith 2

◆§ The gullet has two skins—the outer red, the inner white.

Chullin 43

◄§ The bile and the liver are affixed to the fifth rib.

Sanhedrin 49a

◄§ When the liver is excited, the gall pours a drop over it, and quiets it.

Berachoth 61b

◄§ There is a certain membrane, *chalcholeth,* which keeps the entrails in position.

Chullin 60a

◄§ The entrails are so carefully arranged that if one is misplaced, man cannot live.

Chullin 56b

◄§ The "bag" in which the cerebrum lies is essential for life.

Chullin 45a

◄§ The rectum is supported by three toothlike glands.

Shabboth 82a

◄§ An autopsy will reveal if a perforation was made before or after slaughtering; because if made before, blood will have clung to the needle.

Chullin 51a

◄§ The radial bone of a chicken is one-sixtieth portion of its wings.

Tanchuma Tazriah 8

◄§ If the spinal cord of a slaughtered animal is found to be a pulpy mass, the meat is *terefah* [unfit]; if merely softened, it is kosher [fit for food].

Chullin 45b

◄§ A reed tube was inserted in the perforated windpipe of a lamb, and it recovered.

Chullin 57b

◄§ Two beanlike glands lie at the mouth of the skull [at the end of the cerebellum].

Chullin 45a

◆§ Examination of the brain of a slaughtered fowl will show whether or not the upper membrane had been perforated, for if so, the lower one would have burst on account of the tenderness.

Chullin 56a

◆§ The spinal vertebrae are known as "the knots of the spine."

Shabbath 147b

◆§ The right hip is usually the stronger one.

Chullin 91a

◆§ The index finger of the right hand is usually the most dexterous.

Sifra VaYikrah III, 3

◆§ Among the defects found in an animal after slaughter which render it *terefah* are the following: a pierced gullet or torn windpipe; a pierced membrane of the brain, or of the heart as far as its cells; a broken spine and severed spinal cord; absence of the liver; a pierced or defective lung; a pierced maw, gall-bladder, intestines, or inner stomach; a tear in the greater part of the stomach's outer coating; a fall by the animal from a great height; the breaking of most of its ribs; its mauling by a beast or bird of prey.

Chullin III, 1

◆§ However, if the windpipe is merely slightly pierced or split; if the skull is defective but the membrane of the brain unpierced; if the heart is pierced but not its cells; if the spine is broken but the spinal cord unsevered; if at least an olive's size of the liver remains—the animal does not necessarily become unfit.

Chullin III, 2

◆§ So thorough a knowledge of anatomy was required by the sages that they had to determine, in the case of a slaughtered animal whose lung was found to be dried, whether this had been caused by fright at such a natural phenomenon as thunder

and lightning, or by the act of man, or the roaring of a lion
or similar occurrence.

Chullin III, 2

❧ Tall men are usually slower of perception—first because
their chests are narrow and this diminishes the capacity for
blood and weakens the action of the brain; second because it
requires a longer time for the heart and the brain to cooperate.

Sefer Shaashu'im II

❧ It is difficult for the bladder to discharge its urine when
it is too full because its opening consists entirely of fibers, and
when it becomes overladen they contract and close up the
passage.

Sefer Shaashu'im IX

❧ The stomach has three kinds of fibers—one stretched
lengthwise to receive the food; one placed diagonally to retain
the food until it is digested; and the third stretched across the
width of the stomach to expel the food when digested. There
are six intestines, three upper ones of a delicate nature, and
three lower ones of a coarser nature. The intestine adjacent
to the liver is made of convolutions, so as to detain the food
long enough for the liver to absorb the essence of the food.
The liver, incidentally, absorbs this not through any opening
in the intestines, but by some wonderful energy like that by
which the magnet attracts iron.

Sefer Shaashu'im IX

❧ The kidneys are receptacles for the blood which is not
assimilated into the body. In the breasts of women, blood is
assimilated into milk.

Sefer Shaashu'im VIII, IX

❧ He whose face is flushed is hasty and untruthful; he whose
eyes are sunken in and quick of glance is both deceitful and
resourceful. He whose eyebrows are hairy is a bore and of
morose disposition. A man with a pointed nose and large
nostrils is quarrelsome. One with a round forehead is irritable.

Thick lips are also a sign of bad temper; large ears are proof of foolishness; a short neck is evidence of deceit and envy. A large belly generally goes with an abundance of stupidity. Narrow shoulders bespeak narrow-mindedness; a small palm is an indication of a small mind; and all men who are tall are fools.

Sefer Shaashu'im II, 1

&§ Of all the nerves in the body, the optic nerves are the only ones which are hollow, to allow the power of light to pass through them from the brain to the retina.

Sefer Shaashu'im IX, 1

&§ Teeth come from the surplus of hard food, and their growth is enhanced if the milk which the child drinks is hot— the warmer the milk, the sooner the teeth will appear. Children are not born with teeth normally, because they do not need them while they are sucklings. The incisors appear before the canines and molars, as they come from softer matter, and the molars arrive only when the child begins to eat harder food. The upper molars, being suspended, have three roots each to hold them fast, while the lower ones have but two roots. The milk teeth, coming from softer food, are afterward replaced by the permanent teeth which come from the harder food which the grownup child eats. In old age, the teeth fall out because they dry up and wither like plants.

Sefer Shaashu'im IX

&§ The neck serves two purposes—one to cool off the vapors issuing from the heart before they reach the brain, the other to make the human voice audible. That is why the windpipe is made of cartilage, neither soft like flesh nor hard like bone. Because to make the vibrations of the air audible, they must pass through a medium which is neither too soft nor too hard. That is why when the wind blows against water or rocks, it produces no sound, but when it blows against trees or reeds, it becomes audible.

Sefer Shaashu'im IX, V

৵ Fifty is the best age for retirement, as that is when the strength wanes.

Lekach Tov Bamidbar VIII, 25

৵ An epidemic is determined by the per capita death rate. If in a city of 1500 male population three normally healthy people succumb to a plague daily for three consecutive days, or in a city of 500 one daily for three successive days, it is considered an epidemic.

Taanith 21a

৵ Grief breaks the body.

Berachoth 58

৵ Heart trouble is the worst ailment.

Shabbath 11

৵ Though croup is curable, it may be fatal.

Taanith 19

৵ Croup begins in the intestines and ends in the mouth [choking].

Shabbath 33

৵ Rabbi Elazar bar Jose was cured of croup by a sailor who accidentally used chiropractic methods, but the latter contracted it himself.

Me'ilah 17

৵ One of the causes of gout is stiff shoes.

Pirkei Rabbeinu HaKodesh

৵ Dropsy and gout may be caused by suppressing urination.

Berachoth 25a, 62b

৵ Because the priests continuously walked barefoot on the stone pavement of the Temple, they were subject to intestinal troubles.

Talmud Jerushalmi Shekalim V

❧ Abdominal troubles cause failing of the eyes and palpitation of the heart.

Nedarim 22a

❧ An invalid should not drink cold water.

Yalkut Shimoni Acharei Moth

❧ A slight discharge from the nose and ears is normal, but if heavy, it is not healthy.

Baba Metziah 107a

❧ Susceptibility to epilepsy is hereditary.

Baba Metziah 80a

Angina Pectoris is mentioned in Gittin 69b.

❧ The molars should not be extracted if this is at all avoidable.

Pesachim 113a

❧ A person who swallows a wasp cannot live.

Gittin 70a

❧ Diarrhea may be caused by extreme fright.

Targum Psalms XXIX, 9

❧ To the aged, even a small mound appears like a high mountain.

Shabbath 73b

❧ Dwelling in caves causes a severe skin disease.

Midrash Tehillim Psalm XVII, 14

❧ Bran-broth bloats the animal fed on it.

Baba Metziah 60b

❧ The exertion of climbing can lead to one's becoming overcome by heat. Animals may also suffer from heat prostration.

Baba Metziah VI, 3

Poison can enter one's bloodstream through a scratch on the skin (*Tosefta Terumoth* VII, 14); and one's face is as susceptible to poison as a scratched spot. (Talmud Jerushalmi *Terumoth* VIII, 45).

◆§ Rubbing the hair with earth causes it to fall out.
Nazir VI, 3

◆§ Disease is more prevalent at the change of seasons.
Talmud Jerushalmi *Yebamoth* XV, 14

◆§ Anger causes stomach ailments . . . every quick-tempered, irritable man is a fool.
Kohelleth Rabbah XI, 10

◆§ Swallowing a piece of dry bread without its being softened by saliva in the mouth may cause a wound in the entrails.
Sh'moth Rabbah 24

◆§ There is no trouble greater than blindness.
Midrash Tehillim CXLVI

◆§ Food prepared from a certain species of edible thistles called *Akavis* causes body odor when eaten.
Eichah Rabbah IV, 9

◆§ Certain root-drinks cause impotence.
Tosefta Yebamoth VIII, 4

◆§ He who eats what a mouse has gnawed will lose his memory.
Horayoth 13a

◆§ Up to the days of Jacob, sneezing was a prelude to death; therefore one must now offer thanks after sneezing.
Yalkut Job 927

◆§ Certain afflictions cause loss of vitality.
Yoma 74b

◆§ All wounds produced either directly or indirectly through fire are termed "burns."
Negaim IX, 1

☙§ The flesh which a physician would peel off until he reaches sound flesh is termed "decayed."

Chullin 45b

☙§ Internal injuries may be presumed if an animal falls on a pile of dried bark.

Chullin 51b

Softening of the brain and spinal column is spoken of in *Chullin* 45b; catalepsy in *B'reishith Rabbah* 17; and in *Mechilta Mishpatim* 4, mention is made of a surgeon's causing a patient's death through negligence.

☙§ Death in war is a greater affliction than death from natural causes.

Baba Bathra 8b

☙§ Nausea is accompanied by facial pallor.

Tanchuma B'reishith 12

☙§ There was a case where a patient suffered with fever for three years.

Shir HaShirim Rabbah II, 16

☙§ Living in a cave will cause one's skin to crack.

Shabbath 33b

Inflammatory fever caused by stones in the bladder or kidneys is mentioned in *Baba Metziah* 85a, *Gittin* 69b, *Avodah Zarah* 28a.

☙§ An inflicted wound may cause fever.

Chullin 51a

☙§ Sickness due to a cold caught in a draught is a person's own fault.

Baba Bathra 144b

☙§ For each person who dies a natural death, ninety-nine die through their own negligence.

Talmud Jerushalmi *Shabbath* XIV, 14

◦§ After a confinement, a woman's limbs are shaky, and she does not regain her full strength for twenty-four months.

Niddah 9a

◦§ Fever is more severe in winter than in summer.

Yoma 29a

◦§ Dead flesh does not feel the knife.

Shabbath 13b

◦§ Water, coming in contact with a wound, irritates it.

Yebamoth 120b

◦§ The skin over a fracture retains the discharge [pus] of a broken bone.

Chullin 77a

◦§ All diseases have their origin in the air.

Baba Metziah 107b

◦§ There was no gray-haired person in the town of Mamle; they all were short-lived.

B'reishith Rabbah 59

◦§ Alternate spasms of the head can give the erroneous impression that the one so seized is assenting or dissenting.

Gittin 70b

◦§ Hip-disease is a frequent disorder; severance of the spinal cord is unusual.

Chullin 51a

◦§ Rheumatism was known to and suffered by *midrashic* contemporaries.

VaYikrah Rabbah 19

◦§ There are twenty-four kinds of skin diseases. One of them, called *Raasan,* is accompanied by extreme weakness leading to nervous trembling, and it was with this that the Pharaoh of Egypt was smitten because of his designs against Sarah and Abraham.

B'reishith Rabbah 41

◄§ Skin disease will develop if bleeding is neglected.

Bechoroth 44b

◄§ There were two priestly families in Alexandria—one whose blood-temperature was below normal, and the other above normal. The physician made a compound [theriac] from the blood of each, and with it he cured them.

Shir HaShirim Rabbah 4

◄§ All sicknesses have their effect on the patient's blood.

Baba Bathra 58b

◄§ One should not give a blood transfusion after having eaten fish, fowl, or salted meat; one should not drink milk or eat cheese, eggs, or cress after having given a transfusion.

Nedarim 54b

◄§ A blow, though it may not cause bleeding, may cause a blood-clot.

Shabbath 107b

◄§ There are families whose members bleed little when wounded, and others who bleed profusely.

Yebamoth 64a

◄§ The blood circulates throughout the body.

Midrash Temurah 1

◄§ Man cannot live with less than a *reviis* [$\frac{1}{4}$ of a "log," a liquid measure of the capacity of six eggs, estimated at 108 cubic centimeters] of blood in the body.

Sotah 5a; *Tosefta Kelim* 43; *Chullin* 51a

◄§ If the white corpuscles of the blood outnumber the red, the human being is anaemic and susceptible to all sicknesses; if the red outnumber the white, he is prone to leprosy and similar plagues.

Tanchuma VaYikrah 6

◄§ Blood-types are hereditary.

Niddah 64

◄§ The blood of a goat is similar to that of human beings.

B'reishith Rabbah 84

◄§ Esau's body was completely covered with hair, like a field overgrown with grass.

B'reishith Rabbah XXV, 25

◄§ Hair continues to grow even after death.

Semachoth 4

◄§ Each hair has its own "well" from which it "drinks." When the well dries up, the hair does likewise.

Tanchuma Tazriah

◄§ Rabbi Eleazar ben Azaryah's hair turned gray overnight when he was sixteen years of age.

Talmud Jerushalmi *Taanith* IV

◄§ Letting one's hair and nails grow unkempt is both a symptom of and a prelude to melancholia.

Bamidbar Rabbah 10

◄§ Nails grow only on members of the body which have bones.

Niddah 49

◄§ Hair-cutting retards a patient's convalescence.

Berachoth 57

◄§ A healthy person has strong hair; a weak person weak hair.

Talmud Jerushalmi *Nazir* VI, 3

◄§ Extreme fright may cause a person's hair to fall out, and may lead to permanent baldness.

Sh'moth Rabbah 24

◄§ Famine caused Miriam, daughter of Nakdimon, to lose her hair.

Pesikta Rabbathi 44

◄§ Jonah became bald and also lost his beard after having been confined inside the fish.

Tanchuma Toldoth 12

◄§ Tears of grief are bad for the eyes, but tears of joy are good for them.

Shabbath 151

◄§ Man's eye, ear, and nose are not under his direct control.

B'reishith Rabbah 67

◄§ Man sees through the black, not the white part of the eye-ball; this means the darkest part in the center of the black.

VaYikrah Rabbah 31

◄§ Although there are several sources of secretions in the human head very close to each other, each is different; the fluid of the eyes is salty; of the ears, oily; of the nose, offensive in smell; of the mouth, sweet.

Bamidbar Rabbah 18

◄§ The eyebrows consist of a multitude of hairs. And each has its own individual follicle. For if two hairs were nourished by the same follicle, they would darken man's sight.

Baba Bathra 16a

◄§ Eye-paint [stibium] stops tears, cures a disorder of the eyes. and advances the growth of the eyelashes.

Shabbath 109a

◄§ Lightning may affect the eyesight.

Baba Metziah 78b

◄§ A cataract, or blending of the white part of the eye with the black or the reverse, in a lamb, makes it unfit for the Passover offering.

Talmud Jerushalmi *Pesachim* IX, 36

◄§ Up to the age of forty, the use of stibium improves the eyesight; after that it preserves, but does not improve it.

Shabbath 151b

◄§ Sudden blindness may be caused by dazzling light.

Gittin 69a

◆§ An affection of the eyesight influences the mental faculties.
Avodah Zarah 28b

Another version of the same phraseology is "the muscles of the eye are connected with [or dependent on] the heart."

◆§ The object of sneezing is to free the brain from certain injurious fluids, and the sound is produced by forcing these fluids through a bone perforated like a sieve.
Sefer Shaashu'im IX

◆§ An animal may have double ears with either one or two systems of cartilages.
Bechoroth 40b

◆§ Permanent deafness as the result of a blow cannot be caused unless there is a wound inflicted or a drop of blood shed in the ear.
Baba Kama 86a

◆§ Blowing a horn into someone's ear may deafen him.
Baba Kama 18a

◆§ *Tzumach* [meaning "grown over"] is an animal which has no external ears, or a person with tiny or no auricles.
Tosefta Bechoroth IV, 15, 16

◆§ The natural oil in the ears saves the human being from dying at loud, penetrating noises, because the oil deadens the sound and makes it bearable.
Bamidbar Rabbah 18

◆§ The children of Rabbi Jochanan ben Gudgada all suffered from hereditary deafness, but this was not transmitted to all of their descendants.
Talmud Jerushalmi Terumoth I, 1

◆§ Continual blows on [or ailments of] the ear are dangerous and injurious.
Devahrim Rabbah 10

❧ The mucus of the nose absorbs evil odors and neutralizes them.

Bamidbar Rabbah 18

❧ Sneezing is involuntary, and its after-effects on the body are pleasant.

Berachoth 24

❧ The health of the body depends on the teeth.

Yalkut Shimoni Shir HaShirim 988

❧ First [milk] teeth will be replaced, but those that follow will not [except artificially].

Mechilta Mishpatim 9

❧ An egg can be boiled down to the size of a pill. On being swallowed by the patient it passes unchanged through the body, carrying with it matter which the physician can diagnose.

Talmud Jerushalmi *Nedarim* VI, 39

❧ The limbs of some animals will continue to move convulsively even after decapitation, like the tail of the lizard which continues to move after it has been severed.

Oholoth I, 6

❧ Even though a post-mortem examination is considered a disgrace to the corpse, in certain cases an autopsy may be performed.

Chullin 11b

❧ What is considered the only case on record in ancient literature where a diagnosis was made and verified by a post-mortem examination is the following: Rabbi Yemar diagnosed as ischiagra the ailment causing a sheep to drag its hind legs; Rabbina said it was due to paralysis caused by a solution of continuity of the spinal cord. When the animal was slaughtered, the opinion of Rabbina was corroborated.

Chullin 51a

❧ Rabbi Levi examined a patient suffering from tremor of the head, and diagnosed that he was suffering from softening of the spinal cord. Abaya declared that such cases were not fatal, but that the patients lost their reproductive functions.

Chullin 51a

◆§ The following were considered fatal: perforation of the heart; perforation of the esophagus, stomach, or intestines; rupture or wounding of the spleen; atrophy and abscess of the kidneys.

Chullin 45a, 45b, 2, 55a, b

◆§ Herod preserved a body in honey for seven years.

Baba Bathra 3b

◆§ When burials took place in tombs, it once happened that a sepulchre was visited within three days after the funeral. The supposed corpse was found alive, and he lived twenty-five years thereafter, and had five children before he finally died.

Semachoth VIII

◆§ Certain drugs may cause barrenness.

Yebamoth 65b

◆§ It is impossible to differentiate the sex of the foetus before the end of the fourth month.

Niddah 25b

◆§ Mar Zutra states that although a child born after nine months' gestation is not born until the ninth month is completed, a seven months' child can be born before the seventh month is complete, in fact, after six months and two days' gestation childbirth is possible.

Rosh Hashanah 11a

◆§ Caesarean delivery was named after the Roman Caesar whose birth was accomplished by operation after his mother's death.

Tosfoth Avodah Zarah 10

Childbirth by Caesarean section is spoken of in *Niddah* V, 1.

⋙ The egg laid today was fully developed yesterday.

Beitzah 2b

⋙ The majority of animals secrete no milk unless they have given birth.

Bechoroth 20b

⋙ When a she-donkey was cauterized, her foal was born with a flame-mark.

Vayikrah Rabbah 15

⋙ A hen may be fructified by friction in the dust, and lay eggs.

Beitzah 7a

⋙ One pregnancy may have two confinements, as in the case of the wife of Rabbi Chiyyah, who gave birth to Hezekiah three months after having given birth to Judah.

Niddah 27a, 40a

⋙ Life in an embryo is felt by the mother after three months of pregnancy.

Yebamoth 37a

⋙ Excitement prevents regular menstruation.

Niddah IV, 7

⋙ The formation of the embryo begins from the navel, and it draws nourishment through its navel string.

Yoma 85a, Talmud Jerushalmi *Killaim* VIII, 31

⋙ A feverish flush is one of the premonitory symptoms of regular menstruation, as are constant yawning and sneezing.

Niddah IX, 8

⋙ A woman conceives only shortly after menstruation ends.

Vayikrah Rabbah 14

⋙ The creation of the embryo begins from the navel and it develops on both sides.

Sotah 45b

ᴥᴥ The offspring of extremely dark-complexioned parents will probably be even darker.

Bechoroth 45b

ᴥᴥ A twin-sister was born with Cain, but Abel had two twin-sisters.

B'reishith Rabbah 22

ᴥᴥ When one of a pair of twins has a headache, the other feels the pain as well.

Shir HaShirim Rabbah V, 2

ᴥᴥ As long as a child is in its mother's womb, its mouth is closed and it is nurtured from the umbilical cord.

Tanchuma KiThissa 2

ᴥᴥ Mar Samuel was able to ascertain the age of a foetus.

Niddah 25b

ᴥᴥ An operation can reveal the sex of one whose male or female organs are underdeveloped.

Baba Bathra 126b

ᴥᴥ Circumcision is ordained for the eighth day after birth, because the Almighty wants the child to have sufficient strength.

D'vahrim Rabbah 6

It is worth mentioning that a non-Jewish Canadian surgeon did some research on infants to ascertain why Jewish Law orders circumcision on the eighth day. In an article in a medical journal, he cited the fact that he had discovered that Vitamin K (for pro-thrombin, the coagulating or clotting element in the blood) in a baby's blood increases after birth, reaching its peak on the eighth day, after which it decreases.

ᴥᴥ A weak, sickly infant, or one whose blood is not normal, is not permitted to be circumcised until he is sufficiently strong to stand the operation.

Shabbath 134, 137

◄§ Sleep is the best medicine. It strengthens the natural forces, and diminishes the injurious fluids. The seat of sleep is in the lobes of the brain, and it is akin to apoplexy and epilepsy. Yet it is in the nature of man to have control over his body even in sleep.

Sefer Shaashu'im IX

◄§ Sleep is like food and medicine to the sick.

Pirkei d'Rabbi Eliezer 12

◄§ He who stands up the moment he arouses from sleep is closer to death than to life.

Gittin 70

◄§ The night was created for sleeping.

Eirubin 65

◄§ Too much sleep is inadvisable.

Gittin 70

◄§ Sleep at dawn [because it strengthens the body] is like a steel edge to iron.

Berachoth 62b

◄§ Eight hours of sleep, terminating at dawn, is ideal. One should not sleep either on his face or back, but should accustom oneself to sleep first on the left side, and the rest of the night on the right. After eating, one should wait three or four hours before retiring for the night.

Maimonides, *Hilchoth Dei'oth* IV, 4, 5

◄§ Gout and arthritis may come from sleeping in a bed that is too short.

Pirkei Rabbeinu HaKodesh 3

◄§ Sleep in any kind of a bed except the bare ground.

Berachoth 62b

◄§ One should not sleep alone in a house.

Shabbath 151

◄§ A foot-bath may cure a headache as well as a pain in the eyes.

Sefer Shaashu'im VI

◄§ As the result of an accident, the abdominal viscera protruded through the wound. Reposition of the organs was effected automatically by frightening the patient, which caused the abdominal muscles to relax, after which the external wound was closed by sutures.

Shabbath 82a

◄§ The use of antitoxins derived from the infected animal was advocated by Rabbi Ishmael, who prescribed the lobe of the dog's liver as a cure for one bitten by a rabid dog, despite the protestations of his colleagues who claimed that there was no remedy for such a case.

Yoma 84

In II Kings IV, 38-41, we find the following tale: Elisha returned to Gilgal while there was a famine in the land. When the members of the prophetic order were sitting before him, he said to his servant, "Set on the great pot and make a vegetable stew for the prophets." Then one of them went out into the field to gather herbs and found a wild vine and gathered from it a garment full of wild gourds, and came and cut them up for the pot of vegetable stew, for they did not know what they were. So they poured it out for the men to eat. But while they were still eating of the stew, they cried out and said: "O man of God, there is death in the pot." So they could not eat of it. "Bring meal," he said. Then he cast it into the pot, and said, "Pour out for the people that they may eat." There was now no harm in the pot.

Laboratory tests have shown that meal-protein, when cooked, has a neutralizing effect on the poisonous alkaloid of colocynth, the "gourds of the wild vine" which had been included in the stew.

◄§ A sore throat should be "lubricated" with oil.

Berachoth 36

◄§ Applications of oil, wine, or vinegar are advisable for headache or head-scabs.

Tosefta Shabbath 13

◄§ Shaving off all the hair of the head is sometimes necessary to cure scabs.

Tosefta Pesachim III, 12

◄§ Cooked mangold [a species of beet] is good for the heart and the eyes.

Eirubin 29

◄§ Apple wine that had been aged seventy years cured a case of intestinal trouble.

Avodah Zarah 40

◄§ "Beware of flies that have touched persons afflicted with *raasan* [a severe skin disease accompanied by nervous trembling]." Rabbi Zeira would not even sit where the wind from such a direction would blow, Rabbi Elazar would not enter their tent, and Rabbis Ami and Assi would not even use eggs collected from the street where they resided. Rabbi Chanina said that the people of Babylon were not afflicted with this disease because they ate beets and drank beer made of *cuscuta* [instead of hops]. Rabbi Jochanan said that they were not afflicted with leprosy because they ate beets, drank beer, and bathed in the Euphrates.

Kesuboth 77b

◄§ Whoever visits an invalid takes away one-sixtieth of his pain.

Nedarim 39b

◄§ Visiting the sick has its rules and regulations. One should not visit an invalid during the first or last three hours of the day, nor sit upon the bed.

Nedarim 40a

◄§ When Vespasian was trying to put on his shoes after hearing that he had been made emperor of Rome, he noticed that he could not draw them on, as his feet had swelled. Rabbi Jochanan told him that this was due to the good news he had just heard, because (Proverbs XV, 30): "A good report giveth marrow to the bones." Asked as to the remedy, the rabbi advised him to have a man with whom he was dissatisfied pass before him, because (Proverbs XVII, 22): "But a depressed spirit drieth up the bones." When this was done, Vespasian found that his shoes fit.

Gittin 56b

◄§ Do not sit too much, because sitting affects the abdominal region; do not stand too much, as standing affects the heart; do not walk too much, because this affects the eyes. Spend a third of your time doing each. Standing with something to lean on is preferable to sitting on a seat without a back support.

Kesuboth 111a, b

◄§ Three different types of remedies cure chills, depending on the individual: fat roasted meat and strong wine; bathing in exceedingly hot water; exercise.

Gittin 67b

◄§ A plaster could be placed on a wound and the injured individual could even bathe in warm or cold water, but removal of the plaster before healing would cause an ulcer.

Kiddushin 30b

◄§ Rabbi Zadok was suffering from malnutrition due to constant fasting. He would live on fig juice. He was so emaciated that when he ate something, it could be seen going down his throat. He was eventually cured by drinking on alternate days water mixed with bran and a mixture of water, bran, and flour until his stomach became sufficiently strong to retain food.

Gittin 56b

◄§ Rabbi Judah had eye trouble. His physician, Samuel of Yarchina, wanted to inject some medicine into the rabbi's sore

eyes or smear some salve over them, but his patient declared
that he could not endure the pain [or was allergic to the medi-
cines]. He therefore poured some medicine into a tube, placed
it under the patient's head while in bed, and he was cured
[the fumes penetrated].

Baba Metziah 85b

✍ Youth is regainable. Before Sarah gave birth to Isaac, her
body which was wrinkled with age became smooth, the wrinkles
disappeared, and her beauty returned.

Baba Metziah 87a

✍ Cold water should be applied to a wasp's sting, and hot
water to the sting of a scorpion.

Chagigah 5a

✍ Elisha resuscitated the Shunamite's son, who had heat prostration and died, by covering him and then breathing into his
nostrils and administering artificial respiration. When the lad's
flesh became warm, he walked him up and down until the boy
sneezed seven times, and then recovered.

II Kings, XI

✍ Vinegar has the power to draw blood from meat and contract the blood vessels so that none will ooze.

Pesachim 74b

✍ Medicinal powder placed on a wound will penetrate
through it into the flesh beneath, but if there is no wound, it
will not penetrate.

Sotah 7b

✍ Certain poisons can be neutralized with salt.

Talmud Jerushalmi *Terumoth* VIII, 46

✍ The medicinal properties of the resin or gum and the
leaves of *Chiltis* [asafoetida] differ.

Chullin 58b

ↄᔕ Basking in the sunshine is good for a wound.
B'reishith Rabbah 48

ↄᔕ In the case of a fractured skull, a piece of pumpkin shell was inserted to fill the gap, and the individual lived; a lamb whose windpipe was perforated lived after a reed tube was inserted so that it might breathe; a hen whose leg was dislocated and detached recovered through a support made for it by a reed tube.

Gittin 57b

ↄᔕ Radishes are good for fever . . . which may be caused by eating hot bread.
Avodah Zarah 28b

ↄᔕ Meat and red wine are beneficial after blood-letting.
Shabbath 129a

ↄᔕ Starvation can change a person's appearance beyond recognition.
Pesikta Rabbathi 29

ↄᔕ Pressing the jugular vein may relieve stomach-ache.
Tosefta Shabbath III, 6

ↄᔕ The suburbs of Tiberias, Geder, and Pella were renowned for their salubrious hot springs.
Talmud Jerushalmi and *Eichah Rabbah*

ↄᔕ *Amomum,* an Indian spice, is a medicine for sterility.
B'reishith Rabbah 45

ↄᔕ A bandage should be prepared in advance for the circumcision operation.
Shabbath 134a

ↄᔕ Leek is a remedy for snake-bite.
Tosefta Shabbath XV, 14

ↄᔕ Caraway is a remedy for nausea.
Avodah Zarah 29a

✑ Garlic destroys parasites in the entrails.

Baba Kama 82a

✑ Vinegar may relieve a toothache, but is injurious to healthy teeth.

Shabbath 11a

✑ Gold and silver shells or crowns were used to cover broken or deformed teeth.

Shabbath 65a

✑ Spleen should be chewed and then thrown away, as it is good for the teeth, but bad for the intestines. Leek should be cooked and swallowed without chewing, as it is good for the intestines, but bad for the teeth.

Avodah Zarah 28a, *Berochoth* 44b

✑ The same plants which produce poisonous drugs can produce healing remedies.

B'reishith Rabbah 10

✑ Sometimes a body is not susceptible to the effects of a drug.

Niddah 30b

✑ In the world to come, the leaves of the trees when sucked or pressed will act as a light laxative, and aid digestion.

Talmud Jerushalmi *Shekalim* VI, 50

✑ Blood-letting may relieve asphyxiation or suffocation.

Yoma 84a

✑ Hot water is good for the sting of a thorn.

Avodah Zarah 28b

✑ Burning [cauterization] removes poison from a wound.

Avodah Zarah 28a

✑ Straightening infants' limbs through chiropractic methods was known in the talmudic era.

Shabbath 147b

ᴥᧇ Certain fruits [particularly species of apples] are highly laxative in their effect.

Talmud Jerushalmi *Maasroth* I, 48

ᴥᧇ It is naturally better to have an ulcer on the foot cut, and live, than to let it remain, and die.

Avodah Zarah 10b

ᴥᧇ Fish is healthful for the eyes.

Nedarim 54b

ᴥᧇ The egg of the edible locust, *Chargol*, was carried in the ear as a precaution against earache.

Shabbath VI, 10

ᴥᧇ A cupful of "charmed" drink is less dangerous to health than tepid water.

Baba Metziah 29b

ᴥᧇ Amputation does not mean that life cannot continue.

Chullin 48b

ᴥᧇ Scraping is a means of cleaning the teeth.

Kiddushin 24b

ᴥᧇ Cheerfulness and good health go hand in hand; the word *T'eiv* [Aramaic] which means to be bright and happy also means to feel well.

Daniel VI, 24

ᴥᧇ Collyrium [a red eye-salve] may heal the eye-sore, but dim the eyesight.

Shabbath 78a

ᴥᧇ Better than all the eye-salves in the world is a drop of cold water in the eye in the morning, and bathing hands and feet with warm water in the evening.

Shabbath 108b

◆§ Although wool and flax may not be woven together for clothing, the combination may be used as a bandage for wounds.

Tosefta Killaim V, 23

◆§ It is beneficial to walk, and not lie down, after eating fish, cress, and milk.

Baba Bathra 9a

◆§ Shock treatment was recommended for cases of convulsions and vertigo.

Tosefta Shabbath VII, 21

◆§ The eating of small fish increases man's vigor and vitality.

Berachoth 40a

◆§ Wine and vinegar will reduce swelling caused by a blow.

Shabbath 109a

◆§ A mile walk, or a little sleep, counteracts the effect of wine.

Sanhedrin 22b

◆§ *Itran,* a certain kind of resin, is good for megrim [pain on one side of the head].

Shabbath 90a

◆§ If after eating one has not taken some salt, and after drinking, some water, he will suffer from halitosis by day and choking by night. Drinking water after meals wards off intestinal troubles.

Berachoth 40a

◆§ It is possible to estimate the probable length of time needed for recovery from a wound.

Baba Kama 91a

◆§ Black cumin, although a poisonous drug, is good for heart trouble.

Berachoth 40a

◆§ Egyptian beer acts as a laxative on one suffering from constipation, and constipates the one who does not.

Pesachim 42b

◆§ A lung found overlapping the other need not necessarily be the result of an adhesion caused by a wound, but may be the natural means of healing set up by the body itself.

Chullin 46b

◆§ The proper treatment of an infant is bathing it in warm water followed by rubbing with oil.

Yoma 78b

◆§ The healing of fractures was aided by splints put around them.

Shabbath 53a

◆§ A grain of pepper was held in the mouth as a remedy for halitosis.

Shabbath 65a, *Kesuboth* 75a

◆§ A pregnant woman who has a morbid craving for food must be allowed to eat on *Yom Kippur* [Day of Atonement] until she feels restored.

Yoma VIII, 4

◆§ A form of massage, done on the marble floor of the bathhouse, was termed "breaking the bones."

Derech Eretz X

◆§ There are ten rulers [organs] which regulate the body's vitality.

Bamidbar Rabbah 14

◆§ Dates act as a laxative.

Gittin 70a

◆§ *Shamgaz* was an extremely pungent vinegar used as a restorative.

Avodah Zarah 12b

⋙ Ginger and cinnamon were used as remedies for toothache.
Shabbath 65a

⋙ As a remedy against scurvy, a clove of garlic soaked in olive oil and sprinkled with salt was found effective.
Yoma 84a

⋙ It is not wise to accustom oneself to take medicines, as they will eventually lose their potency.
Pesachim 113a

⋙ Proper diet is of paramount importance in the care of an invalid.
Berachoth 57b

⋙ For quotidian fever [recurring daily] large quantities of water are beneficial; for tertian fever [recurring every other day] blood-letting will help; for quartan fever [two days between paroxysms] eat red meat broiled on glowing coals, and drink diluted wine; for chronic fever, constant bathing plus complete immersion, and plenty of rest, is the prescription.
Gittin 67b

⋙ A piece of wheat-straw is utilized by the physician in cases of mouth hemorrhage. If it adheres to the blood, the flux is from the lungs, and is curable. If it does not adhere, it is from the liver, and there is no cure.
Gittin 69a

⋙ Unripe dates in vinegar will stop the flow of blood from a wound; the scraped root of cynodon and the parings of bramble will repair the flesh.
Avodah Zarah 28a

⋙ A remedy for catarrh is a boiled combination of gum-ammoniac, sweet galbanum, white honey, and white wine.
Gittin 69b

◄§ An abscess is the forerunner of fever; it should be lanced crosswise when softened.

Avodah Zarah 28a

◄§ Purple aloe mixed with wine may relieve and cure an abscess.

Gittin 69b

◄§ For palpitation of the heart, take three barley cakes soaked in curdled milk, followed by diluted wine.

Gittin 69b

◄§ For asthma, three wheat cakes soaked in honey, followed by undiluted wine.

Gittin 69b

◄§ Honey or other sweets relieve faintness due to fasting.

Yoma 83b

◄§ Mint to the quantity of three eggs; one of cumin; and one of sesame are good for angina pectoris. For indigestion—100 grains of long pepper in wine daily for three days. For tapeworm—one-quarter of a log [measure] of wine with a bay leaf.

Gittin 69b

◄§ Fresh poley in water for diarrhea, dried poley in water for constipation. An injection of three drops of oil of tar, three drops of leek-juice, and three drops of white wine is efficacious for hip disease.

Gittin 69b

◄§ Any remedy for earache should be lukewarm, neither hot nor cold, and the ear should be kept out of a draft.

Avodah Zarah 28b

◄§ Abdominal operations were performed after a sleeping potion had been administered.

Baba Metziah 83b

Joseph ben Meir ibn Zabara (Barcelona, 1140–1200) was learned in religion, astronomy, mathematics, logic, botany, geography, mineralogy, zoology, music, and poetry, as well as in medicine, physics, psychology, philosophy, and physiognomy. In addition to his many theological, philosophical, literary, and medical works (there are several quotations in this volume from his *Sefer Shaashu'im*), he wrote a remarkable poem called *"Battei Ha'Nephesh"* ("Seats of the Soul"), which is a model of succinctness and comprehensiveness. In rhymed prose, the preface tells of the four elements in nature, the four humors in the human body, the three vital forces which exist in the vegetable and animal kingdom, and the soul which puts man in an individual category.

This is followed by the poem in acrostic form, giving an exposition of the Creation, the four elements, the three functions of the brain, and the five senses. He then describes, all poetically and concisely, the muscles, teeth, windpipe, gullet, lungs, stomach, intestines, and liver. He traces the progress of the food along the alimentary canal from the time of its mastication until it is turned by the peculiar function of the liver into blood and the three humors: red bile, black bile, and phlegm; how the blood carried by the veins to the different parts of the body is assimilated into the body while the residue goes to the kidneys and thence to the bladder where it is transformed into urine. He points out the importance of urine for both diagnosis and prognosis; and follows the progress of the unassimilated food until it leaves the body—also showing the functions of the intestines, the liver, the stomach, the spleen, and the testicles.

He traces the structure of the heart and its importance in character, and concludes with an account of the pulse and its significance in the art of healing—followed by a religious prayer (with which he also begins his poem).

HYGIENE

Jewish Law, and its interpretation by the ancient sages, is concerned not only with the religious or moral aspect of behavior, but also with the physical. As stated in the Talmud (*Avodah Zarah* 20b) by Rabbi Pinchas ben Jair (who lived in the second half of the second century of the Common Era), "Physical cleanliness leads to spiritual purity"; and as Rabbi Hillel (first century) remarked (in *Va'Yikrah Rabbah* 34): "It is a religious duty to pay attention to hygiene. For if someone is paid to clean the statues of kings, how much more should I, who am created in the divine image and likeness, take care of my body!" It is also stated in the Talmud (*Shabbath* 50b): "One should wash his face, hands, and feet every day out of respect for his Maker."

When Rabbi Akiba (at the beginning of the second century) was imprisoned by the Romans (*Eirubin* 21b), Rabbi Joshua used to bring water to him daily. The jailer cut the water ration, as he believed the prisoner was utilizing it to soften the ground in order to dig a hole for escape. When Rabbi Akiba received the negligible remaining amount, although it was not even sufficient to quench his thirst, he would not let a drop pass his lips until he had washed his hands, as he considered cleanliness of paramount importance.

Neglect of one's health is regarded as a sin (*Nedarim* 10a). And this applies to communal as well as individual needs. Control of infectious diseases was instituted by biblical law (some 3,300 years ago, as prescribed in the Book of Leviticus, particularly chapters XIII, XIV, and XV), calling for isolation and quarantine as well as avoidance of crowds in time of plague or pestilence (*Baba Kama* 60b).

The unique immunity of Jewish families to the widespread plagues in the Dark Ages led to accusations on the part of their contemporaries that "black magic" was their talisman, yet nothing protected them except their observance of the laws of cleanliness which were incorporated into their religion.

The following quotations on the subject of hygiene are from these sources:

APPROXIMATE DATE	SOURCE
1st-5th Century, C.E.	*Mishnah* and *Talmud* (*Berachoth, Chullin, Terumoth, Me'ilah, Nedarim, Menachoth, Succah, Baba Metziah, Shabbath, Gittin, Kesuboth, Tamid, Yoma*)
2nd and 3rd Centuries, C.E.	*Tosefta* to *Shabbath*
1st and 2nd Centuries, C.E.	*Testament of Rabbi Eliezer the Great*
2nd Century, C.E.	*Ahvoth d'Rabbi Nathan*
2nd Century, C.E.	*Pirkei Rabbeinu HaKodesh*
1st-3rd Centuries, C.E.	*Midrashim* (*Midrash Rabbah, Shochar Tov, Kallah Rabbathi, Sifra, Derech Eretz, Yalkut Shimoni*—13th century collection of ancient *Midrashim*)
11th Century, C.E.	*Sefer Raziel HaMalach* (legendary origin traced to days of Adam and Noah)

Approximate Date	Source
12th Century, C.E.	Maimonides (Moses ben Maimon)
12th Century, C.E.	*Sefer Shaashu'im* (Joseph ben Meir ibn Zabara)

◦§ The first thing to be done upon arising in the morning is to wash the hands because of the germs which have gathered there during sleep.

Testament of Rabbi Eliezer the Great

◦§ If the eye could see all the invisible dangers lurking in the air [germs, etc.] no creature could exist . . . there are thousands to the left and tens of thousands to the right.

Berachoth 6

◦§ No matter what a person touches, he gets germs on his hands, but there are also beneficial bacteria which combat their effect.

Shochar Tov 17, Yalkut Shimoni Tehillim XLII, 6

◦§ Although the flesh of an animal bitten by a snake or a rabid dog may be permissible from the legal standpoint of Kashruth, it is forbidden from the standpoint of possible danger to health.

Chullin 58

◦§ The breath of a sick person contains germs of his illness.

Testament of Rabbi Eliezer the Great

◦§ All perspiration is poisonous except that of the face.

Talmud Jerushalmi Terumoth VIII, 5

◦§ Perspiration that is the result of sickness, bathing, and work is beneficial to the body.

Ahvoth d'Rab Nathan 41

◦§ The skin of a dead animal may have been contaminated by the disease from which it perished, and may infect one wearing shoes made from it.

Chullin 94

⋖§ The garments of a person afflicted with disease may transmit the disease to others.

Sifra VaYikrah XIII, 47

⋖§ Quarantine is essential for certain diseases, and for those who come in contact with the sufferers.

Talmud Jerushalmi *Shekalim* VIII, 5

⋖§ Croup is infectious, as is dysentery.

Me'ilah 17, *Nedarim* 41

⋖§ When infectious diseases are rampant, remain at home and do not venture out on the street.

Midrash Ruth 1

⋖§ Clothes worn during the day should not be worn during the night.

Menachoth 43

⋖§ One should never expectorate where people pass.

Derech Eretz Rabbah 10

⋖§ After bathing in warm water, one should rinse with cold water; one should not rinse with warm water after bathing in cold.

Kallah Rabbathi 10

⋖§ The human being cannot live without air; if he is confined in an airless place, he cannot breathe, and will die.

Sefer Raziel HaMalach 13

⋖§ The body is sustained by its blood, and the blood by air.

Midrash HaGadol B'reishith 4

⋖§ A house that is not sufficiently spacious is not fit to be called a dwelling.

Succah 3

⋖§ Unfortunate is the house whose windows open to the dark side [north].

Sh'moth Rabbah 14

◅§ Windows should be constructed wide on the interior and narrow on the exterior so as to draw in the air.

VaYikrah Rabbah 31

◅§ Sun-motes are therapeutic.

Nedarim 8

◅§ A clean, attractive, freshened-looking home revivifies an invalid.

Nedarim 40

◅§ Gnats, flies, and fleas are the curse of the earth.

B'reishith Rabbah 20

◅§ Because the tribe of Levi kept its houses clean and sanitary, it was not troubled with flies, gnats, fleas, vermin, all of which are dangerous [spread disease].

D'vahrim Rabbah

◅§ Every house should have a bathroom and toilet as well as a dining room.

Berachoth 8, Baba Metziah 107, Shabbath 25

◅§ Spices were used to freshen the air in a bathroom.

Berachoth 53

◅§ The hands should always be washed before leaving the toilet.

Pirkei Rabbeinu HaKodesh

◅§ One who wants to avoid intestinal disorders should not delay attending to the call of nature.

Gittin 70

◅§ Regularity in elimination is attainable by attending to the call of nature every morning and evening.

Berachoth 62

◅§ Proper environment has its effect on the sick. Rabbi Akiba visited one of his disciples who was ill, and swept and sprinkled the house, after which the student recovered.

Nedarim 40a

◆§ A pestilential disease known as *corrompement* in French may be due to bad food or foul air. If caused by foul air, all patients suffering from it will show the same symptoms; if caused by bad food, each individual patient will show specific symptoms.

Sefer Shaashu'im IX

◆§ Because of unsanitary conditions, all sickness comes from the air. If not for the unhealthful air, even those killed could be restored to life.

Baba Metziah 107a

◆§ Coins should not be placed in the mouth because they may have been touched by persons suffering from contagious diseases.

Maimonides *Yad HaChazakah, Rotzeach* XII, 4

◆§ There is a celestial sanitation department: the wind and the rains are the sweepers and sprinklers marching before the Lord.

Chullin 60a

◆§ The floors were sprinkled for cooling and perfuming the air.

Tosefta Shabbath XVI, 3

◆§ Some flies are dangerous because of their sting, while others transmit diseases.

Shabbath 121b, *Kesuboth* 77b

◆§ Rinse your cup before and after drinking from it.

Tamid 27b

◆§ Martha, daughter of Boethus, was walking in the street during the famine caused by the siege of Jerusalem. The dirt infected her foot, and caused her death.

Gittin 56a

◖§ Abstention from bathing is a privation.

Yoma 77a

◖§ The washing of the hands before a meal was introduced for the sake of uniformity, to make it a habit.

Chullin 106a

◖§ Those who eat food with unwashed hands endanger their health because they are full of dangerous germs.

Yoma 77b

◖§ The face, hands, and feet should be washed every day.

Shabbath 50b

◖§ He who washes his face and does not dry it well, will get a scab [eruption].

Shabbath 113b

◖§ Uncleanliness of the head may. lead to blindness; uncleanliness of clothes may lead to scabs which may result in idiocy; uncleanliness of the body may lead to skin diseases.

Nedarim 81a

◖§ An unwashed hand touching the nose may generate a polypus; an unwashed hand touching the ear may cause deafness; an unwashed hand touching the eye may cause blindness, and deserves to be cut off.

Shabbath 108b, 109a

◖§ There is certain water which is salubrious to drink, but not good for washing; other water which is good for washing, but not for drinking. Well-water is good for both purposes.

Shochar Tov II, 23

◖§ The water of the Pool of Siloah [near Jerusalem] is pure and sweet; that of the Euphrates is turbid and foul.

Introduction to *Eichah Rabbah*

◖§ More people died from drinking the water of the Euphrates than were killed by Nebuchadnezzar; hence the open-

ing verse of Psalm CXXXVII: "By [because of] the waters of
Babylon we wept . . ."

Shochar Tov 137

◅§ Samuel, well-versed in medicine, drank only boiled water.

Talmud Jerushalmi *Terumoth* VIII, 5

13

DIET

Health is largely dependent on diet, and it is a religious duty to keep healthy, in line with the biblical command: "And you shall guard your souls [bodies]" . . . so as to be a complete human being and so as to serve the Maker properly and fully "with all one's heart, with all one's soul [body, life], and with all one's might."

Throughout biblical, talmudic, midrashic, and later literature, emphasis is placed on rules of health, hygiene, and diet. In this treasury of Jewish curiosities, the reader will frequently encounter quotations from Maimonides. No individual since the days of the *Tannaim* and *Amoraim* possessed the keen analytical intellect and general all-round knowledge and ability of this genius of whom it was so aptly said: "From Moses [the Law-giver at Sinai] to Moses [the Law-expounder], there arose none like unto Moses."

A brief outline of his life and accomplishments is therefore presented here.

Moses ben Maimon (Moses Maimonides), referred to as the *Rambam* from the Hebrew initials of his name, was born in

Cordova, Spain, on March 30, 1135. Descended from a long line of distinguished scholars, his ancestry traceable to Judah ha-Nasi, compiler of the *Mishnah,* and consequently to King David, he was known in non-Jewish circles as "the Jewish Aristotle" because of his profound philosophical prowess and his earnest attempts to reconcile Aristotelian philosophy with Judaism.

His father, Maimon ben Joseph, was a learned Talmudist, astronomer, and mathematician, and was his principal teacher in his early years. As a youth, Moses studied Talmud, logic, metaphysics, mathematics, astronomy, natural sciences, and medicine. When he was thirteen years of age, Cordova was captured by the fanatical Mohammedan Almohades, and Moses and his family—faced with the choice of embracing Islam, death, or exile—chose the latter. For twelve years they led a nomadic existence, wandering throughout Spain. In the year 1160 they went to Fez, North Africa, but after living there precariously for five years, they journeyed to Acre, Jerusalem, and finally to Fostat (Cairo) where they settled.

There Moses, disdaining to earn his livelihood through religion, as he considered it a sin "to utilize the words of the Torah as a spade with which to dig" (*Pirkei Ahvoth* IV, 5), adopted the medical profession. After several years of practice, his authority in medical matters was firmly established, and he was appointed private physician to Saladin's vizier, who recommended him to the royal family.

Maimonides declined a similar position offered to him by Richard the Lion-Hearted (Richard I of England) because of the persecution and massacre of the Jews of York and other English towns during his reign.

It was the practice of Maimonides to begin his therapy with a simple treatment—endeavoring *to cure by a prescribed diet* before administering drugs.

In the year 1158, Maimonides composed a *Treatise on the Jewish Religion,* and shortly thereafter a book on terms of logic. In 1168, he completed his *Commentary on the Mishnah,* a masterpiece of lucidity, knowledge, and comprehensiveness, one of whose important sections is the *Shemonah Perakim, (Eight Chapters)*, a remarkable philosophical and ethical synthesis of Judaism and Hellenism. It contains among other valuable material his "Thirteen Articles of Faith"—a concise yet comprehensive creed of Jewish belief recited daily to this very day by the Orthodox.

Twelve years later he issued his fourteen-volume compendium of The Talmud—*Mishneh Torah, Yad ha-Chazakah*—(Repetition of The Law—The Strong Hand)—a complete codification of biblical and rabbinical law and religion, prefaced with an outline known as *Sefer ha-Mitzvoth* (The Book of Commandments), tracing all of the 613 cardinal commandments to sources in the Pentateuch.

In 1190 he published his *Moreh Nebuchim (Guide for the Perplexed)* to harmonize Judaism with Aristotelian philosophy and to unify reason and faith, which he believed taught one truth.

Moses Maimonides wrote many additional books on philosophy, theology, Jewish Law, medicine, and astronomy, and conducted considerable correspondence with Jewish leaders in many lands, answering their questions on religious law and ritual.

An idea as to his multitudinous activities may be gained from this excerpt from a letter written to Samuel ben Judah ibn Tibbon, who translated the *Guide for the Perplexed* from its Arabic original into Hebrew. This letter is dated September 30, 1199, at Cairo:

"I dwell at Mizr [Fostat] and the Sultan resides at Kahira [Cairo]; these two places are two Sabbath days' journey (about three miles) distant from each other. My duties to the Sultan are very heavy. I am obliged to visit him every day, early in the morning; and when he or any of his children, or any of the inmates of his harem are indisposed, I dare not quit Kahira, but must stay during

*the greater part of the day in the palace. It also frequently
happens that one or two royal officers fall sick, and I must
attend to their healing. Hence, as a rule, I repair to Kahira very early in the day, and even if nothing unusual
happens, I do not return to Mizr until the afternoon.
Then I am almost dying with hunger ... I find the ante-
chambers filled with people, both Jews and non-Jews,
nobles and common people, judges and bailiffs, friends
and foes—a mixed multitude who await the time of my
return.*

*"I dismount from my animal, wash my hands, go forth
to my patients, and entreat them to bear with me while I
partake of some slight refreshment, the only meal I take
in the twenty-four hours. Then I go forth to attend to my
patients, and write prescriptions and directions for their
various ailments. Patients go in and out until nightfall,
and sometimes even, I solemnly assure you, until two hours
or more in the night. I converse with and prescribe for
them while lying down from sheer fatigue; and when night
falls, I am so exhausted that I can scarcely speak.*

*"In consequence of this, no Israelite can have any pri-
vate interview with me, except on the Sabbath. On that
day, the whole congregation—or at least the majority of
the members—come to me after the morning service, when
I instruct them as to their proceeding during the whole
week; we study together a little until noon, when they de-
part. Some of them return, and read with me after the
afternoon prayers until evening prayers. In this manner I
spend that day.*

*"I have related to you only a part of what you would
see if you were to visit me."*

Moses ben Maimon passed away in Cairo on December 13,
1204, mourned by Jew and non-Jew alike. He was buried in
Tiberias, in the Holy Land.

The *Rambam* is a recognized authority on Jewish Law, and

his influence on Jewish thought has been profound and lasting. His praises were sung by the Arabic poet and cadi, Al-Sa'id ibn Surat al-Mulk, in the following ecstatic manner:

> "Galen's art heals only the body,
> But Abu Imram's [Maimonides'] the body and the soul.
> With his wisdom he could heal the sickness of ignorance.
> Were the moon to submit to his art,
> He would deliver her of her spots at the time of the full moon,
> Cure her of her periodic defects,
> And at the time of her conjunction save her from waning."

Maimonides' "Daily Prayer of a Physician" could well become the stand-by of every individual taking the Oath of Hippocrates:

> "I begin once more my daily work. Be Thou with me, Almighty Father of Mercy, in all my efforts to heal the sick. For without Thee, man is but a helpless creature. Grant that I may be filled with love for my art and for my fellowmen. May the thirst for gain and the desire for fame be far from my heart. For these are the enemies of pity and the ministers of hate. Grant that I may be able to devote myself, body and soul, to Thy children who suffer from pain.
>
> "Preserve my strength, that I may be able to restore the strength of the rich and the poor, the good and the bad, the friend and the foe. Let me see in the sufferer the man alone. When wiser men teach me, let me be humble to learn; for the mind of man is so puny, and the art of healing is so vast. But when fools are ready to advise me or to find fault with me, let me not listen to their folly. Let me be intent upon one thing, O Father of Mercy, to be always merciful to Thy suffering children.
>
> "May there never rise in me the notion that I know

enough, but give me strength and leisure and zeal to en-
large my knowledge. Our work is great, and the mind of
man presses forward forever. Thou has chosen me in Thy
grace, to watch over the life and death of Thy creatures.
I am about to fulfill my duties. Guide me in this im-
mense work so that it may be of avail."

The following sources are quoted—with approximate dates
of their origin:

Approximate Date	Source
1st-5th Century, C.E.	*Mishnah* and *Talmud* (*Taanith, Yoma, Pesachim, Succah, Berachoth, Shabbath, Kesuboth, Gittin, Niddah, Chullin, Baba Kama, Avoda Zarah, Nedarim, Sanhedrin, Yebamoth, Sota, Eirubin, Baba Bathra*)
1st-3rd Centuries, C.E.	*Midrashim* (*Eichoh Rabbah, Temurah, Ruth Rabbah, Sh'moth Rabbah, Midrash B'reishith, Tanchuma, Yalkut Shimoni*—13th century collection of ancient *Midrashim*)
2nd and 3rd Centuries, C.E.	*Tosefta, Sifra*
2nd Century, C.E.	Ben Sira
11th Century, C.E.	*Sefer Raziel ha-Malach* (legendary origin traced to days of Adam and Noah)
12th Century, C.E.	Maimonides (Moses ben Maimon)
12th Century, C.E.	*Sefer Shaashu'im* (Joseph ben Meir ibn Zabara)
13th Century, C.E.	*Zohar* (authorship attributed to Simeon ben Yochai of the 2nd century)

꙳ He who denies himself proper food is a sinner.

Taanith 11

꙳ Fasting weakens the body and blackens the teeth.

Eichah Rabbah 1, *Chagigah* 22, *Nazir* 52

꙳ Crying drives away the appetite.

Eichah Rabbah 1

꙳ Eating to satiety brings sleep.

Yoma 18

꙳ Children eat more than adults because they need food for both sustenance and growth.

Sefer Shaashu'im IX

꙳ Food should be appetizing as well as nourishing.

Yoma 74

꙳ Rabbi Judah, either because of feeble health or fastidiousness of diet, ate only during the daytime, and never at night.

Talmud Jerushalmi *Pesachim* X, 1

꙳ The administrator of King Agrippa ate only one meal a day.

Succah 27

꙳ Talking while eating may cause choking, as may eating while lying on one's back or reclining to one's right.

Taanith 5, *Pesachim* 108

꙳ Cutting one's food and eating it is better than biting off pieces and swallowing them.

Berachoth 74

꙳ One should not bite off a piece of food and return either it or the remaining portion to the dish, or give it to someone else—from the standpoint of both etiquette and health.

Tosefta Berachoth 85

❧ One should eat to live, as the body cannot live without food.

Midrash Terumah

❧ Overeating causes sickness.

Ben Sira 37

❧ Food that is tempting is easily digested.

Sefer Raziel HaMalach 13

❧ A meal without soup is no meal.

Berachoth 44

❧ Up to the age of forty, solid foods are better than liquids [foods which require no chewing] and vice versa thereafter.

Shabbath 152

❧ Sweets are best after a meal.

Ruth Rabbah III, 7

❧ Dates, roasted grains, and nuts are good for dessert.

Pesachim 119, *Berachoth* 17

❧ A change of diet leads to bowel diseases.

Kesuboth 110b

❧ A properly balanced diet, avoidance of overeating, and attention to the calls of nature on time, prevent intestinal trouble.

Gittin 70

❧ A desire for food does not always indicate that the patient is on the road to recovery.

Sefer Shaashu'im VIII

❧ Sickness may be caused by withholding desired food or drink [making the mouth water].

Sh'moth Rabbah 16

❧ More people die from overeating than from hunger.

Shabbath 33a

◄§ Eat a third of your capacity, drink a third, and leave the remaining third empty. Then if you become angry, there is room for the stomach to expand.

Gittin 70a

◄§ The person who overeats invites sickness.

Gittin 70a

◄§ One should not eat meat twice a day.

Yoma 75

◄§ Venison is the easiest flesh to digest.

Yalkut Shimoni Shalach 743

◄§ Salt sweetens meat.

Berachoth 5

◄§ Chewing food is essential to health.

Niddah 65a, *Shabbath* 152a

◄§ Of all edibles, only water and salt are not included in the category of food [nourishment].

Berachoth 35b

◄§ One should not eat meat unless he has a special appetite for it.

Chullin 84a

◄§ Weight-reducing may give a feeling of physical comfort, but this is not to be confused with the wasting-away that results from consumption.

Sifra B'chukothei 2, IV

The value of calcium in the diet is evident from the expression used in Genesis XLIX, 12: "From milk comes the whiteness of teeth."

◄§ Bread satisfies, but does not exhilarate.

Berachoth 35b

⋘ Bread with salt in the morning and plenty of water will banish all illnesses.

Baba Kama 92b

⋘ Meal regulation is important to health: eat when hungry, drink when thirsty.

Berachoth 62b

⋘ Eating or drinking while standing shatters man's body.

Gittin 70a

⋘ When traveling, one should eat sparingly, as otherwise disorder of the bowels may result.

Taanith 10b

⋘ Small fish in brine are good to eat after fasting.

Avodah Zarah 29a

⋘ Fish is bad for those suffering from eye ailments, but wholesome after they recover.

Nedarim 54

⋘ The danger of eating certain sea-food out of season was known in talmudic times: Shibbuta, a kind of mullet, may cause leprosy in the month of Nissan (spring).

Pesachim 112b

⋘ Before the Deluge, human beings were vegetarians.

Sanhedrin 59b

⋘ Eggs and milk may replace mother's milk to sustain a child's health.

Yebamoth 42b

⋘ Cheese that is one day old is most healthful.

Shabbath 134

⋘ Milk from a kosher animal is white, from a non-kosher one, greenish; the former will curdle into cheese, the latter will not.

Avodah Zarah 35

◄§ The properties of milk whiten teeth [calcium content].
Midrash B'reishith XLIX, 12

◄§ Bright teeth come from drinking milk.
Eichah Rabbah

◄§ Warm milk from morning to night is a remedy for sickness which causes coughing and spitting blood.
Kesuboth 60, *Baba Kama* 80, Talmud Jerushalmi *Sotah* IX, 6

◄§ Raw vegetables should not be eaten in the early morning, as they then cause halitosis.
Berachoth 44b

◄§ Vegetables eaten raw cause pallor.
Berachoth 44b

◄§ It is better to eat vegetables and not fear creditors, than to eat duck and have to hide from them.
Pesachim 114a

◄§ Raw [insufficiently cooked] beets can kill a healthy man.
Eirubin 28b

◄§ Certain herbs stimulate the appetite.
Shabbath 140b

◄§ Garlic, cucumbers, onions, and leek are bad for a pregnant and nursing woman and for the child.
Sifra B'haalothcha

◄§ Peeled garlic, peeled onions, or shelled eggs left exposed overnight become injurious.
Niddah 17a

◄§ Eating lentils once in thirty days keeps croup away; but eating them daily causes halitosis.
Berachoth 40a

◄§ Sweet apples are a remedy for almost every ailment.
Zohar III, 74

◆§ Abba Saul could tell from the condition of bones in a grave the kind of diet indulged in by their owner before his demise.

Niddah 24

◆§ Wine drunk during a meal will not intoxicate, but wine drunk after a meal will.

Talmud Jerushalmi *Pesachim* X, 6

◆§ The aftermath of a drunkard's joy during drinking wine is sorrow; when the exhilarating effects of the wine vanish, grief enters.

Tanchuma Sh'mini

◆§ Breakfast is the most important meal of the day, as it has thirteen advantages: it protects from heat, cold, wind, evil spirits; brightens the intellect of the fool; helps one win a lawsuit; helps one learn, helps one teach; makes his words listened to and retained by his listeners; his flesh does not give excessive heat [causing him to perspire needlessly]; makes him have affection for his wife and not lust after a strange woman; and it also kills intestinal parasites. To these, some add—it removes jealousy and substitutes love.

Baba Bathra 107b

◆§ Foods of laxative effect—such as grapes, figs, mulberries, pears, melons, certain species of cucumbers and melopepons should be eaten at the beginning of a meal, and one should wait a bit before eating the regular food thereafter. Foods which are binding, such as pomegranates, quinces, apples, should be eaten at the conclusion of the meal.

If the menu contains both fowl and beef, the fowl should be eaten first; if eggs and fowl, the eggs should be eaten first; lean and fat meat—the lean first—the general rule being that the lighter food should always precede the heavier.

In the summer, cool foods should be eaten, and the use of spices should be avoided; in the winter, warm foods should be eaten, and they may be liberally spiced if desired.

Certain foods are particularly injurious to the system—such as large, salted, old fish; stale, salted cheese; certain species of mushrooms; aged, salted meat; unfermented wine; foods which have become stale and odoriferous; and all foods which have a vile odor or are particularly bitter. They are all like poison to the body.

There are other foods which while not dangerous, are not especially wholesome, and these should be eaten only in moderation and infrequently—such as large fish, old cheese, milk more than twenty-four hours old, flesh of a large bull or he-goat, beans, lentils, peas, barley-bread, mustard, radish, unleavened bread [matzoth], cabbage, leek, onions. These should be eaten sparingly, and only in the winter. Pumpkins and similar gourds should be eaten only in the summer.

Figs, grapes, and nuts are exceptionally wholesome, either fresh or dried. Unripe fruits are like a sword piercing the body. Honey and wine are bad for youngsters, but excellent for the aged, particularly in winter time. During the summer a normal diet should be about two-thirds of what is eaten during the winter.

The individual who is wise controls his appetite, and refrains from eating any food which is harmful unless it is required for curative purposes.

Regular, punctual elimination is desirable and essential for well-being. Constipation is a warning of approaching serious ailments. As long as a man works hard, does not eat to his full capacity, as long as his eliminative organs function smoothly and properly, no ailment will visit him, and his strength will remain and increase. But he who sits idle, takes no exercise, and is constipated, although he may eat good food and take medicinal precautions, will suffer pain all his life and his strength will fade. Gluttony is as deadly as poison, and is the basis of most illness; for most diseases are caused either by improper food or eating to excess.

Maimonides, *Yad HaChazakah, Hilchoth Dei'oth* IV, 6-15

14

THE BIBLE

To include all of the curiosities in Sacred Scripture would require not one chapter, not one book, but many volumes. There is such a limitless expanse of subject matter that many lifetimes of many scholars would fail to encompass the untold millions of interpretations to be derived from each sentence, each phrase, each word. Each letter of the Bible, too, has its manifold meanings.

For instance, in four words one letter in each is suspended above the line in the Scrolls of the Bible. In Judges XVIII, 30, the name "Menashe" has the "n" (Hebrew "noon") suspended, undoubtedly as a token of reverence for "Moses," as the Hebrew letter "n" was added to "Moshe" (Moses) to make it read "Menashe." This verse refers to the wickedness of Jonathan, son of Gershom (who was a son of Moses)—and since the tribe of Menashe had an unsavory reputation anyhow, one more culprit was assigned to it. The other three words with suspended letters are in Psalm LXXX, 14, and Job XXXVIII, 13, 15.

We find that what is probably the shortest prayer ever recorded is in the Bible—the plea of Moses for the restoration of health to his sister, Miriam (Numbers XII, 13): "O God! Heal her, I beseech Thee!" (In Hebrew, this sentence consists of merely five short words, totaling a mere 11 letters!)

Then again we find that the longest word in the Bible—*Mahershalalchashbaz* (Isaiah VIII, 3) is actually a coined term consisting of four Hebrew words meaning "speedy booty, sudden spoils," reminiscent of the English word, *antidisestablishmentarianism* and the German *Constantinopolitanischerdudelsackpfeifermachergesellschaft,* meaning "an association of Constantinople bagpipe players."

Jacob ben Asher of the 13th/14th century points out that the commandment to observe *Shabbath* (the Sabbath) in Exodus XX, 8-11, refers to the 7th day of the week; that it begins with the 7th letter of the Hebrew alphabet ("Zahyin"); that it appears in the 7th verse of the Ten Commandments; and that it proclaims rest for 7 classes of creatures.

It is quite evident, therefore, that it is humanly impossible to cull from the sea of the Bible a complete collection of oddities cast up by its waves. Yet no collection of curiosities could be complete without a category on the Bible, and for this reason some miscellaneous items have been included, quoted from the following sources:

Approximate Date	Source
1st-5th Centuries, C.E.	*Mishnah* and *Talmud* (*Sotah, Megillah*)
1st-3rd Centuries, C.E.	*Midrashim* (*Midrash Rabbah*)

THE FIVE BOOKS of Moses contain 304,825 letters, as follows:

Genesis	78,084
Exodus	63,529
Leviticus	44,790
Numbers	63,530
Deuteronomy	54,892

The letter occurring most frequently is *Yood* (tenth in the alphabet)—31,530 times; the one used least is the Final *Phai*—834 times.

*   *   *

All of the letters of the Hebrew alphabet are contained in verse 13 of Chapter III of the Book of Esther.

*   *   *

The word *mishteh* (feast, or banquet) occurs twenty times in the Book of Esther, equal to the total number of times it occurs in the rest of the Scriptures (Old Testament).

*   *   *

The Book of Esther contains the longest biblical verse—Chapter VIII, verse 9—consisting of 43 words in Hebrew. The shortest verses in the Bible are I Chronicles I, 1—"Adam, Seth, Enosh"—and I Chronicles I, 25—"Eber, Peleg, R'u"—each consisting of three words totaling nine letters. There are also other three-word sentences in other Books of the Bible (as, for instance, Genesis XLIII, 1 and XLVI, 23) but they have more than nine letters.

*   *   *

The smallest chapter of the Bible is Psalm CXVII, and the longest is Psalm CXIX.

*   *   *

According to the *Dictionary of Phrase and Fable* by E. C. Brewer, LL.D., the English version of the Old Testament contains 929 chapters, 23,214 verses, 592,439 words, and 2,728,800 letters. The word *and* occurs 35,543 times.

*   *   *

Various English editions of the Bible have been given nicknames because of peculiar typographical errors:

The Idle Bible—in which "the idole shepherd" (meaning "foolish") is printed idle *(Zechariah XI, 17).*

The Bug Bible—Psalm XCI, 5: "Thou shalt not be afraid of buggies [bogies] by night," is printed bugges.

The Treacle Bible—in which the word balm *is translated as "treacle."*

The Wicked Bible—the word not *is omitted from one of the Ten Commandments, rendering it: "Thou shalt commit adultery."*

The Printers' Bible—in which King David complains that the "printers" (instead of "princes") "have persecuted me." (Psalm CXIX, 161)

*   *   *

There are certain words or word-forms occurring only once each in the Scriptures, called *Hapax Legomena*. There are 414 absolute ones in the 39 books of the Old Testament, plus an additional 887 of other unique forms which, however, are traceable to familiar roots or stems. The Books of Joshua, Obadiah, and Haggai are the only ones not having any, whereas the most occur in Isaiah and Job—60 in each.

◈§ The first word of the Book of Lamentations is *Eichah*, "woe," for it deals with the woes of Israel when it went into exile. And its letters represent the reasons for the exile. The *Aleph* (1) symbolizes the denial of the Almighty, Who is One; the *Yood* (10) symbolizes denial of the Ten Commandments; the *Chaf* (20) symbolizes denial of circumcision, which law was given after twenty generations from Adam (to Abraham); and the *Hai* (5) symbolizes denial of the Five Books of Moses [the Torah].

Eichah Rabbathi I, 1

◈§ The Torah Scroll given to Moses by the Almighty was composed of white fire, written upon with black fire, sealed with fire, and swathed with bands of fire.

D'vahrim Rabbah 3

ᴥᕂ According to one opinion, the engraving on the Two Tablets was in a square; the Ten Commandments were engraved four times on each side, thus readable no matter how turned.

Talmud Jerushalmi *Sotah* VIII, 22

ᴥᕂ The letter *Sahmech* [which is like a circle surrounded by space] was suspended in the Ten Commandments on the Two Tablets by a miracle.

Megillah 2b

ᴥᕂ The first time the letter *Sahmech* (fifteenth letter of the Hebrew alphabet) occurs in the Bible is in Genesis, II, 21. For when woman was created, temptation [*Satan*—which begins with a *sin*—the same sound as *Sahmech* and interchangeable therewith] came into the world.

B'reishith Rabbah 17

15

HOSPITALITY

Hospitality is considered a *mitzvah* (religious duty or commandment). Hence according to biblical law, even strangers are protected against oppression and are assured of the same treatment accorded to natives and citizens, even being invited to participate in the festivals and to share in the tithe distributed among the poor. (Exodus XXIII, 9, Leviticus XIX, 34, Deuteronomy XVI, 14, XXV, 19).

It is good manners and proper procedure to set food and drink before one who has come from a journey before anything else is done (*Va'Yikra Rabbah* 34). In only one instance was a breach of hospitality lauded rather than condemned—in the case of Jael who slew Sisera (Judges IV, 18-21, V, 24-27) after having given him food and drink—because of the tyrannical persecution endured by her compatriots at the hands of the Canaanites. Lot (Genesis XIX, 1-8) risked his life and the honor of his daughters rather than transgress the laws of hospitality. Paragons of hospitality were Abraham and Job, and the *Midrashim* are replete with legends as to the lengths to which they went. And Ben Sira (Wisdom of Sirach) devotes

180

many verses to the duties of the host and guest toward each other. It is pointed out in the Talmud, however (*Pesachim* 49a), that the guest should not take undue advantage of hospitality; the parasite who took every opportunity to indulge in meals at other people's homes was denounced and despised.

The quotations are from the following sources:

APPROXIMATE DATE	SOURCE
1st-5th Centuries, C.E.	*Mishnah* and *Talmud* (*Shabbath, Taanith, Berachoth, Baba Bathra, Derech Eretz Zuta, Kiddushin, Pesachim*)
1st-3rd Centuries, C.E.	*Midrashim* (*Midrash Rabbah, Yalkut Shimoni*—13th century collection of ancient *Midrashim*)
12th/13th Century, C.E.	*Sefer Chassidim* (Judah ben Samuel of Regensburg)

◄§ Hospitality to strangers [guests] is even more meritorious than receiving the glory of the *Shechinah* (Divine Presence).

Shabbath 127a

◄§ The doors of the houses of Abraham and Job were open at all four corners, so that strangers approaching from any direction might find ready access.

B'reishith Rabbah 58, 7; *Yalkut Job* 917

◄§ Job always had forty tables spread for travelers and twelve for widows.

Yalkut Job 917

◄§ Rab Huna, when about to take his meal, would open his door and say: "Anyone who is hungry may come in and eat."

Taanith 20b

◄§ It is meritorious to sit long at the table so as to give an opportunity for the belated poor to come in and partake of the meal.

Berachoth 54b

◄§ In Jerusalem, it was customary to display a flag at the door to indicate that the meal was ready and anyone might enter and eat.

Baba Bathra 93b

◄§ It is the duty of the host to be cheerful during meals so as to make guests feel comfortable and at home.

Derech Eretz Zuta 9

◄§ The guest should not be watched too attentively at the table, as it may embarrass him and he will refrain from eating fully.

Sefer Chassidim 105

◄§ It is commendable for the host himself to serve at the table, to show his willingness to satisfy his guests.

Kiddushin 32b

◄§ It is the duty of the guest to comply with all of his host's requests.

Pesachim 86b

◄§ It was the custom in Jerusalem to place all of the courses on the table at once, so that the fastidious guest might choose anything he desired, and not be compelled to eat something he did not like.

Eichah Rabbah IV, 4

◄§ The guest was expected to leave a little food in his plate to show that he had had more than enough. But if the host asked him to finish his portion, he did not have to leave any in the plate.

Sefer Chassidim 870-878, 883

16

MISCELLANY

Miscellaneous Oddities

This is a group of items which for one reason or another do not fit specifically into any special category but are presented here for their general interest. Sources of quotations from ancient Hebrew literature are as follows:

APPROXIMATE DATE	SOURCE
1st-5th Centuries, C.E.	*Mishnah* and *Talmud* (*Terumoth, Baba Bathrah, Berachoth, Sanhedrin, Shabbath, Peah, Kesuboth, Beitzah, Sotah, Killaim, Chagigah, Niddah, Avodah Zarah, Arakhin, Yoma, Yebamoth, Sheviith, Gittin, Nedarim, Kiddushin, Shevuoth, Succah, Horayoth, Bechoroth, Pesachim, Eirubin, Rosh Hashanah, Taanith, Ahvoth*)
2nd Century, C.E.	*Ahvoth d'Rab Nathan*
2nd Century, C.E.	*Tosefta*

APPROXIMATE DATE   SOURCE
1st-3rd Century, C.E.   *Midrashim (Yalkut Shimoni*—13th
                                              century collection of ancient
                                              *Midrashim,   Pesikta,   Midrash
                                              Rabbah)*

ONE OF THE main pillars of the Jewish faith consists of the Dietary Laws, mentioned in the Bible some 3,500 years ago, and explained and codified in the Talmud. They prohibit, among other things, the eating of milk and meat together, and provide for a specified interval of time to elapse after the eating of meat, before taking milk or milk products. On February 28, 1935, the New York *American* printed the statement of a group of British medical men that "Drinking milk within two hours after eating meat is highly detrimental to the digestive system."

The *Shamir,* one of the ten marvels created at twilight before the first Sabbath, was a unique wonder which ceased to exist after the destruction of the Temple. The size of a grain of barley, it could split the hardest substance. Iron cracked open when in its vicinity. The only way it could be preserved was by wrapping it in spongy balls of wool and placing it in a lead box filled with barley bran. With the aid of the Shamir, Moses inscribed the names of the tribes on the precious stones in the High Priest's breastplate, and Solomon used it for splitting the stones used in constructing the Temple, as metal implements were prohibited. Opinions differ among the sages as to whether the *Shamir* was of animal, vegetable, mineral, or chemical nature.

(From the Talmud and *Midrashim*)

Remarkable examples of brevity are contained in two paragraphs in the Prayer Book. The fifth stanza of *Ma'oz Tzur,* a hymn forming part of the *Chanukah* ceremony, gives the complete story of the Maccabean struggle against the Syrio-Greeks and the miracle of the oil, in a mere twenty-four words. In 52 words, a prayer for *Purim* gives the full story of the Book of Esther which in the original consists of 167 verses, making five chapters.

❧ Wherever an Egyptian fled [at the Red Sea], the sea ran against him and submerged him.

Yalkut Sh'moth 237

Simplification of regulations into generic commandments was indulged in by various individuals, according to the Talmud (*Makkoth* 24a): 613 commandments were given to Moses on Mount Sinai; King David reduced them to eleven (Psalm XV); Isaiah to six (Isaiah XXXIII, 15); Micah to three (Micah VI, 8); Isaiah again to two (Isaiah LVI, 1); and Amos (V, 6) to one—"Seek Me and live." This is reminiscent of the statement of Hillel, who was asked to give the essence of the Torah, and answered: "What is hateful to you, do not do to your fellowman . . . The rest is commentary."

❧ One who has no work to do should indulge in a hobby, because idleness leads to idiocy.

Ahvoth d'Rab Nathan 11

The *Magen David* (Shield of David) is a hexagram formed by the combination of two equilateral triangles. No mention is made of it in the Talmud, its earliest use as a Jewish symbol probably being its appearance on a third-century tombstone in Tarentum, Italy. From about the sixteenth century on, it superseded the *Menorah* (Candelabrum) as the symbolical ornament of Judaism, and it has been adopted as the official emblem on the flag of the State of Israel. Many religious and mystic reasons have been advanced for its significance, one of them stating that the middle hexagon represents the Sabbath, the six corners representing the six other days of the week. In cabala, it signifies the link between the material world and the supernatural world with its forces.

∾§ A monument was once erected to a dog that had saved some human lives. Some shepherds had curdled milk for their meal, and in their absence a serpent had eaten of it, instilling poison into it. The dog, which had witnessed the act, began to bark when the shepherds returned and proceeded to eat of it, disregarding his warning. The dog there upon hastened to consume all that was in the dish, and fell down dead, having thus saved his masters' lives. The shepherds buried the faithful hound, and erected "The Dog's Monument" to him.

Pesikta B'shallach 79, Talmud Jerushalmi *Terumoth* VIII, 46

One of the most notorious forgeries in history, and despite its proved falsehood still an accepted weapon of many anti-Semitic groups, is *The Protocols of the Elders of Zion,* published in Russia in 1905. It purports to give reports of an alleged international Jewish congress aimed at Jewish world domination. Many eminent authorities have presented conclusive evidence to show that it is a complete fabrication.

∾§ Among the seven attributes taken away from Adam and his descendants after his expulsion from the Garden of Eden were celestial beauty, length of life, and high stature.

B'reishith Rabbah 12

Although *matzoth* (unleavened wafers) are made of wheat flour, they may also be made of rye, barley, spelt, or oats. In any event, the only other ingredient is water, and the dough is kneaded hastily and baked immediately, so as to prevent any fermentation.

∾§ Even one retired or exempt from taxes is bound to contribute toward the maintenance of local institutions.

Baba Bathra 55a

∾§ One is not permitted to eat until he has fed his animals.

Berachoth 40a

The ashes of the Red Heifer (*Parah Adumah*) which were utilized in a purification ritual in ancient Israel, are claimed by some scientists to have had a disinfectant power, because cedar-wood and hyssop, both of which have medicinal properties, were burned together with the heifer and blended with its ashes. A peculiar point of Jewish Law is involved in its use: it purified the unclean yet rendered unclean those who handled it.

◅§ Fifth columnists infiltrating a land will cause its downfall.

Sanhedrin 104a

◅§ Weapons, armaments, and essential materials may not be sold to a real or a potential enemy.

Tosefta Avodah Zarah II

The word *mazel* ("luck") occurs only once throughout Sacred Scriptures, and in its plural form—in II Kings, XXIII, 5, where it refers to constellations or signs of the Zodiac. The exclamation, *Mazel Tov* ("Good Luck" or "Congratulations"), is derived from it.

◅§ The kindling-wood in Jerusalem was of the cinnamon tree.

Shabbath 63a

◅§ Foliage of the cinnamon-tree was food for goats.

Talmud Jerushalmi *Peah* VII, 20

Shechita, the ritual method of slaughtering animals for food, is the most humane, as it induces most rapidly and reliably complete anemia of the brain with loss of consciousness and sensation, and because the cutting of the tissues with the extremely sharp and perfect blade is in itself painless. Dr. David I. Macht, American physiologist and pharmacologist, studied the effect of arteriotomy (severing the vessels of the throat) with that of other methods of slaughter on toxicity of both blood and muscle tissues. He proved that when animals were killed by bleeding after arteriotomy, muscle extracts studied by special pharmacological methods were much less toxic than those obtained from animals killed by a blow on the head or other injury to the brain, by general anesthetic, by the inhalation of poison gases, or by electrocution. Meat from *Shechita* remains fresh longer, is more resistant to putrefaction and formation of ptomaines and other poisonous substances, and forms an unfavorable culture medium for bacteria.

* * *

The Kingdom of the *Chazars* in the Crimea had separate judges for adherents of Judaism, Christianity, and Mohammedanism. In the middle of the eighth century its king, the Khagan Bulan, and a large portion of the nobility, adopted Judaism, and in subsequent years there were several Jewish kings, of whom the Khagan Joseph was the last.

* * *

Sirens, the mythical sea-maidens who entice sailors with their songs, are mentioned in *Sifra Sh'mini* IV, 3.

In dancing, one lifts up one foot and rests the other.
Talmud Jerushalmi *Beitzah* V, 63

If the serpent had not been cursed, each man would have had two faithful serpents who would have acted as his servants, bringing him precious gems, jewels, and pearls.
Sanhedrin 59b

The game of chess was immortalized with all of its rules and a descriptive commentary in a poem by Abraham ibn Ezra (1093–1167) which is probably the oldest European account of this intellectual pursuit.

One should cover his mouth with his hand when yawning.
Berachoth 24b

Faithlessness in the house is like a worm in poppy plants.
Sotah 3b

"Euphemism," the substitution of an inoffensive or mild expression for one that may offend or suggest something unpleasant, is known in the Talmud as *Lashan Sagi Ne'hor,* "expression of bright light," because the blind are referred to as "men of much light." A cemetery, for example, is known as *Beth Olam* ("House of Eternity") or *Beth Chaim* ("House of Life").

❧ Rue may not be grafted on wild cassia, as this would be combining an herb with a tree—a violation of Jewish Law.

Killaim I, 8

❧ There must be at least thirty-six righteous men in each generation, as otherwise the world would not continue to exist.

Sanhedrin 97b

The *Fiscus Judaicus* was a poll-tax imposed on the Jews in the Roman Empire after the destruction of the Second Temple, for the benefit of the temple of Jupiter Capitolinus at Rome, in substitution for the half-shekel required by Jewish Law for maintenance of the Temple Service in Jerusalem.

* * *

The statement in the Revelation of John (Chapters 1, 21, and 22) that "I am the Alpha and the Omega, the beginning and the end, the first and the last," is the Hellenized form of a talmudic saying: "The seal of the Almighty is Truth." Truth, in Hebrew, is *emeth,* composed of the first, the middle, and the last letters of the Hebrew alphabet. "Whatever decree bears the seal of the Lord, Truth, is immutable; for *aleph* is the first, *mem* the middle, and *tov* the last letter of the alphabet," it is related in *B'reishith Rabbah* 81, "this being the Name of the Almighty, according to Isaiah XLIV, 6 (and explained in the Jerushalmi Talmud *Sanhedrin* 1), 'I am the first [having had none from whom to receive the kingdom]; I am the middle, there being none who shares the kingdom with Me; and I am the last, there being none to whom I shall hand the kingdom of the world.' "

Note that the first two letters of the word, *emeth* form the word, *eim,* "mother," the beginning of life; and the last two

letters form the word, *meith*, "death," the end of life . . . imply-
ing that the world exists solely through truth. In addition, the
numerical value of *emeth* is 441, which is diminished to 9 by
ignoring the ciphers (4 plus 4 plus 1). In other words, just as
"the seal of the Almighty is Truth," it represents "9."

And just as Truth is immutable, so is the number "9" never
lost. Multiply it by any other number, or even by itself and
the sum of the answer will always be 9. (Examples: $9 \times 9 = 81$;
8 plus 1 equals 9; $9 \times 152 = 1,368$; 1 plus 3 plus 6 plus 8
equals 18, and 1 plus 8 equals 9).

Add 9 to any figure. The answer (when reduced to simple
digits with the elimination of the ciphers) will always be the
same as the number to which 9 was added. (Examples: 9 plus
$175 = 184$: 175 is 1 plus 7 plus 5, equalling 13; 1 plus 3 equals
4; 184, the answer arrived at by adding 9 to 175—is 1 plus 8
plus 4, equalling the identical 13, or 4 when reduced. 9 plus
12 equals 21; 12 is 1 plus 2, equalling 3; 21, the answer arrived
at by adding 9 to 12, is identical.

We can divide 9 only into numbers whose total is 9 (the
simple digits without the ciphers). Subtract 9 from any figure,
and the answer will have the identical total as the number from
which it was subtracted. In other words, "9" never loses its
identity, always remains unchanged and complete—because it
represents "emeth," Truth, the seal of the Almighty, which is
unchangeable and everlasting.

◄§ The eagle is the king of birds.

Chagigah 13b

Borderstones, pegs, or stakes were set into the ground at
the roadside to prevent vehicles from trespassing on private
property.

◄§ The fish we call "sole" was called "sandal" in talmudic
times, due to the similarity in shape.

Talmud Jerushalmi *Niddah* III, 50

Fish were the only living creatures not included on the passenger-list of Noah's Ark.

*   *   *

The Hebrew word for "air" (*avir*) is not mentioned in the Bible.

◄§ The habit of pronouncing many-syllabled words in briefer form [like "Wooster" for *Worcester,* "Chumley" for *Cholmondeley,* "Lester" for *Leicester,* etc.] apparently was commonplace centuries ago as well. For Caius Caligula, Roman Emperor, was referred to as "Casgalgas."

Tosefta Sotah XIII, 6

◄§ Iron bars were not to be sold to the Romans, because they forged weapons out of them.

Avodah Zarah 16a

◄§ Sandals were worn in the summer, and shoes in the winter.

Baba Bathra 58a

The Hebrew word for "altar" is *mizbeach,* composed of four letters: *Mem* for *Mechilah* (forgiveness); *Zahyin* for *Z'chus* (justification; protecting influence of good conduct and merit); *Beth* for *B'rachah* (blessing); and *Cheth* for *Chaim* (life). One of the miracles associated with the altar in the Temple, as mentioned in *midrashic* literature, is that the continuous fire which burned upon it never marred or destroyed the copper with which its stones were overlaid.

◄§ Only a flute solo was used for closing a tune, because it makes a pleasant finale.

Arakhin II, 3

The musical notes or symbols to scriptural reading, called Cantillation, placed both above and below the words, also have vital grammatical significance. They specify the exact accent of each word, and also constitute a means of deeper penetration into the meaning of the sentence as an entity, as well as its component parts and individual words.

◄§ Figures resembling a basket, palm leaves, or shears on a signet ring are of commercial use, not of idolatrous worship.
                    Talmud Jerushalmi *Avodah Zarah* III, 42

◄§ The glare of the sun [on a cloudy day] is stronger than the solar heat itself, comparable to a jar of vinegar [the odor is stronger through a slight opening than when the cover is completely removed]. The dazzling rays of the sun [through breaks in the clouds] are more concentrated than complete sunlight, comparable to the intensity of water through a small aperture. Sinful imagination is worse than the sin itself, just as the stench of roasting meat is more objectionable than the smell of the meat itself. The heat at the end of the summer is more unbearable than the heat of the summer itself, like a hot oven [in which it is easier to kindle a fresh fire]. Fever in the winter is worse than in the summer, just like a cold oven [more wood is required to heat it], so fever in the winter, when air and body are cold, must be greater. Studying old subjects is more difficult than learning new ones—like cement made of cement [more difficult to mix than if made of fresh sand].
                    Yoma 28b, 29a

The founders of the Hasmonean dynasty—Mattathias and his five sons—are known as the Maccabeans, a name coined from the first letters of the four-word quotation from Exodus XV, 11, which Judah adopted as his slogan: "Who is like unto Thee among the gods, O Lord!" The initial letters of the Hebrew words form, "Maccabee." *Macab* also means "hammer," and since Judah and his followers struck hammerlike blows at their enemies, some authorities believe this to be the origin of the term (and the last letters of Abraham, Isaac, and Jacob in Hebrew are "M-k-b").

◄§ Only fellow-citizens should be elected to public office.
                    Yebamoth 45b

◄§ A meal without salted preserves is not worthy of being termed a meal.

Berachoth VI, 7

Among the Jews of Egypt in the fifteenth century, coffee was so popular that it was known as "the Jewish drink." It was introduced into England, incidentally, by a Jew named Jacob, at Oxford, in 1650.

*   *   *

On *Chanukah* it is customary to play all sorts of games. Among them is one utilizing a *dreidel* (teetotum, or spinning-top). On each of its four sides there is a Hebrew letter representing the amount won or lost when the top comes to a stop. These letters also form the word, *Goshnah*, meaning "to Goshen" (Genesis XLVI, 28), to which Jacob sent the "original" Judah (a forecast for Judah the Maccabee). These letters also are an abbreviation of a description of the *Chanukah* event leading to its celebration—"a great miracle transpired there."

◄§ Age takes precedence when sitting down at a festive meal.

Baba Bathra 120a

Sometimes a positive is equivalent to a negative. The Hebrew phrases, *Baruch Mordecai* ("blessed be Mordecai") and *Arur Haman* ("accursed is Haman"), are identical in their *Gematriah* ("Numerical Value")—502.

◄§ Oiling a plant is merely like appointing a watchman; it does not advance its growth, merely protects it.

Sheviith II, 4

◄§ Secret letters may be written with a solution of gall-nut. The recipient pours untanned ink over the writing, and it becomes legible.

Talmud Jerushalmi *Gittin* II, 44

In *Shir HaShirim Rabbah* (I, 2) pastilles (lozenges) or pills of sugar are mentioned; *Nedarim* VI, 10, speaks of "asparagus";

"isopolity" (civic rights granted to strangers) is found in *Pesikta Rabbah* 15; "iskundre" or "iskodar," a Persian chess or checker game, is mentioned in *Kiddushin* 21b and *Shevuoth* 29a; "icon" (idol or statue) occurs often in talmudic and *midrashic* texts, as do "astrology," "athlete," "philosopher," "gypsum," "dragon," to mention but a few words of Greek of Latin origin. In all of these cases, the words utilized are identical in pronunciation with the original form, and they represent but a few examples of foreign words appearing verbatim in the Aramaic tongue.

◄§ One of a magician's [or juggler's] tricks is to pull ribbons of silk out of the nose.

Sanhedrin 67b

Ball-playing is mentioned in *Tosefta Shabbath* X, 10.

◄§ At wedding parties the guests were entertained not only by music, but also with riddles.

Gittin 68b

◄§ Dinner music was furnished by an orchestra of four instruments.

Sotah 48a

◄§ No organ was used in the Temple in Jerusalem, because its music interfered with the sweet melody of the Levites.

Talmud Jerushalmi *Succah* V, 55

From the boundaries of the cities allotted to the Levites (Numbers XXXV, 5), the talmudic sages deduced that walking on the Sabbath is permitted for any distance within a city, and for 2,000 cubits in any direction beyond its boundaries.

◄§ A chariot drawn by four mules abreast was called a *tetramuli* [a coined compound which does not appear in Greek dictionaries].

Sh'moth Rabbah 3

Although the Talmud consists of 63 tractates, it is popularly known as the *shas*—a word-abbreviation taken from the first two letters of *Shishah Sedarim*, the "Six Orders" into which both the *Mishnah* and Talmud are divided: *Zeraim, Mo'ed, Nezikkin, Nashim, Kodoshim,* and *Tahoroth.*

◄§ Commemorative medals or coins were issued for special occasions.

Yalkut Joshua 17

◄§ A sorcerer is powerless when lifted off the ground.

Talmud Jerushalmi *Chagigah* II, 77

◄§ In the desert [on a cloudy day] you can recognize the arrival of the Sabbath by the actions of the ravens; in marshland, by the *arone,* a species of plants which closes its leaves at nightfall.

Shabbath 35b

◄§ The father of the husband and the father of the wife are no more kinsmen than is a basket to a barrel.

Sanhedrin 28b

The Talmud and other ancient Jewish literature often refer to the seventy nations of the world, based on the seventy descendants of Noah enumerated in the tenth chapter of Genesis.

◄§ Although salt is cheap and pepper dear, the world can exist without the latter, but not without the former.

Talmud Jerushalmi *Horayoth* III, 48

Moth-holes gave trouble in talmudic days, too. In *Shabbath* 75a, we are told of a curtain in the Tabernacle attacked by moths.

◄§ It was customary to give a maiden twelve months to provide herself with a trousseau.

Kesuboth 57b

The original statute of limitations is outlined in Deuteronomy XV, 2, whereby restitution of property pledged and money borrowed is ordained for every seven years.

◆§ The average man's daily walk is ten parasangs [Persian mile—approximately three modern miles].

Pesachim 93

◆§ The members of the tribe of Naphtali were noted for their fleetness of foot.

Yalkut Shimoni B'reishith XLIX, 21

The Samaritans inscribe an abbreviated version of the Ten Commandments on the doorposts of their dwellings instead of the two paragraphs from Deuteronomy VI and XI used in the traditional Jewish *Mezuzah* (encased parchment scroll).

◆§ The inhabitants and the animals of a city which has many steps and inclines suffer for at least half their lives and die prematurely.

Eirubin 56

◆§ Babylon, which is mostly lowland, had a very high infant mortality rate.

B'reishith Rabbah 37

◆§ The land of Israel, which has a high altitude, has good air and excellent water.

Midrash Sh'moth XXIII, 76

◆§ The north wind clears the atmosphere.

Yalkut Shimoni Haazinu

Shibboleth, defined by Webster as a "watchword, criterion, or test," actually means an ear of corn or grain. It was the password whereby the Gileadites distinguished their members from the Ephraimites (Judges XII, 6), as the latter could not pronounce the *sh* sound, and rendered it *Sibboleth*.

◆§ A boy of thirteen is required to fast all day on *Yom Kippur*, whereas a girl is required to do so at the age of twelve.

Yoma 82a

✒ Fruits placed in the earth from which they originate will be preserved.

B'reishith Rabbah 90

According to the *Sefer Yetzirah* (The Book of Creation), a mystical cabalistic word on cosmology attributed variously to Abraham the Patriarch, Rabbi Akiba, and other authors, every form of existence, from matter to eternal unfathomable wisdom, is an emanation of the Infinite Being, the Almighty.

✒ Up to the time of Abraham, it was impossible to distinguish old age from youth in appearance.

Sanhedrin 107b

✒ There is a worm called *pah,* indigenous to figs, which is dangerous, and known to have caused death.

Shabbath 90a

✒ According to Rabbi Eliezer, in the month of *Tishri* [the month in which *Rosh Hashanah* occurs], the world was created, Abraham and Jacob were born and died [Isaac was born on Passover]; on *Rosh Hashanah* [the 1st of *Tishri*] Sarah, Rachel, and Hannah were informed of the coming birth of their children; Joseph was released from the dungeon; the slavery of the Israelites terminated [in *Nissan* they were redeemed]; and the future redemption will occur in *Tishri.* However, according to Rabbi Joshua, all of these events occurred in the month of *Nissan,* with the exception of those concerning Sarah, Rachel, and Hannah, Joseph's release from prison, and the cessation of the Egyptian bondage.

Rosh Hashanah 10b 11a

✒ Leaves of stems of onions kept in the ground for a long time exude a poisous fluid.

Eirubin 29b

✒ Pregnancy of the cat lasts for fifty days—and its counterpart in the vegetable kingdom is the mulberry tree [its fruit ripens fifty days after blossoming].

Bechoroth 8a

⇨ The sages considered the curse of Achiyah preferable to the blessing of Balaam. Because Achiyah said (I Kings XIV, 15): "For The Lord will smite Israel as a reed shaken in the water," whereas Balaam said (Numbers XXIV, 6): "As cedars beside the waters." The reed bends with the wind, but stands erect again when the wind ceases. But the winds uproot the cedar.

Taanith 20a

⇨ What may seem to be a curse may be a blessing in disguise. On the wedding day of his daughter, Rabban Gamaliel expressed the wish that he might not see her return to his house. At the birth of her son, he hoped that she might continually wail. When she asked him why he had "cursed" her on these two joyous occasions, he pointed out that they were blessings, not curses. Because she would not return to live in her father's home if her married life were happy; and if her son was strong and healthy, she would continually wail that the child did not eat or drink enough and was late for school.

B'reishith Rabbah 26

The famous sculpture of Moses by Michelangelo, as well as those by other medieval sculptors and contemporary paintings as well, depict two "horns" of light emanating from his forehead. These have given corroboration to the ridiculous theory among the ignorant that "Jews have horns." The artistic misconception was due to an accidental or premeditated error in both the Aquilas (Greek) and the Vulgate (Latin) translations of the Bible, in which the phrase, *"Kahran or pahnav"* ("The skin of his face shone") (Exodus XXXIV, 29, 30, 35) is translated, "His head had horns." The Hebrew words for "shone" and "horn" are identical, except that "shone" is a verb in the past tense, and "horn" is a noun. Also, the word *or* in Hebrew means both "light" and "skin," and although they sound alike, they are spelled differently. The mistranslation might have been due to the ancient scholars' desire to link Moses with Egyptian and Babylonian horned deities.

*   *   *

Pilpul, a method of talmudic study, means a penetrating investigation and disputation of a subject, leading to a logical conclusion. The word is derived from *pilpel,* which means not only "to season" and "to spice," but also "to dispute violently" in a metaphorical sense. The Talmud and later literature are replete with pilpulistic examples.

One curious instance from the Middle Ages concerns the additional month (Adar II) which is added to the Hebrew calendar in a leap year. The question is, how is it that if two boys were born on two successive days of the same year, the one born a day later than the other attained before the older one the legal age required for his becoming a *Bar Mitzvah* (confirmed). The *pilpul* points out that one boy was born on the 29th day of Adar I, the other being born on the 1st day of Adar II. In their thirteenth year, which was an ordinary one (not a leap year), there was naturally only one month of Adar. Hence the younger boy, born on the 1st of Adar II, reached his religious majority on the 1st of Adar, whereas the elder one, born on the 29th of Adar I, did not reach his legal maturity until the 29th of Adar in the thirteenth year.

*   *   *

The Talmudists had a system of shorthand called *Notarikon,* or *Notrikon,* a word derived from the Latin *notaricum* (from *notarius*)—meaning "a shorthand writer." Individual letters of a word or phrase, through this method, stand for complete ideas, or form the abbreviation of other words. For example, the first word of the Bible is *B'reishith*—and each letter of that word represents a word in itself:

Beth for *barah*—"He created";
Raish for *rakiah*—"the firmament";
Ahlef for *eretz*—"the earth";
Shin for *shamayim*—"the heavens";
Yood for *yam*—"the seas"; and
Tov for *t'hom*—"the abyss."

Thus, *"B'reishith"* stands for: "He created the firmament, the earth, the heavens, the seas, the abyss."

The word *Pardes,* "Paradise," also signifies the four main methods of interpreting Torah:

Pai for *p'shat*—the literal meaning;

Raish for *remez*—by analogy;

Dahleth for *d'rash*—through exposition;

Sahmech for *Sod*—the hidden, inner significance.

A misinterpretation has arisen in one instance. In certain editions of medieval Passover Hagadahs, there is a woodcut depicting a huntsman pursuing a hare. There is a mnemonic word, *Yaknehaz* which represents the order of benedictions at *Kiddush* (sanctification prayer) on a festival evening occurring on Saturday night: "Wine, Sanctification, Candlelight, Separation of the Sabbath from the weekday routine, and blessing over the coming of a new holiday.

However, when this word *Yaknehaz* is pronounced, it sounds like the German sentence, *"(Er) jagt den Haas (en)"*—"He chases the hare." And that is what the medieval artist assumed, either seriously or in jest, that the word signified.

Manna

While the divine ambrosia of Greek and Roman mythology had many distinctive qualities, it was like common food compared with the miraculous manna on which the Israelites subsisted during the forty years of wandering in the Wilderness.

This resembled a grain of linseed (or coriander). Despite its solid form, it melted in the sun, and therefore had to be gathered before sunrise. No matter how much one collected, the quantity was exactly one *omer* (measure) for each individual, but on Friday mornings, the portions were double because none fell on the Sabbath. It had to be eaten the day it was gathered, as it became wormy if left overnight; but that which was collected on Friday remained fresh on the Sabbath.

Each night, the north wind swept the ground clean, and then light rain washed it. When the ground dried, it was covered with a layer of dew like a frozen mass, which formed a tray, upon which the manna fell, and was then covered with another layer of dew. The righteous found it at the entrance to their tents, so that they had no difficulty in gathering it. Those of lesser faith had to walk to collect it, and the wicked had to go a long distance from the camp for it. According to another version, the diligent gathered it in the field, the less diligent just outside their tents, and the lazy ones had it fall into their hands.

Only the Children of Israel could enjoy it; and if a heathen stretched out his hand for it, it slipped from his grasp. Another *midrashic* writer claimed that it tasted sweet to the Israelites, and bitter to the heathen.

When the manna melted, it formed streams from which deer and other animals drank, and the taste of the manna was evident in their flesh, the only way non-Israelites could recognize its taste, for the streams themselves were bitter to them. To each individual, the manna tasted like the food of which he was thinking; to the adult it had the flavor of food for the adult, to the suckling it tasted like its mother's milk.

It was completely nutritious, and was absorbed thoroughly by the body, leaving no waste-matter. The manna itself had a fragrant aroma, and served the Israelite women as perfume.

The flask of manna which Aaron the High Priest sealed for the edification of future generations disappeared from the Temple at its destruction, and will be restored by Elijah before the coming of the Messiah.

—from talmudic and *midrashic* literature

Abraham, according to tradition, instituted *Shacharith,* the morning prayer, as it is written: "And Abraham arose, early in the morning," and the sages state that "there is no early rising except for prayer." Religious ritual declares that there are five days on which it is compulsory to arise particularly early

to pray, and it is interesting to note that the last letters of
these five occasions form an acrostic which coincides with Abraham's name (in Hebrew—"AVRaHaM") and this tradition:

Hoshana Rabba (Last of the Intermediate days of
       Tabernacles) .... A
Tish'a B'Av (Fast of the 9th of Av) V
Yom Kippur (Day of Atonement) .... R
Rosh Hashanah (New Year's) .... H
Purim (Feast of Lots) .... M

ALPHABETICAL CALENDAR
FOR EASY REMEMBERING

The Fast of the 9th of Av
    always occurs on the same weekday as the 1st day of
    Passover
The 1st day of *Shevuoth*
    always occurs on the same weekday as the 2nd day of
    Passover
The 1st day of Rosh Hashanah
    always occurs on the same weekday as the 3rd day of
    Passover
Simchath Torah
    always occurs on the same weekday as the 4th day of
    Passover
Yom Kippur
    always occurs on the same weekday as the 5th day of
    Passover
Purim, which precedes Passover, has
    always occurred on the same weekday as the 6th day of
    Passover

In Hebrew, it is particularly easy to remember these events,
because they are mnemonics based on the letters of the alphabet. The Fast of the 9th of Av (*Tish'a b'Av*) begins with the
last letter of the alphabet—as opposed to "1," the first letter of
the alphabet, representing the first day of Passover.

Shevuoth begins with the penultimate letter of the alphabet, as opposed to "2."

Rosh Hashanah begins with the third from the last letter, as opposed to "3."

Simchath Torah, represented by *K'riyath Ha'Torah*, Reading of the Torah, which is concluded and recommended on this holiday, begins with the fourth from the last letter, as opposed to "4."

Yom Kippur, represented by *Tzom* (fasting), begins with the fifth from the last letter, as opposed by "5."

And *Purim* begins with the sixth from the last letter, as opposed by "6."

17

THE MARVELOUS TALES OF
RABBAH BAR BAR CHANA

The Talmud, like any other comprehensive classic, abounds in figures of speech. While many of them may also be taken in their literal sense, it is quite evident that statements often reflect exaggeration for the sake of emphasis.

For example, Rabbi Jose (*Baba Bathra* 75b) declares that he had seen Cyprus in the days of its prosperity, and it had 180,000 markets for sauces. Upon King Solomon's marriage to Pharaoh's daughter, she introduced him to 1,000 different kinds of musical instruments (*Shabbath* 56b). King Solomon (*Menachoth* 29a) made ten candelabra for the Temple; for each he set aside 1,000 talents of gold which he refined in a crucible until they were reduced to the weight of one talent of absolute purity. There was an organ in the Temple which produced 1,000 kinds of melody (*Arakhin* 11a). King Solomon uttered 3,000 proverbs upon each and every matter in the Torah, and for every matter of the Scribes he gave 1,005 reasons (*Eirubin* 21b). The keys of the treasury of Korach were so numerous that it required three hundred white mules to carry them; they were made of leather, not metal, hence considerably lighter in weight (*Pesachim* 119a). In Rome there were 365 streets, each street having 365 palaces, each palace having 365 rooms—each of which contained enough wealth to feed the world. (*Pesachim* 118b).

In addition, at the time of the writing of the major portion of the Talmud and *Midrashim,* certain teachings were prohibited by the occupying powers. The sages often had to resort to fantastic and ambiguous parables in order to convey thoughts and lessons to their students. Among the rabbis who indulged in flights of fancy to demonstrate his teachings was Rabbah Bar Bar Chana, Babylonian *Amora* of the third century, who lived during the Neo-Persian dynasty which issued many restrictive measures against the Jews. For instance, while he was answering an *halachic* question, a Zoroastrian priest entered the room and extinguished the lamp, as that day was a festival of Ormuzd on which Jews were forbidden to have fire in their houses (*Gittin* 16b, 17a).

Sinbad the sailor, Baron von Münchhausen, Paul Bunyan, and other tellers and heroes of tall tales had nothing on Rabbah Bar Bar Chana, of whom one of his contemporaries remarked: "All of Bar Bar Chana's talk is nonsense [drivel]!" Yet fantastic as they seem, these stories all had ethical or political significance. They are given here as related in *Baba Bathra* 73a to 74b, without any attempt at interpretation or elucidation, and merely for their curiosity value. In some instances, scientific teachings are easily evident beneath the cloak of fantasy.

⤳ Once a wave lifted me up so high that I could see the base of a small star. Had I been lifted any higher, the heat of the star would have burned me.

⤳ I saw a gazelle a day old, yet as big as Mount Tabor, which is four parasangs in size. Its neck stretched out three parasangs, and the width of its head was one-and-a-half parasangs. When it excreted, the Jordan was obstructed.

◦§ At one time I was on a ship and saw a fish covered with sand and meadows. We thought it an island on which we landed, made a fire, and baked and cooked. But as soon as the back of the fish became hot, it turned over. Had our ship not been standing by, we would all have drowned.

◦§ Once on board ship I noticed a fish into whose nostrils a mud-worm had crawled. The fish died, and was washed up on shore by the sea. Sixty coast towns were demolished by its weight. It had enough flesh to feed sixty towns, and sixty other towns salted the remainder. From one eyeball, they filled three hundred jars with oil. Twelve months later, when I returned there, I saw that its bones had been sawed into building material for rebuilding all of the destroyed towns.

◦§ I once saw a bird standing in water up to its ankles, and its head reached the sky. We thought the water was shallow and wanted to wade in it to cool off. But we heard a voice warning us: "Do not enter, because seven years ago a carpenter dropped his axe here and it has not yet reached bottom—not only because the water is so deep, but also because the current is so strong." (Rabbi Ashi identified the bird as the *ziz*, a fabulous bird of the fields.)

◦§ An Arabian merchant once took me to a place where the earth and the sky meet. I put my basket there, and after praying noticed that it had disappeared. "Are there thieves here?" I inquired. "That is the sphere of the sky that turns daily," was the reply. "Wait here until tomorrow at the same time, and you will find it."

Rabbi Judah of India told this tale:

◦§ Once while aboard ship I saw a precious stone encircled by a snake. A diver went to fetch it, but the snake opened its mouth and threatened to swallow the boat. A raven came and decapitated the snake and all the water turned into blood. Another snake appeared, touched the carcass with the gem, and it was revivified, again threatening to swallow the ship. A bird flew down, bit off its head, took the gem, and threw it on the ship. It fell on some salted birds, which immediately came back to life. They flew away with the jewel.

Rabbi Ashi said that he had heard the following from Huna bar Nathan:

✌§ Once while in the desert they had a leg of meat and put it on the grass while searching for firewood. When they returned, the leg had resumed its original uncut shape. They roasted it. When they returned to that spot twelve months later, the coals on which it had been roasted were still gleaming. Amemar remarked to Rabbi Ashi that the grass was *samtrie* ["dragon's-blood," which has the power of healing] and the coals were "broom-brush" [which burns for a long time after it has been ignited].

18

A DOZEN DIGITS

Ever since primitive man learned to count on his fingers, numbers have had special significance. Among various peoples and religions, they have even assumed sacred proportions, some being considered lucky, others unlucky. This is not true, however, in Judaism, which abhors superstition and actually legislates against it. There is no such thing as an "unlucky 13," for instance. In fact, the divine attributes of the Almighty are numbered as 13, and that is also the age at which a boy becomes a *Bar Mitzvah* (reaches his religious majority). Any aura of sanctity or taint of profanity adhering to numbers in Jewish literature and thought is the result of accumulated folklore. Yet because numbers are so all-important in every phase of life, the following selections have been grouped into a sheaf of twelve, the dominant thought in each revolving around the numerals one through twelve. This material has been gathered from the following sources:

APPROXIMATE DATE	SOURCE
1st-5th Centuries, C.E.	*Mishnah* and *Talmud* (*Shabbath, Yoma, Sanhedrin, Chullin, Pesachim, Megillah, Kethuboth, So-*

APPROXIMATE DATE   SOURCE

          tah, Bechoroth, Niddah, Nedarim,
          Berachoth, Chagigah, Succah,
          Kiddushin, Derech Eretz, Baba
          Bathra, Kinnim, Gittin, Baba
          Metziah, Baba Kama)

2nd Century, C.E.   *Ahvoth d'Rab Nathan*

1st-3rd Centuries, C.E.   *Midrashim (Otzar Midrashim, Tan-*
          chuma)

ONE

৶৶ A non-believer once asked Shammai to convert him, provided he could teach him the entire Torah while standing on
one leg. Shammai, who was quite impatient, drove him away.
When he approached Hillel with the same request, Hillel said:
"That which is hateful to thee, do not do to thy neighbor. This
is the whole Law, the rest is Its commentary."

                  Shabbath 31a

৶৶ Not one thing is created in vain by the Almighty. He
created the snail as a remedy for a scab; the fly for the sting of
a wasp; the gnat for the bite of a serpent; the serpent for
healing the itch [or head-sores]; the spider for the sting of a
scorpion.

                  Shabbath 77b

৶৶ The entire world is preserved for the sake of one righteous
man, as it is written (Proverbs X, 25): "The righteous man is
an everlasting foundation."

                  Yoma 38b

৶৶ Man was created singly—as an individual—to teach that
he who destroys one soul is considered as if he had destroyed
the entire world; he who preserves one soul is considered as
though he had preserved the entire world. And further, for

the sake of peace, so that no man can say: "My father was greater than yours!"

Sanhedrin 37a

&ะ The Almighty's greatness is evident in many things. An example is that with one die a man mints many coins and all are exactly alike. Whereas the Lord, with one die, impressed the same image [of Adam] on all men, yet not one of them is like his neighbor.

Sanhedrin 37a

TWO

&ะ The Almighty permitted man to create two things after Creation. One was fire, which through divine inspiration Adam drew forth by striking two stones together; the other was the mule, which was produced by cross-breeding.

Pesachim 54a

&ะ If speech is worth one *selah* [coin], silence is worth two.

Megillah 18a

THREE

&ะ The Almighty loves three kinds of individuals: one who does not become angry; one who does not become drunk; one who does not love himself [praise his own virtues].

Pesachim 113b

&ะ Three species of creatures hate each other: dogs, roosters, sorcerers. Three love each other: strangers, slaves, crows.

Pesachim 113b

&ะ Three creatures grow stronger as they grow older: the fish, the serpent, and the pig.

Shabbath 77b

&ะ Food remains undigested in the stomach of the dog for three days, because the Almighty knows that its food is scanty.

Shabbath 155b

~§ Three maladies are remedied by dates: a troubled mind, constipation, hemorrhoids. Dates are excellent after the morning and evening meal, but harmful in the afternoon. They are best at noon.

Kethuboth 10b

~§ Three things weaken man's strength: fear, travel, sin.

Gittin 70a

~§ Three things are pleasant to their possessor: the pleasure of a place in the eyes of its inhabitants, a woman in the eyes of her husband, and a purchase in the eyes of its buyer.

Sotah 47a

~§ It takes three years for the following to give birth: the wolf, the lion, the bear, the leopard, the hyena, the elephant, the ape, and the long-tailed ape.

Bechoroth 8a

~§ Three types of individuals become prematurely aged: the man who lives on an upper floor, a poultry-raiser, and a man whose commands are not carried out.

Otzar Midrashim 166

~§ During the first three months of pregnancy, the child lies in the lower part of the womb; during the next three months it occupies the middle part; and during the last three it is in the upper part. Before parturition, it turns over and this causes birth-pains. Those caused by a female child are more severe than those caused by a male.

Niddah 31a

~§ There are three partners in every child: the Almighty, the father, and the mother. The father's share consists of all that is white, which includes the bones, veins, nails, brain, and the white of the eye; the mother's share consists of all that is red— the skin, flesh, hair, and the black part of the eye; the Almighty's share consists of the breath, the soul, the physiognomy, sight, hearing, speech, motive power, understanding, wisdom.

When man departs from this world, the Lord removes His share, leaving only those of the father and mother.

Niddah 31a

FOUR

◄§ There have been four women in the world's history who could truly be termed "beautiful," aside from Eve, who was not born, but was created: Sarah, Abigail, Rahab, Esther.

Megillah 15a

◄§ One cup of wine is good for a woman; two make her disgraceful; three are demoralizing; and four are brutalizing.

Kethuboth 65a

◄§ Four kinds of people are considered as if dead: the pauper, the leper, the blind man, and the childless one.

Nedarim 64a

◄§ There are four causes of premature aging: fear, anger, a shrewish wife, war.

Midrash Tanchuma, Chaye Sarah

◄§ Four individuals were named before their birth: Isaac, Ishmael, Josiah, Solomon.

Jerushalmi Berachoth I, 6

◄§ Four languages are ideal for four purposes: Greek for poetry [song]; Latin for war [military affairs]; Aramaic for lamentation; Hebrew for speech [or prayer]. And some add Assyrian [modern Hebrew square characters] for correspondence.

Jerushalmi Sotah VII, 2

FIVE

◄§ Five things contain a sixtieth part of five other things: fire is a sixtieth of hell; honey a sixtieth of manna; the Sabbath a sixtieth of the rest in the world to come; sleep a sixtieth of death; a dream a sixtieth of prophecy.

Berachoth 57b

☙§ Five things should be killed even on the Sabbath: the Egyptian fly, Nineveh hornet, Adiabenean scorpion, the serpent, and the mad dog.

Shabbath 121b

☙§ A mad dog is recognized by five symptoms: its mouth gapes wide, it slavers, its ears hang down, its tail is curled between its legs, and it slinks along the side of the road. And some add that it barks, but its voice is not heard.

Yoma 83b

☙§ The sacred fire upon the altar had five unusual characteristics: it crouched there like a lion; shone like the sun; its flames had substance; it consumed liquids as though they were dry materials; it emitted no smoke.

Yoma 21b

☙§ There are five sorts of terror which the strong have of the weak: the fear of the lion of the gnat, the elephant of the mosquito, the scorpion of the spider, the eagle of the swallow, and the leviathan of the stickleback.

Shabbath 77b

SIX

☙§ Six things are a certain cure for sickness: cabbage, beetroot, water distilled from dry moss, the maw and matrix [or pancreas] of an animal, the lobe of the liver.

Berachoth 44b, 57b

☙§ There are six kinds of tears—three good, three bad. The bad ones are those caused by smoke, grief, constipation; the good ones are those caused by fragrant herbs, laughter, aromatic spices.

Shabbath 151b, 152a

☙§ Of six human characteristics, three are angelic and three beastly. Human beings have intelligence, walk erect, and converse in the holy tongue like angels; they eat and drink, generate and multiply, and relieve nature like animals.

Chagigah 16a

◄§ The horse is distinguished by six characteristics: it is wanton; delights in the strife of war; is high-spirited; despises sleep; eats much; voids little.

Pesachim 113b

SEVEN

◄§ Seven things are hidden from the knowledge of man: the day of death; the day of relief from troubles; the depth of eternal justice; the future reward or punishment; that which is in his fellow-man's heart; the restoration of the Kingdom of David; the date of the fall of the Kingdom of Persia.

Pesachim 54b

◄§ The seven shepherds mentioned in Amos V, 5, are: Adam, Seth, Methusaleh, David, Abraham, Jacob, Moses.

Succah 52b

◄§ The seven prophetesses were Sarah, Miriam, Deborah, Hannah, Abigail, Huldah, Esther.

Megillah 14a

◄§ Moses was born and died on the seventh day of the month of *Adar,* and it was on this day as well that the manna ceased to fall.

Kiddushin 38a

◄§ There are seven stages of transgression: evil thought, scoffing, arrogance, cruelty, idleness, causeless hatred, malevolence.

Derech Eretz Zuta 6

◄§ Seven men form an unbroken chain from Creation to our own time: Methusaleh saw Adam; Shem saw Methusaleh; Jacob saw Shem; Amram saw Jacob; Ahijah the Shilonite saw Amram;

and Ahijah was seen by Elijah the Prophet who, according to tradition, is still alive.

Baba Bathra 121b

❧ While a ram has but one voice while alive, it has seven voices after its death: its horns make two trumpets; its leg-bones make two flutes; its skin makes a drum; its larger intestines yield strings for the lyre; its smaller ones yield strings for the harp.

Mishna Kinnim III, 6

❧ Seven children were born circumcised: Adam, Seth, Noah, Jacob, Joseph, Moses, Job.

Midrash Tanchuma, Noach

EIGHT

❧ Eight additional letters point the way toward the use of decent language. When the Lord commanded Noah to take the animals into the ark, instead of saying "unclean," which has an indecent connotation, He said, "those which are not clean" (Genesis VII, 2, 8), thereby employing eight additional letters to avoid indecency.

Pesachim 3a

❧ The last eight verses of the Torah, according to one tradition, were written by Joshua, and according to another by Moses himself, at the Almighty's dictation.

Baba Bathra 15a

❧ There are eight things which are harmful in excess, but beneficial in limited quantity: travel, intercourse, accumulation of wealth, strenuous labor, wine, sleep, hot baths, bloodletting.

Gittin 70a

NINE

❧ A man takes more pride in one measure raised by his own efforts than in nine raised by his neighbor's exertions.

Baba Metziah 38a

❧ Nine individuals entered Paradise alive: Enoch, son of Jared; Elijah the Prophet; the Messiah; Eliezer, servant of Abraham; Hiram, King of Tyre; Ebed-Melech the Ethiopian [officer at Zedekiah's court who saved Jeremiah]; Jabez, son of Rabbi Judah the Prince; Bathia, daughter of Pharaoh who saved Moses; Serach, daughter of Asher. Some include Rabbi Joshua ben Levi, and exclude Hiram, King of Tyre.

Derech Eretz Zuta I

TEN

❧ Ten things cause hemorrhoids: cane leaves, tendrils of the vine, foliage of the vine, the palate of cattle, the backbones of fish, half-cooked salted fish, lees of wine, wiping with three injurious, irritating substances.

Berachoth 55a

❧ Ten things lead to a convalescent's relapse: eating beef, fat meat, broiled meat, flesh of birds, roasted eggs; shaving; eating cress; drinking milk; eating cheese; a full bath. Some sages also include eating nuts, and others add cucumbers.

Berachoth 57b

❧ If there are ten men of leisure who are able to attend the synagogue at any time in a place, it is large enough to be called a town; otherwise it is considered a village.

Megillah 3b

❧ Ten terms are used to denote a prophet: ambassador, faithful, servant, messenger, seer, watchman, seer of vision, dreamer, prophet, man of God.

Ahvoth of Rab Nathan 34

❧ Ten things [out of the ordinary course of nature] were created during twilight at the first Sabbath eve: the well which accompanied the Israelites through the wilderness; manna; the rainbow; the shape of the written characters; the art of writing [or the stylus]; the two Tables of stone on which the Ten Commandments were engraved; the grave of Moses; the cave in which Moses and Elijah stayed; the speech of Balaam's donkey; the opening of the earth which engulfed Korach and his followers. To which some add Aaron's staff which blossomed, the destroying spirits, and Adam's garments.

Pesachim 54a

In *Pirkei Ahvoth* V, the enumeration deletes the grave of Moses and the cave in which Moses and Elijah stayed, and substitutes the rod of Moses and the *Shamir* (utilized to cut the stones for the Temple, since no metal implements were employed). To which some sages add the destroying spirits, the sepulchre of Moses, the ram which Abraham sacrificed instead of Isaac, and tongs made with tongs.

⊷§ Ten miraculous features bear witness to the sanctity of the Temple in Jerusalem: no woman ever miscarried because of the smell of the hallowed flesh; the hallowed flesh never turned putrid; no fly was seen in the slaughter-house; no pollution befell the High Priest on *Yom Kippur;* no disqualifying defect was ever found in the *omer* [measure of new barley offered on the second day of Passover] or in the two loaves [the first fruits of the wheat harvest offered on *Shevuoth*], or in the shewbread; though the congregation stood closely pressed together, there was ample room for them to prostrate themselves; never did a serpent or scorpion injure anyone in Jerusalem; nor did any man ever fail to find lodgings in Jerusalem; rain never quenched the fire of the woodpile on the altar; the wind never overcame the column of smoke arising therefrom.

Yoma 21a

⊷§ King David included in the Book of Psalms those composed by ten elders: Adam (Psalm CXXXIX); Melchizedek (CX); Abraham (LXXXIX); Moses (XC); those of Heman, Jeduthun, and Asaph; and those of the three sons of Korach.

Baba Bathra 14b, 15a

⊷§ Ten things of strength were created, but that which follows them is stronger: a mountain is strong, but iron hews it in pieces; fire weakens iron; water quenches fire; the clouds carry off water; the wind disperses the clouds; the living body resists the wind; fear enervates the body; wine abolishes fear; sleep overcomes wine; and death overpowers them all. But it is also taught that even death can be overcome, in Proverbs X, 2: "Charity [righteousness] delivereth from death."

Baba Bathra 10a

ᕔᔕ Manifestation of the Holy Spirit is described in ten ways: proverb, interpretation, riddle, saying, oracle, glory, decree, burden, prophecy, vision.

Ahvoth of Rab Nathan 34

ᕔᔕ Ten individuals coveted that to which they were not entitled, and they did not achieve it: the serpent, Cain, Korach, Balaam, Achithophel, Doeg, Absalom, Adoniyahu, Uzziahu, Gechazi.

Chuppath Eliayahu, Otzar Midrashim 177

ELEVEN

ᕔᔕ The giver of a *perutah* [smallest coin] to a poor man receives six blessings; and if he speaks a kind word while doing so, he realizes eleven blessings.

Baba Bathra 9b

ᕔᔕ Eleven were anointed with the holy oil: five kings—Saul, David, Solomon, Joash, Jehuachaz; and six priests—Aaron, his four sons, and Zadok.

Pirkei Rabbeinu Ha'Kodesh, Otzar Midrashim 514

TWELVE

ᕔᔕ The day consists of twelve hours, and that was the length of time Adam spent in the Garden of Eden. During the first hour, dust was collected from all parts of the world; during the second it was made into a lump; during the third his limbs were formed; during the fourth his body was animated; the fifth, he stood upon his legs; the sixth, he gave names to the animals; the seventh, he associated with Eve; the eighth, Cain and a twin sister were born; the ninth, he was ordered not to eat of the forbidden tree; the tenth, he succumbed to temptation; the eleventh, he was judged; during the twelfth, he was banished from Eden.

Sanhedrin 38b

᠍᠍ A creature which has no bones in its body does not live more than twelve months.

Chullin 58a

19

A TRIP THROUGH THE TALMUD

In the last part of the fifteenth century and the early part of the sixteenth, Jacob ibn Solomon Chabib, Spanish Talmudist, wrote his *Ein Yaakob* (*Well of Jacob*)—a collection of the Aggadic passages of the Talmud. His purpose was twofold: to familiarize the Jewish public with the ethical spirit of talmudic literature, and to refute the charges brought against the Talmud by non-Jewish opponents and converts.

The following pages contain representative material from the *Ein Yaakob*.

✤ A harp hung over the head of King David. At midnight, a northerly wind blew through its strings and caused it to play, thus awakening him to study the Torah until dawn.

Berachoth 3b

✤ The Written and the Oral Torah is one—inseparable and interdependent—and given to Moses on Mount Sinai in Its entirety. For it is written (Exodus XXIV, 12): "And I will give thee the tables of stone, with the Torah and the Commandments which I have written to teach them." "The tables of

stone" refer to the Ten Commandments; "The Torah" refers
to the Five Books of Moses; "the commandments" refers to
the Mishnah; "which I have written" refers to the Prophets
and Hagiographa; "to teach them" refers to the Gemarah (Talmud). Hence—Biblical text teaches that all were given to Moses
on Sinai.

Berachoth 5a

❧ When the Almighty enters a Synagogue and does not find
ten men (religious quorum) present, His anger is kindled, as it
is written (Isaiah L, 2): "Why have I come and no man was
there, why have I called and there is none to answer?"

Berachoth 6b

❧ The first human being to thank the Almighty was a woman.
"Since the day the Holy One, Blessed is He, created the world,
there was no man who thanked Him until Leah came and
thanked Him, saying (Genesis XXIX, 35): 'This time I will
thank The Lord.' "

Berachoth 7b

❧ There are 903 kinds of death in the world, corresponding
to the numerical value of the Hebrew word *totza'oth,* meaning
"escape through death" (Psalm LXVIII, 21). The most difficult
of them is croup, which is like trying to tear a thorn from a
ball of wool; the easiest is the divine kiss [the way Moses died],
which is like removing a hair from milk.

Berachoth 8a

In this connection, in the *Agadath B'reishis (Mishpatim* 172)
it is stated that there are 83 diseases which are incurable, based
on the numerical value of *mach'a'lah* (disease) in Exodus XV,
26: "I will inflict none of the *mach'a'lah* on you which I have
inflicted on the Egyptians, for I, the Lord, am your Physician."

❧ King Hezekiah hid the Book of Remedies, so that people
might not rely solely upon medicinal aid, but would pray to
the Almighty as well.

Berachoth 10b

◆§ When Elazar ben Azaryah, because of his profound knowledge and other qualifications, was appointed head of the Talmudic Academy, he was only eighteen years of age. Miraculously, his hair turned gray overnight, so that he appeared as
a man of seventy, so as not to embarrass his elders.

Berachoth 28a

◆§ In a certain place a vicious wild ass used to injure the
inhabitants. When they showed Rabbi Chanina ben Dosa the
cave in which it was hiding, he placed the sole of his foot on
the narrow entrance and when the animal came forth, he struck
it so that it perished. Rabbi Chanina carried it on his shoulder
to the academy and said to the students: "My sons, see—it is
not the wild ass that kills, but sin that kills." They all then
exclaimed: "Woe to the man who is met by a wild ass, but
woe to the wild ass when it meets Rabbi Chanina ben Dosa!"

Berachoth 33a

◆§ Og, giant King of Bashan, tried to destroy Israel. He uprooted a mountain three parasangs in extent and raised it
above his head to cast it upon the camp of Israel. But the Almighty sent an army of ants who bored a hole in it, causing
it to fall over his head and rest on his shoulders. He tried to
throw it off, but his teeth protruded and riveted it upon him.
This explains the passage in Psalms III, 8: "Thou hast broken
the teeth of the wicked," for Rabbi Simeon ben Lakish says:
"Do not read 'thou hast broken,' but [by a play on words],
'Thou hast caused his teeth to branch out.'"

Berachoth 54b

◆§ It is a dictum that "every dream is realized according to
its interpretation." An elderly man once said that there were
twenty-four places in Jerusalem for the interpretation of dreams;
once he had a dream and went to each one and each gave him a
different interpretation—all of which were fulfilled.

Berachoth 55b

◦§ Three things restore the mind of man: melody, scenery, and fragrance. Three things develop the mind of man: an attractive dwelling, a pleasant wife, and elegant furniture.

Berachoth 57b

◦§ Ben Zoma contrasted modern man with his primitive ancestors: "Behold! How much labor Adam, the first man, had until he had bread to eat. He had to plow, sow, reap, sheave, thresh, winnow, clean, grind, sift, knead, and bake, and only then was he able to eat. But I arise in the morning and find all this done and prepared for me. And how much labor Adam had before he could clothe himself! He sheared the sheep, bleached the wool, dispersed it, spun it, wove, dyed, and sewed —and only then did he find garments in which to clothe himself. But I arise in the morning and find everything done for me!"

Berachoth 58a

◦§ The following parable, on a completely different matter, contains a hint of the theory of evolution:

When the Romans forbade the study of the Torah, Rabbi Akiba instituted congregations and lectured to them publicly. When he was asked if he were not afraid, he answered: "A fox, walking by the banks of a river, noticed the fish swimming agitatedly. 'Why are you running to and fro?' he asked. 'Because we fear the nets set for us,' they replied. 'Then come up on the shore,' said the fox, *'and live with us just as my ancestors lived with your ancestors.'* The fish then sarcastically exclaimed: 'You are called the wisest of beasts? If we are in danger in our own element, how much greater would be our danger in the element in which we perish!' And so it is with us. If when we study the Torah which is our life we are in such fear of danger, how much greater would our danger be if we ceased to study the Torah!"

Berachoth 61b

◦§ A man should never show preference for one child over his other children. Because for the sake of two *selaim* [coins] worth of silk which Jacob gave to Joseph in preference to his other sons, the brothers became jealous and brought about the migration of Israel to Egypt.

Shabbath 10b

◄§ Rabbi bar Mechasia in the name of Rabbi Chama bar Guria who spoke in the name of Rav, said: "Rather any sickness than sickness of the bowels; rather any pain than pain of the heart; rather any disorder than that of the head; rather any evil than that of an evil wife."

Shabbath 11a

◄§ The same Rabbi said: "If all the seas were ink, if all the reeds were pens, if the entire expanses of Heaven were sheets of parchment, and if all men were scribes—it would not suffice to write the machinations of political government, as it is written in Proverbs XXV, 3: 'As the height of the heavens and the depth of the earth, so is the heart of kings unsearchable.' "

Shabbath 11a

◄§ It was the custom of the house of Rabban Gamaliel to send white clothes to the laundry three days before the Sabbath; but dyed garments were given even on Friday. From this it is inferred that white garments are more difficult to wash than colored ones. Once Abaye took dyed clothes to the laundry and asked what the charge would be. When he was told that they would not cost more than for white ones, he replied, "The Rabbis realized that long ago!"

Shabbath 19a

◄§ The badger whose skin was utilized for the Tabernacle existed in the days of Moses. It was a unique creature, and had but one horn on its forehead. It was assigned to that purpose exclusively, becoming extinct after the Tabernacle had been completed.

Shabbath 28b

◆§ King David would study the Torah throughout the Sabbath. On the Sabbath when he was to die, the Angel of Death came and stood before him, but was unable to take him because the king never ceased studying. The Angel then went to an orchard behind the palace and shook the trees violently. When the king went to investigate the cause of the disturbance, the Angel of Death took his life.

Shabbath 30b

◆§ Hillel was renowned for his patience. A man once wagered four hundred *zuzim* that he could cause him to lose patience. One Friday afternoon, when Hillel was washing, he shouted at Hillel's door until the latter wrapped himself in his cloak and came out. "Why are the heads of the Babylonians round?" the tester queried. Hillel, although he realized the question was a foolish one, replied in all seriousness, "Because they do not have trained midwives." The man departed, but returned shortly thereafter and went through the same procedure. This time he asked: "Why are the people of Palmyra weak-eyed?" Hillel replied: "Because they live in sandy country." The questioner left again, but returned once more and interrupted Hillel's bath by asking, "Why do the people of Africa have such broad feet?" To which Hillel replied, "Because they live in marshy land." The man then told Hillel that he had many more questions, but feared to ask them because the sage might become angry. Hillel told him to ask all he wanted to. Then the man said, "Are you really Hillel, called Prince of Israel?" Hillel replied in the affirmative. "Then," said the questioner irritably, "I pray that there may not be many more in Israel like you." "Why?" Hillel smilingly inquired. "Because," answered the other, "I have lost four hundred zuzim because of you." "Be cautious of your temper," Hillel replied. "Better it is that you lose four hundred zuzim, and even four hundred more, than that Hillel should lose his temper and patience!"

Shabbath 31a

◄§ If a man eats and does not drink, his food will turn to blood and this is the beginning of stomach trouble. If he eats and does not walk four cubits, his food will rot and this is the beginning of bad breath. He who must ease himself and eats before doing so is like a stove which was heated upon its ashes; this is the beginning of evil body odor. Washing in warm water and not drinking anything is like heating a stove from without and not from within. Washing in warm water but not having taken a shower with cold water thereafter is like an iron put into the fire but not tempered with water thereafter. Washing without oiling oneself is like pouring water on a barrel.

Shabbath 41a

◄§ It happened once that a man's wife died, leaving him a nursing son. He was so poor he could not afford a wet-nurse. Miraculously his breast became like a woman's and he nursed his son. In commenting upon this, Rabbi Joseph said that this man must indeed have been great to merit such a miracle. Abaye, on the other hand, said he must have been exceedingly wicked, because he did not merit the ability to earn enough to pay for nursing, but the order of nature had to be changed for him.

Shabbath 53b

◄§ There was once a man who married a woman with only one hand, and this fact was not discovered until her death. Rabbi Judah declared that she was modest indeed because her husband did not discover her defect until she died. But Rabbi Chiyyah answered that it is natural for a woman to be modest and hide such things, but that her husband was the truly modest one not to have discovered her deformity throughout her life.

Shabbath 53b

◄§ When one puts on his shoes, he should put the right one on first, and then the left shoe; when he removes them he should take the left shoe off first, and then the right one. When one washes himself, he should wash the right side first and then the left; when he anoints himself, he should anoint the right side first and then the left. Whoever anoints the entire body, should anoint the head first, as the head is the king of all the bodily organs.

Shabbath 61a

🌿 According to Rabbi Huna, if one is traveling through a desert and does not know what day is the Sabbath, he should count six days and observe the seventh. He based his opinion on the order of the Creation of the world. Rabbi Chiyyah, on the other hand, believed he should first observe one day as the Sabbath, and then count six days. His opinion is based on the fact that Adam was created on Friday, and observed the Sabbath first.

Shabbath 69b

🌿 The rabbis told of a man named Joseph who honored the Sabbath, and who had a wealthy neighbor. The latter was told by the Chaldean soothsayers that Joseph would eventually acquire his entire riches. The neighbor sold his estate and bought a large diamond with the proceeds. He put the gem in his turban. While crossing a bridge one day, the wind blew the turban into the water, and a fish swallowed the diamond. This fish was caught and brought to the market on a Friday. The fisherman, informed that Joseph would buy a fish in honor of the Sabbath, took it to him and he purchased it. When the fish was cut up, the jewel was found, and Joseph sold it for thirteen purses of gold dinarim.

Shabbath 119a

🌿 The Roman emperor once asked Rabbi Joshua ben Chanina why Sabbath meals have a special flavor. The rabbi replied that the Jews have a certain seasoning called *Sabbath* which they throw into the food, imparting this special taste. When the emperor asked for the seasoning, Rabbi Joshua replied: "Only he who keeps the Sabbath is helped thereby; it does not help him who does not keep the Sabbath."

Shabbath 119a

⋖§ Rabbi Simeon ben Elazar declared that every commandment for which Israel was ready to become martyred, such as circumcision and the rejection of idolatry, is still strictly observed; whereas every commandment for which they might not have to lay down their lives, such as *tephillin,* is but feebly observed.

Shabbath 130a

⋖§ The Elisha who lived in the days of the *Tannaim* was called "the man of wings" by reason of a miracle wrought for him. The Roman government had issued a decree calling for severe punishment for anyone wearing *tephillin.* Elisha was walking one day, and a *Quaestor* [military inquisitor] saw him wearing his phylacteries. The officer pursued him and Elisha fled. And when he overtook him, Elisha removed the *tephillin* and held them in his hand. When asked by the *Quaestor* what he was holding, he replied: "Wings of a dove." The officer forced him to open his hand. The *tephillin* had disappeared and in their place were the wings of a dove. The rabbis later asked why he had chosen a dove's wings, and the answer was that because in Psalm LXVIII, 14, Israel is compared to a dove. And just as the dove defends itself with its wings, so Israel defends itself with the Torah.

Shabbath 130a and 49a

⋖§ Circumcision should take place on the eighth day after the child's birth unless the infant's health does not warrant it. Abaye said that his mother had told him that if an infant appears red all over its body, it is an indication that the blood is not properly absorbed within the body's organs, and circumcision should be delayed until the blood is properly absorbed; if the infant has a yellow or greenish appearance, it indicates that it is anaemic, and circumcision should be postponed until the child's blood is richer. Rabbi Nathan remarked that he once went to one of the towns at the sea, and a woman whose first and second sons had died because of circumcision brought her third son to him. When he noticed that the infant was exceedingly red, he told her to postpone the circumcision—and when the child was circumcised after its appearance was normal, it lived. Another time he came to Cappadocia in Asia Minor, where a similar case was presented to him, but this time the child had a greenish appearance. They waited with the circumcision until the child had sufficient blood, and the child lived. In both instances, the grateful parents named their children Nathan the Babylonian in his honor.

Shabbath 134a

⋑§ The sages often spoke in riddles. When Rabbi Judah asked Rabbi Simeon ben Chalafta why they were not privileged to see him on the Festival as his ancestors were accustomed to see his, Rabbi Simeon answered: "The hillocks became mountains; the intimate became strangers; two have become three." By this he meant that because of advancing age little difficulties become great: a road looks like a mountainous ascent; because of old age, friends become estranged as they can no longer meet each other; and one's two legs must be assisted by a third—a staff.

Shabbath 152a

⋑§ According to Rabbi Joshua ben Levi, he who is born on the first day of the week will be either entirely good or entirely wicked [the choice being up to the individual], because two opposites, light and darkness, were created on the first day. He who is born on the second day of the week will be quarrelsome; the division of [disagreement between] the waters took place then. He who is born on the third day will be rich and voluptuous; grass, which is abundant but not distinctive, came forth on the third day. He who is born on the fourth day will be a scholar and a luminary; on this day the heavenly luminaries were set in place. He who is born on the fifth day will be charitable; on this day the fish and the fowl were created, and they are supplied their needs by the Almighty. He who is born on the sixth day will be zealous in his pursuit and observance of the Sabbath. He who is born on the Sabbath will be called greatly pious, yet he will also die on the Sabbath, for it was violated for his sake when he was born.

Shabbath 156a

◆§ Rabbi Chanina, however, declared that it is not the *day* which forecasts or influences an individual's life, but rather the constellation in ascendancy at the hour of his birth. He who is born in the hour of the sun will be bright, will eat and drink of his own, will be unable to conceal secrets, will not be a successful thief. He who is born in the hour of Venus will be rich, hot-tempered, and voluptuous. He who is born in the hour of Mercury will be intelligent and wise. He who is born in the hour of the moon will be burdened with sickness, will build and destroy, destroy and build, will not eat or drink of his own, and will be able to conceal secrets. He who is born in the hour of Saturn will find disappointment in all of his expectations. He who is born in the hour of Jupiter will be righteous. He who is born in the hour of Mars will be a shedder of blood.

Shabbath 156a

Both Rabbi Joshua ben Levi and Rabbi Chanina, as can be seen from the two preceding quotations, believed that man's wisdom and riches were dependent upon destiny. But Rabbi Jochanan, Rab, Samuel, Rabbi Akiba, Rabbi Nachman, to mention but a few of the overwhelming majority whose opinion differed from theirs, insisted that Israel's fate is not dependent on the influence of stars or constellations . . . that each individual through proper observance, behavior, and prayer can even alter his fate or destiny. The following two tales illustrate this:

ఴ Samuel was once sitting with the astrologer, Abalat, and the latter remarked that one of the men passing by on his way to the field would not return, for a serpent would bite him and he would die. Samuel replied that if he was an Israelite, he would return. When the man returned later, Abalat examined the pack on his back and discovered a serpent cut in two. Samuel asked the man what meritorious deed he had performed that day. The man answered that the workers usually pooled their bread, but that day he had noticed one man who had none. When mealtime drew near, he insisted on collecting the bread, and when he reached the poor soul who had none, he pretended to take a portion from him, so as not to embarrass him, and all shared together, with no one knowing what had transpired. "That," said Samuel, "explains the statement (Proverbs XI, 4): 'But righteousness delivers from death'—not only from an unnatural death, but from a natural one as well."

Rabbi Akiba had been told by the Chaldeans that his daughter would die from the bite of a serpent when she entered the garden. One day she took off her head-dress on entering the garden, and its brooch pierced the eyes of a snake on the fence, killing it unnoticed. When she picked up the head-dress the next morning, the dead snake was hanging from it. Rabbi Akiba asked her what meritorious deed she had performed the previous day. She replied that a poor man came to the door of the house late in the afternoon. The whole family was occupied with the meal, and she was the only one who heard him. She gave her portion to him. "That," said Rabbi Akiba, "explains what is meant by 'but charity [the Hebrew word for righteousness, *Tzedakah*, also means charity] delivers from death,' not only from an unnatural death, but also from a natural one."

Shabbath 156a, b

ఴ With argument and logic, anything can be proved, but it need not necessarily be the truth. It is told of Rabbi Meier

that he could give so many apparently logical reasons to prove
that a levitically unclean thing was clean that it would appear
to be so; and that he could give so many reasons to prove a
levitically clean thing unclean that it would appear to be so.
And it is said that there was once a distinguished scholar in
Jamnia who could prove by 150 reasons that a reptile [which
is unclean] was clean.

Eirubin 13b

⋖§ For two and a half years the school of Shammai disputed
religious questions with the school of Hillel—one contending
that it would have been better if man had not been created,
the other claiming it is better that man has been created than
if he had never been. At the end of the disputation, they
counted the number of opinions, and it was found that the
majority concurred that it would have been better for man
not to have been created; but that since he had been, it was
his duty to examine his actions and to be scrupulous concerning them.

Eirubin 13b

In the penitential prayers on *Yom Kippur* there is a verse
that states, according to the tabulation of the sages, happy is
the man who was not born. This may be based on the total
number of *mitzvoth*—613. Of these, 365 are prohibitory ("Thou
shalt not") and 248 are mandatory ("Thou shalt"). In other
words, since one who has not been born is *incapable* of *violat-
ing* 365 commandments, he is actually *fulfilling* them, and the
sum of these is greater than the 248 commandments requiring
positive action.

⋖§ The dove which Noah released from the Ark returned with
an olive leaf. This, according to Rabbi Jeremiah ben Elazar,
symbolized the creature's distrust of man. For the dove said to
the Almighty: "Sovereign of the universe! May my food be
bitter as the olive leaf, but direct from Your hand, rather than
sweet as honey and from the hand of mortal man."

Eirubin 18b

◄§ The Cave of *Machpelah,* where Abraham buried Sarah and where he later was interred with the other Patriarchs, derives its name from the Hebrew word meaning "double." Rab and Samuel had different explanations as to the origin of the name. One said it was so called because it was like one house within the other; the other said it was like a house with an upper story. The latter opinion is correct etymologically, but why, then, is the former derivation also possible? Because of the "doubles" [couples] whose sepulchre it is: Adam and Eve, Abraham and Sarah, Isaac and Rebecca, Jacob and Leah.

Eirubin 53a

◄§ The origin of the saying, "When wine enters, secrets escape," is based on the numerical value of both words—*Yayin* [wine] and *Sod* [secret], each equivalent to 70.

Eirubin 65a

◄§ A man's character is recognized by the way he conducts himself in three circumstances: the way he drinks, the way he conducts business, the way he controls his temper.

Eirubin 65b

◄§ One may cure himself by any means except by resorting to idolatry, adultery, or murder.

Pesachim 25a

◄§ Those who engage in commerce should remember that the oak trees [from which the gall-nut is gathered] are an indication of mountainous terrain; palm trees indicate valleys; reeds indicate rivers; sycamores indicate lowlands.

Pesachim 53a

◄§ It was said of Jochanan ben Narbai that his repast consisted of three hundred calves and three hundred jars of wine; and that he would have as dessert forty *seahs* [measures] of young pigeons. [This is explained by the commentators, however, to mean that he trained the young priests, and they ate at his table.]

Pesachim 57a

◄§ Arrogance removes wisdom from the wise and prophecy from the prophet; anger does likewise. In fact, even were such a one predestined to be great, his greatness would vanish.

Pesachim 66b

◄§ The belief in Resurrection is deduced from various biblical passages, including Deuteronomy XXXII, 39: "I shall kill and I make alive . . . I wound and I heal." First the Almighty makes alive that which He has killed, then He heals that which He has wounded.

Pesachim 68a

◄§ The sages always sought virtue even in calamity. Rabbi Ulla said that Israel was exiled to Babylon because there they might eat dates [which were extremely inexpensive] and thus, by not worrying about livelihood, be able to devote more time to study of the Torah.

Pesachim 87b, 88a

◄§ Rabbi Akiba enjoined his son to observe seven rules: (1) Do not attempt to study where it is crowded; (2) do not live in a city whose leaders are scholars (and therefore cannot provide for its inhabitants); (3) do not enter your home suddenly [unannounced]; (4) do not go barefooted; (5) rise early in the summer and eat before the heat is oppressive, and in the winter before you get cold [this may also be translated as, "eat a hearty breakfast because of the heat and the cold"]; (6) make your Sabbath [meal] [as plain] as the weekday one, so as not to be dependent on others; (7) strive to be associated with him who is fortunate.

Pesachim 112a

◄§ The sages could be as self-critical as they were discerning. When it was taught that there are three types of individuals to whom life is not life—the sympathetic, the quick-tempered, and the fastidious—Rabbi Joseph remarked that he possessed, unfortunately, all three characteristics.

Pesachim 113b

❧ The *Urim* and *Thummim* (Numbers XXVII, 21) in the High Priest's breastplate were so called because they "illuminated" their decisions [gave them clearly, not ambiguously]; and because they "completed" their decisions [gave them fully, not partially]. [This indicates that they were unlike the oracles of pagan nations, whose "opinions" or "decisions" were totally in riddles, and often in contradictory form.]

Yoma 73b

❧ A mad dog should be killed [not by hand but] by a projectile, for whoever touches it becomes dangerously ill, and whoever is bitten by it, dies.

Yoma 84a

❧ A man is forbidden to sleep in the daytime longer than the sleep of a horse, which is equivalent to sixty respirations.

Succah 26b

❧ Jonathan ben Uzziel learned and taught with such intensity and fiery zeal that "it was said that every bird which flew overhead was instantly burned."

Succah 28a

❧ Observance of commandments entails both inherent and external fitness. A dry *lulab* (palm branch used on the Festival of Tabernacles) is not valid because it does not fulfill the requisite of being "beautiful," and a stolen *lulab* is not valid because it would be fulfilling the commandment through a transgression.

Succah 30a

❧ At the conclusion of the first day of *Succoth* at the ceremony of the water libation, candelabra were lighted in the Temple Court; and the illumination was so great that there was not a courtyard in Jerusalem which was not brightened.

Succah 51a

❧ The Basilica Synagogue in Alexandria was so large that it had a pulpit in the center on which the sexton stood, with a scarf [flag] in his hand. When the service reached a portion requiring the answer of "Amen" by the congregation, he waved the scarf and the people responded "Amen."

Succah 51b

◄§ At first the evil inclination [temptation] is as thin and fragile as the thread of a spider's web; but in the end it is as thick and strong as a wagon-rope.

Succah 52a

◄§ There are seven names applied to the evil inclination: The Almighty calls it "evil"; Moses calles it "obdurate"; David calls it "unclean"; Solomon calls it "enemy"; Isaiah calls it "stumbling-block"; Ezekiel calls it "stone"; Joel calls it "hidden."

Succah 52a

◄§ When King David started to dig the foundation for the Temple, the waters of the deep rose and threatened to inundate the world. He then composed the fifteen *Songs of Degrees* [*Ascents*] (Psalms CXX-CXXXIV) and checked its flow. Another version is that when he was digging the foundation of the altar, the waters of the deep rose and threatened to inundate the world. King David then asked if anyone knew whether it was permitted to inscribe the Holy Name on a piece of clay and cast it into the water. Achithophel reasoned that since it is permitted to erase the Holy Name in water in order to bring peace between husband and wife (Numbers, Chapter V), it is certainly permitted to bring peace to the entire world. David then wrote the Name on a piece of clay and dropped it into the water which subsided sixteen thousand cubits. When he noticed this, he uttered the fifteen *Songs of Degrees* and the water rose fifteen thousand cubits, thus leaving it one thousand cubits deep. From this it is inferred that the thickness of the earth [to the waters of the deep] is one thousand cubits. And if one asks why it is that water rises even when one does not penetrate that far, it is because this water comes from the source of the River Euphrates.

Succah 53a, b

◆§ There are three keys [to human aid] which the Almighty holds in His own hand and does not entrust to any agent: The keys of rain, confinement, and resurrection; to which should be added the key of sustenance [livelihood].

Taanith 2a, b

The Hebrew word for "key" is *mafteach*. The first letter, *Mem*, stands for *Matar* (rain); the second, *Pai*, for *Parnassah* (livelihood); the third, *Tov*, for *Techiyah* (resurrection); and the fourth, *Cheth*, for *Chayah* (life, or confinement).

◆§ Three men made unreasonable demands of the Almighty. Two were answered favorably—Eliezer, servant of Abraham, and Saul, son of Kish. The third, Jephthah the Gileadite, was answered in the same unreasonable manner as that of his request.

Taanith 4a

◆§ One should not converse while eating, as the food may enter the windpipe in front of the gullet and lead to disastrous effects.

Taanith 5b

◆§ What is meant by the passage (Proverbs XXVII, 17): "Iron sharpens iron"? Just as one piece of iron can sharpen another piece of iron, so two scholars when studying together sharpen each other's intellect. And with regard to this comparison, just as a small piece of wood kindles a larger one, so does a lesser scholar brighten the wits of a greater one. That is what was meant by Rabbi Chanina when he said: "I have learned much from my teachers, more from my colleagues, and most from my disciples."

Taanith 7a

◆§ When Rabbi Ada bar Ahaba was asked to what he attributed his longevity, he replied: I was never angry in my house; I never superseded one of superior knowledge; I never thought of divine subjects in unclean places; I never walked four cubits without studying Torah or without phylacteries; I never slept in the house of study, either for a regular sleep or a nap; I never rejoiced when my neighbor was in misfortune; I never called my fellow-man by an opprobrious nickname.

Taanith 20b

◄§ Rabbi Chanina ben Dosa once noticed his daughter in a despondent mood before the Sabbath, because she had accidentally poured vinegar into the Sabbath lamp instead of oil. "He who ordained that oil should burn," he remarked, "can ordain that vinegar should also burn." It is said that the vinegar in the lamp burned all night and all day until the end of the Sabbath.

Taanith 25a

◄§ King Ptolemy once took seventy-two elders of Jerusalem and placed them in seventy-two separate rooms without informing them why. He then visited each chamber and ordered each elder to translate the Torah by heart, into Greek. The Almighty inspired all of them simultaneously, so that they all thought alike; and when their work was completed, all seventy-two had given the same translation to fifteen passages which were either obscure, might lead to misinterpretation, or be offensive to the monarch. [This translation, done around 270 years before the current era, is known as the Septuagint.]

Megillah 9a, b

◄§ The sages indulged in metaphoric and hyperbolic eulogies at the death of prominent colleagues. For instance, "When Rabbi Abahu died, the pillars of Kisri shed tears; at Rabbi Jose's death, the gutters of Sepphoris were overrun with blood; when Rabbi Jacob bar Acha died, the stars were seen in daytime; for Rabbi Assi, the trees were uprooted; for Rabbi Samuel bar Isaac, and also for Rabbi Chiyyah, stones of fire fell from Heaven; for Rabbi Menachem bar Simai, all the images were obliterated and became smooth as if passed over by a roller; for Rabbi Tanchum ben Chiyyah, a similar statement was made; for Rabbi Isaac bar Eliashib, seventy breaches were made; for Rabbi Hamnunah, hailstones fell from heaven; when Rabba and Rabbi Joseph died, the bridge-arches of the Euphrates collapsed; for Abaye and Rabba, those of the Tigris caved in; when Rabbi Mesharshia died, the trees brought forth thorns."

Mo'ed Katan 25b

ଈୡ Ten things were created on the first day: heaven and earth, chaos and desolation, light and darkness, wind and water, the length of the day and the length of the night . . . all deduced from the first five sentences of Genesis. Chaos [*Tohu*] is the green [or yellow] circle which surrounds the world, and from it darkness descends upon the world. Desolation [*Vohu*] refers to the smooth [or unformed] stones sunk in the great deep from which waters gush forth. Although the sun was not set in the heavens until the fourth day, from the first day there was celestial light so bright Adam could see by it from one end of the world to the other, but this light was concealed after Adam sinned, to be kept for the righteous in the future.

Chagigah 12a

ଈୡ With ten things was the world created: wisdom and understanding; knowledge and strength; might and rebuke; righteousness and justice; mercy and compassion. These attributes are proved by scriptural quotation and explanation.

Chagigah 12a

ଈୡ One school of thought attempted by biblical reference to prove that the heavens were created first and the earth thereafter, while other sages theorized the other way around. But the general opinion is that both were created simultaneously, and the conflicting opinions are reconciled by assuming that, for the purposes of narration, at Creation the heavens preceded the earth, but when the Almighty expanded the universe, the earth preceded the heavens.

Chagigah 12a

◦§ Isaiah the Prophet was tried on trumped-up charges before a court of false prophets convened by Menashe, and sentenced to death. He uttered the *Tetragrammaton* [Holy Name] and was swallowed by a cedar tree. They sawed the cedar through, and when the saw reached Isaiah's mouth, he perished —a punishment for his having said (Isaiah VI, 5): "And in the midst of a people of unclean lips do I dwell."

Yebamoth 49b

◦§ All of the other prophets "saw" the Almighty through a dim speculum, whereas Moses "saw" Him through a lucid one. [The word used is *Ispaclariah—specularia* or *lapis specularis*—window-glass.]

Yebamoth 49b

◦§ A man is not considered a man unless he has a wife; nor is he considered a man unless he owns real estate. This is based on the biblical statements (Genesis V, 2): "Male and female He created them, and called their name man," and (Psalms CXV, 16): "The Heavens are the heavens of the Lord, but the earth hath He given to the children of man."

Yebamoth 63a

◦§ "The fool [obscene person] says in his heart: 'There is no God.'" (Psalm XIV, 1) This refers to the inhabitants of Barbaria and Mauretania who walk nude in the streets, for none is more detested and abhorred before the Lord than he who walks abroad naked.

Yebamoth 63b

◦§ The prayers of the righteous are symbolized by a shovel. Because just as the shovel turns the grain from place to place at the threshing floor, so do the prayers of the righteous turn the Almighty's dispensations from anger to mercy.

Yebamoth 64a

◦§ One who feigns blindness, a swollen belly, or simulates a hump [in order to receive alms] will not leave this world until he actually suffers from such ailments.

Kethuboth 68a

❧ Bribery need not be money or gifts; it may also be deeds and words. Rabbi Samuel was once on a ferry crossing a river. About to fall, he was saved by a man's helping hand. "Why are you so attentive?" he innocently asked. The man replied: "I have a lawsuit coming up before you." The rabbi responded: "I am disqualified from acting as your judge." Similarly, Amemar once disqualified himself because a man involved in a lawsuit before him removed some feathers clinging to his hair; and Mar Ukba because a man politely stepped up and covered some saliva on the ground before him—both rabbis claiming that they had been "bribed" by the contestant's kind attention.

Kethuboth 105b

❧ Rabbi Chiyyah bar Joseph said that at Resurrection, the righteous will survive fully clothed, proving his theory by the analogy that since wheat which is buried in the earth comes forth with many "cloaks," the righteous who are buried covered with their shrouds will surely be resurrected in that state.

Kethuboth 111b

❧ Marvels of the utopian age [possibly the atomic?] are expressed quite definitely: wheat will sprout forth and rise like palms on mountain tops, and there will be no hardship in harvesting it as the Almighty will cause a wind to blow upon it and make its flowers fall off; man will go out into the field and bring back handfuls of corns from which he will support himself and his family; wheat will be as large as two kidneys of a big ox, and this should not be astounding, as it once happened that a fox made its den in a turnip which when weighed was found to be sixty Zipporian pounds, and there was once a mustard plant so big it yielded nine measures of mustard and from its wood a potter's hut was built; and there was a cabbage so high a ladder had to be used to ascend to its top; one grape will be brought in a wagon or ship and placed in the corner of a house—from which the entire support of the house will be obtained, and its stalks will yield wood for the cooking fire; each grape will yield at least thirty kegs of wine, requiring an entire colony to pick it from the vine.

Kethuboth 111b

✥ The phrase describing the Promised Land as one "flowing with milk and honey" may also be accepted in its literal sense. Rami bar Ezekiel noticed in B'nei B'rak goats eating under fig trees from which honey dripped, and at the same time milk dropped from the goats. Rabbi Jacob ben Dosi declared that he once took a walk from Luda to Oni, a distance of three miles, and as he walked, his ankles dipped in fig-honey. Resh Lakish said that he saw the milk and honey which flowed in Sepphoris, which was a distance of sixteen miles. Rabbi Bar Bar Chana also attested to this, and where he saw the honey and milk flowing would cover a distance twenty-two miles in length and sixteen miles in width. Peaches were shown to Rabbis Chelbo, Avira, and Jose bar Chanina which were as large as the five-*seah* pots used in Bethania.

Kethuboth 111b, 112a

✥ Compulsory military service caused Abraham to be punished in that his descendants were enslaved in Egypt for 210 years, for he gave military training to the scholars in his household, taking them away from their studies.

Nedarim 32a

✥ Rabbi Gamda gave four *zuzim* to some sailors, asking them to bring him something valuable. Not being able to purchase anything valuable for such a small sum, they brought him an ape. On the way, it ran into a hole, and when they dug after it they found it lying on a rare and expensive pearl, which they brought and gave to him.

Nedarim 50b

✥ Four different winds blow each day, and the northerly one accompanies them all. For were it not for this wind which goes along with each, the world would not be able to exist for even one hour.

Gittin 31b

❧ Titus reviled and blasphemed the Almighty, but was punished by one of His most insignificant creatures, a gnat. The insect flew up his nostrils and gnawed at his brain for seven years. One day as he was passing a blacksmith's forge, he discovered that the noise of the hammer had a soothing effect. He secured relief for thirty days, but thereafter the gnat became accustomed to the din. When an autopsy was performed on the body of Titus, they discovered in his brain a gnat as big as a swallow or pigeon, with a mouth of copper and claws of iron.

Gittin 56b

❧ Among the historic men of muscle, like Samson the mighty, was Bar Deroma, who lived at the time of the Roman invasion. He could jump a mile and kill in that leap whatever was in his path.

Gittin 57a

❧ It was a custom in Bettar when a child was born for the parents to plant a young cedar tree for a boy, and a pine tree for a girl; and when the child was married, the wedding canopy would be made out of its wood.

Gittin 57a

❧ Non-Jewish poor must be supported along with those of Israel; non-Jewish sick must be visited along with those of Israel.

Gittin 61a

❧ When Rabbi Judah stated that a hated wife should be divorced, and Rabbi Jochanan declared that hated is he who divorces his wife, the two conflicting opinions were reconciled: the latter statement refers to one's first marriage, while the former refers to a second marriage—this being based on Rabbi Elazar's comment on the text from the Prophet Malachi, "Even the altar sheds tears when a man divorces his first wife."

Gittin 90b

◆§ Proper matchmaking is as difficult as the miracle of splitting the Red Sea [after the Exodus from Egypt].

Sotah 2a

◆§ It is better for a man to be thrown into a fiery furnace than to be the means of bringing another to shame publicly.

Sotah 10b

◆§ When Scripture states that at the age of 120, the natural strength of Moses was not abated, it was proved by the fact that when he ascended from the plains of Moab to Mount Nebo, there were twelve steps, and he surmounted them in one stride.

Sotah 13b

◆§ Blue was the color selected for the thread of the fringes *(tzitzith)* because blue resembles the sea, the sea resembles the heavens, and the heavens resemble the Divine Throne.

Sotah 17a

◆§ A foolish "saint" is a supposedly pious man who sees a woman drowning but does not want to rescue her because she is unclothed.

Sotah 21b

◆§ Joseph was given permission to leave Egypt to bury Jacob because of a "deal" he had made with Pharaoh. When the latter had appointed Joseph to be his viceroy, Pharaoh's astrologers objected on the grounds that a slave bought for twenty pieces of silver was not qualified to rule, particularly since he did not possess the regal quality of understanding all of the seventy languages of the world. That night, the angel Gabriel taught Joseph these tongues. This legend is bolstered by Psalm LXXXI, 6: "He appointed it in Joseph for a testimony, when he went forth over the land of Egypt; 'where I heard a language I knew not.'" The verse begins and ends with the Hebrew letter *Ahyin*, which is the number "70." When Joseph demonstrated his knowledge before the court, Pharaoh did not comprehend Hebrew, and made Joseph swear that he would not reveal this deficiency to anyone. At Jacob's death, Joseph reported to Pharaoh that he had sworn to his father that he would bury him in the Cave of Machpelah. When Pharaoh asked him to get a release from that oath, Joseph agreed on condition that he would then ask for release from the oath he had made to the king, whereupon Pharaoh gave his consent to Joseph to leave, as he did not want his secret revealed.

Sotah 36b

◄§ Each commandment mentioned in the Torah is secured [strengthened] by 48 covenants, with 603,550 guarantors [the entire nation of Israel at Mount Sinai].

Sotah 37b

◄§ Four classes of people will not merit receiving the *Shechinah* [Divine Presence]: scorners, liars, hypocrites, tale-bearers.

Sotah 42b

◄§ The Canaanite warriors attempted to instill fear into their adversaries' hearts in a battle by swinging their shields, sounding their trumpets, shouting, and galloping with their horses. [This is reminiscent of the tactics of the Japanese in World War II, and the North Koreans thereafter.]

Sotah 42b

◄§ The city of Luz, where the purple thread used for the *tzitzith* [fringes] was dyed, could not be destroyed by either Sennacherib or Nebuchadnezzar, and even the Angel of Death was powerless against it. When its old inhabitants desired to die, they went outside of the city.

Sotah 46b

◄§ Whatever part of the world the first man, Adam, decreed should be inhabited, became inhabited; and whatever land he decreed should not be inhabited, remained unpopulated.

Sotah 46b

◄§ One who does not marry before the age of twenty will spend the rest of his life either in sin or in contemplating committing sin.

Kiddushin 29b

◄§ The penultimate letter of *Gachon* in Leviticus XI, 42, is the halfway mark of all the letters in the Torah (Five Books of Moses); the words, *Darash-doresh* in Leviticus X, 16, are the midway mark of all its words; the 33rd sentence of the 13th chapter of Leviticus represents half the verses. The middle letter of *Ya'ar* (a three-letter word in Hebrew) in Psalm LXXX, 14, is the halfway mark of all the letters in the Book of Psalms; the 38th sentence of the 78th Psalm is the midway mark of all of its verses. The Book of Psalms, incidentally, contains eight passages more than the Torah, and Chronicles eight less.

Kiddushin 30a

◄§ Whoever is not well-versed in Scripture and *Mishna* is considered uncivilized, and is disqualified as a witness. He who eats in the street is likewise disqualified.

Kiddushin 40b

◄§ Ten measures of various things came down to the world, and were divided as follows: Wisdom—nine to the land of Israel and one to the rest of the world. Beauty—nine to Jerusalem. Wealth—nine to Rome. Poverty—nine to Babylon. Haughtiness—nine to Elam. Bravery—nine to Persia. Vermin—nine to the Medeans. Sorcery—nine to Egypt. Plagues—nine to the swine. Unchastity—nine to the Arabs. Impudence—nine to Meshan [*Mesene*]. Talk—nine to women. Blackness—nine to the Ethiopians. Sleep—nine to servants.

Kiddushin 49b

◄§ Discreet silence is a sign of distinguished birth.

Kiddushin 71b

◄§ Exchange marriages were practiced by the Babylonians in the town of Birka.

Kiddushin 72a

◆§ Bad habits come to those whose occupations put them in contact with women—such as goldsmiths, dyers, pressers and cleaners of women's garments, hand-mill cleaners, peddlers, weavers, barbers, launderers, phlebotomists [those who practice bleeding], masseurs, tanners.

Kiddushin 82a

◆§ It is forbidden to raise a dangerous dog or keep a defective ladder in one's house.

Baba Kama 15b

◆§ Thorns and broken glass should not be thrown away indiscriminately, but should be buried at least three spans below the surface of the ground.

Baba Kama 30a

◆§ Rabbi Chanina ben Dosa was as modest as he was pious and gifted. When events turned out the way he had predicted, he attributed this to faith alone, insisting, "I am neither a prophet nor the son of a prophet."

Baba Kama 50a

◆§ One should not raise a dog unless it is kept on a chain, but it is permitted in a frontier town if the animal is chained during the daytime and left unchained only at night.

Baba Kama 83a

◆§ The coins of Jerusalem had David and Solomon engraved on one side, and Jerusalem on the reverse; those of Abraham had an old man and woman on one side, and a young couple on the other.

Baba Kama 97b

◆§ Stealing a *perutah* [about half a cent] is just as shameful as any other theft.

Baba Kama 119a

◆§ The adequacy of a contribution depends on the standard of living. Rabbina, who was a treasurer of charity, once accepted golden chains and rings for charity from the women of Mechuza. When reminded that there is a law which states that charity collectors may accept only small donations from women without their husbands' knowledge, he replied: "For the people of Mechuza, this is considered a small donation."

Baba Kama 119a

§ One should not talk with his mouth differently from what he thinks.

Baba Metziah 49a

§ Inquiring the price of an article without having the money to pay for it is a form of cheating.

Baba Metziah 58b

§ There is no absolution for an adulterer, for one who exposes his fellow-man to shame publicly, and for one who applies vile names to his neighbor.

Baba Metziah 58b

§ One should always be on guard not to deceive his wife, for just as her tears are frequent, so are her sensibilities easily offended.

Baba Metziah 59a

§ A wife's advice should always be taken on household matters.

Baba Metziah 59a

§ A measuring rope will not be accurate in all seasons of the year, as it will shrink when dry.

Baba Metziah 61b

§ Demolition of a building even as holy as the Temple is advisable if it threatens to collapse.

Baba Bathra 3b

§ Jeremiah was the author not only of the book bearing his name, and the Scroll of Lamentations [*Eichah*], but also of the Book of Kings.

Baba Bathra 15a

✒ A man should not be held responsible for the things he says when he is sorely distressed.

Baba Bathra 16b

✒ A precious gem was suspended around Abraham's neck, and when a sick man looked upon it, he was cured. At Abraham's death, the Almighty sealed it in the sphere of the sun. Hence the proverb: "When the sun rises, the afflicted are healed."

Baba Bathra 16b

✒ Rabbi Baanaah, who measured the Cave of Machpelah where Adam and Eve and the patriarchs and matriarchs are interred, saw merely the heels of Adam, and they appeared to him like two globes of the sun, so dazzling was their brilliance. In appearance and beauty, all are as inferior to Sarah as an ape is to man; Sarah is equally inferior to Eve, and Eve likewise to Adam. And the appearance of Adam may be compared the same way in contrast with that of the *Shechinah*.

Baba Bathra 58a

✒ A will in the form of a riddle, wherein a man had bequeathed to his sons a barrel of earth, a barrel of bones, and a barrel of stuffing [padding] respectively, was solved by Rabbi Baanaah as referring to real estate, cattle, and household furniture.

Baba Bathra 58a

✒ In the future, the Almighty will make a banquet for the righteous from the flesh of the Leviathan; the rest will be distributed for sale among the markets of Jerusalem; a *succah* will be made from its skin, the remainder of which will be spread on the walls of Jerusalem and its brightness will illuminate the entire world.

Baba Bathra 75a

✒ A disciple who was told that in the future gems and pearls of gigantic dimensions would be available, sneeringly remarked that this is impossible as one had never been found even as large as a turtle dove's egg. He later was on a boat and saw angels sawing gems and pearls thirty cubits square, which were being reserved for placing at the gates of Jerusalem.

Baba Bathra 75a

ᴈᴓ Commissioners should be appointed to superintend weights, measures, and prices to protect the public from swindlers.

Baba Bathra 89a

ᴈᴓ The name of Abraham's mother was Amthalai, daughter of Karnebo; Haman's mother was Amthalai, daughter of Urbitha; David's mother was Natzebeth, daughter of Edal; Samson's mother was Z'lalpunith. The Babylonian city of Eibra-Zeira of Cutha is the city of Ur-Kasdim [mentioned in the Bible as the place from which Abraham emigrated].

Baba Bathra 91a

ᴈᴓ A flake of bran is exceedingly light, yet even lighter in value is a groom who resides in the house of his father-in-law; still lighter is the guest who brings along an uninvited companion; and even lighter is he who answers a question before having heard it in its entirety.

Baba Bathra 98b

ᴈᴓ The majority of children take after their mothers' brothers.

Baba Bathra 110a

ᴈᴓ Scripture does not give reasons for its laws, because the two laws for which reasons were given—that a king should neither acquire many wives nor many horses (Deuteronomy XVII, 17)—were the very ones broken by King Solomon, wisest of men, who thought himself above the law by arguing that the reasons advanced would not apply.

Sanhedrin 21b

ᴈᴓ Just as the hammer breaks the stone into innumerable pieces, so may a biblical passage be interpreted for a multitude of arguments.

Sanhedrin 34a

❧ Divine justice steps in where a human court is powerless to convict a criminal because of lack of witnesses and the inadequacy of their evidence. He who should be stoned meets his death by falling from a roof or being trodden by a wild beast; he who should be burned dies by fire or by the bite of a snake; he who should be slain by the sword is either executed by the government or murdered by another; he who should be hanged dies either by drowning or suffocation.

Sanhedrin 37b

❧ Man was created last so that if he becomes proud and overbearing, it may be said to him: "Even the mosquito was created before you." And also that no one could claim the Lord had a partner in Creation.

Sanhedrin 38a

❧ Man was created singly so that no one may claim he is better than his neighbor, as all are the first man's descendants.

Sanhedrin 38a

❧ Nadab and Abihu were consumed by two cords of fire which emanated from the Holy of Holies, separated into four cords, and entered their nostrils, consuming them inwardly, but leaving their bodies and garments unscorched.

Sanhedrin 52a

❧ The Seven Noachide Commandments [given to the sons of Noah and applying to all humanity before the Ten Commandments were revealed on Sinai] concerned courts of law, blasphemy, idolatry, adultery, murder, robbery, and the prohibition against eating a part of the living body of an animal.

Sanhedrin 56a

❧ A child is not able to call "mother" or "father" until it has eaten wheat.

Sanhedrin 70b

◆§ The Lord will not pardon the father who marries off his young daughter to an old man, or his young son to an old woman.

Sanhedrin 76a

◆§ The ancient judicial system in Israel consisted of courts of twenty-three judges in every city, two higher courts of twenty-three members each—one at the gate of the Temple Mound and the other at the gate of the Temple Court—and the *Sanhedrin* [the Supreme Court] of seventy-one judges in the Temple Treasury. Citation of traditional precedents was the usual procedure, and if no precedent was available, a majority vote decided the case.

Sanhedrin 88b

◆§ A sudden command to do something violently opposed to one's nature may cause insanity.

Sanhedrin 89b

◆§ The following have no share in the world to come: he who denies Resurrection; he who denies the divinity of the Torah; an atheist [Epicurean]; he who reads heretical books; he who utters magical charms over a wound; he who pronounces the Name of the Lord as written in Hebrew with its proper letters.

Sanhedrin 90a

◆§ Some Egyptians once haled Israel before Alexander of Macedon, demanding restitution for the wealth which the Israelites had taken with them at the Exodus (Exodus XII, 36). To which Gebiha ben Pasisa replied, as long as they believed in the truth of the biblical text [to which they agreed], they should first pay the wages of the 600,000 men who labored for the 430 years of enslavement (Exodus XII, 40), whereupon the Egyptians dropped their claim.

Sanhedrin 91a

◆§ On another occasion, the descendants of Ishmael and those of Keturah demanded the land of Canaan, as mentioned in the

Bible (Genesis XXV, 12) as they had a share in it with Israel. However, the same advocate [Gebiha ben Pesisa] quoted the fifth verse of that chapter, which states that Abraham gave all that he had unto Isaac, but to the sons of Abraham's concubines he gave gifts and sent them away. "If a father made a bequest to his children and separated them during his lifetime, how can the heirs have a claim against one another?"

Sanhedrin 91a

◄§ On the day that Nebuchadnezzar cast Chananyah, Mishael, and Azaryah [Shadrach, Meshech, and Abed-Nego] into the fiery furnace, six miracles occurred: the furnace floated upward; it broke; its foundation was crumbled by the heat; the golden image fell on its face; four kingdoms of the monarch were burned; Ezekiel restored to life the dead of the Valley of Dura.

Sanhedrin 92b

◄§ The ten lost tribes of Israel were exiled to Africa.

Sanhedrin 94a

◄§ Education was so popular and widespread in the days of King Hezekiah that from Dan to Beersheba an ignorant man could not be found; nor even a child from Gabbath to Anti-patris [between which legend states there were 600,000 town-ships] who was not acquainted with the technical laws of puri-fication.

Sanhedrin 94b

◄§ Abishai once rescued King David from the Philistines by suspending the power of gravity and causing David to remain in mid-air.

Sanhedrin 95a

◄§ Sennacherib found one of the boards of Noah's Ark. Rely-ing on what he believed were its magical properties, because through it Noah was saved, he vowed to sacrifice his two sons if he succeeded in destroying Israel. But they overheard him, and murdered him instead, as related in II Kings, XIX.

Sanhedrin 96a

ᴥ§ In Messianic times, the leaves of trees will be a cure for every sickness.

Sanhedrin 100a

ᴥ§ The city of Shechem was designated for trouble. For it was there that Dinah [daughter of Jacob] was assaulted, Joseph was sold by his brothers, and the kingdom of David was divided.

Sanhedrin 102a

ᴥ§ Balaam was lame in one leg and blind in one eye.

Sanhedrin 105a

ᴥ§ Love disregards the rules of dignified conduct, and causes men to do things ordinarily left to servants.

Sanhedrin 105b

ᴥ§ Ruth, ancestress of King David, was the daughter of Eglon, who was the grandson of Balak, King of Moab.

Sanhedrin 105b

ᴥ§ Balaam, Job, and Jethro were all advisers to Pharaoh [of the Exodus]. Balaam gave the advice to drown all the Israelite children, and he was killed; Job, who kept silent, was punished with tribulations; Jethro, who fled, was rewarded by having his descendants placed among the *Sanhedrin*.

Sanhedrin 106a

ᴥ§ Four hundred hypothetical questions concerning the levitical cleanlinesss of an airplane [turret or tower that flies in the air] were propounded.

Sanhedrin 106a

ᴥ§ Gechazi put a magnet over the golden calves made by Jeroboam, and they were suspended in mid-air.

Sanhedrin 107b

ᴥ§ Not less than six and not more than twelve days can a man live in fever without taking any food.

Sanhedrin 108b

◄§ One-third of the Tower of Babel was burned, one-third was swallowed by the earth, and one-third is still in existence.

Sanhedrin 108b

◄§ These are some of the sins of the Sodomites: they abolished free trade; they would stand a wealthy man under a tottering wall, push the wall, and then rob him of his money; or they would deposit balsam with him and return at night to rob him because the aroma of the balsam [which was usually kept in treasure-boxes] would reveal the hiding place of his wealth; he who possessed one ox had to pasture all the city's cattle one day, while he who had none had to pasture them two days; he who passed the river on a boat had to pay one *zuz,* and he who passed afoot had to pay two *zuzim;* if a man had a row of bricks, or had left garlic or onions in the sun to dry, each one came and took one, saying, "I am not causing you any damage by taking merely one."

The justice meted out in the Sodomite courts was as follows: if a person struck his neighbor's wife and she miscarried, the woman was given to the assailant and he should return her when she would again become pregnant! If one cut off the ear of his neighbor's donkey, the donkey was given to the striker until it grew back again! If one wounded his neighbor, the assaulter was compensated for bleeding him! He who crossed a river on a bridge had to pay four *zuzim,* and he who waded across had to pay eight! And if the latter refused to pay the charge, they struck him until he bled, and then charged a physician's fee for bleeding, plus the original eight *zuzim!* They had a bed for strangers. If the newcomer was too long for the bed, they shortened him; and if he was too short, they stretched him. If a poor man came to town, each inhabitant gave him a *dinar* on which his name was engraved. But they refused to sell him any food, and when he died of hunger each took his coin back. A girl once supplied a poor man with bread which she used to hide in a pitcher when she went for water. Her "crime" was discovered; they smeared her body with honey and put her on the roof, so that bees came and stung her to death.

Sanhedrin 109a, b

◆§ The first word of the Fourth Commandment in the Decalogue, regarding the Sabbath, is "Remember," as given in the Book of Exodus, and "Observe" in the Book of Deuteronomy. Yet both of these words were uttered by the Almighty in a single word—something transcending the power of the human mouth to speak and the ear to hear.

Shebuoth 20b

◆§ The oath taken in court must be administered in the language understood by the one taking it, and he must be cautioned in advance as to its seriousness and implication.

Shebuoth 38b, 39a

◆§ When Adam saw that the days were growing shorter after his expulsion from the Garden of Eden, he thought that because of his sin darkness would gradually return the world to desolation and chaos, and that this was the decree of death meted out to him. He sat and prayed for eight days. After the winter solstice [December/January] he noticed that the days were again growing longer, and realized that this was the cycle of the world. He therefore established these eight days as an annual holiday in praise of heaven. But his descendants made them into holidays for idols.

Avodah Zarah 8a

◆§ The first "Wanted!" posters were displayed in Rome. When the government desired the capture of Rabbi Meier for disobedience to its edicts, his picture was engraved on the gates of the city, with the statement that anyone seeing him should turn him over to the authorities.

Avodah Zarah 18b

◄§ The sun stood still for Joshua [Joshua X, 13] a full twenty-four hours, but these were not consecutive, as there were intervals between its going and stopping.

Avodah Zarah 25a

◄§ King David's crown was so heavy that he could not wear it. It was suspended over his head by a magnet so that it appeared as if he were wearing it.

Avodah Zarah 44a

◄§ If a cripple is cured by visiting an idol in a temple, it is not the idol that has cured him, but the fact that the sickness has run its course.

Avodah Zarah 55a

◄§ No decree shall be promulgated unless the majority of the people can comply with it.

Horayoth 3b

◄§ Just as sacrifices make atonement, so are the priestly garments symbolical of atonement: the coat atoned for murder; the breeches for adultery; the mitre for pride; the girdle for evil thoughts; the breastplate for injustice; the Ephod for idolatry; the robe for slander; the golden plate for impudence.

Zevachim 88b

◄§ The design of the Ark, the Table, and the Candelabrum of the Tabernacle was shown to Moses in a pattern of fire.

Menachoth 29a

◄§ Seven letters of the Hebrew alphabet have crownlets [flourishes, ornaments] when written in the Torah, and Rabbi Akibah could interpret countless rules from each one.

Menachoth 29b

◄§ Man is required to utter one hundred blessings daily.

Menachoth 43b

◆§ When the members of the *Sanhedrin* convened, they sat in a semicircle, so that each one could see the other.

Chullin 5a

◆§ The donkey of Rabbi Phineas ben Yair would refuse to eat grain from which the levitical portion had not been taken off.

Chullin 7a, b

◆§ A scholar who sees no improvement in his studies over a period of five years will never progress.

Chullin 24a

◆§ Rabbi Simon ben Chalafta was a researcher and experimenter, and studied the habits of ants, among other things.

Chullin 57b

◆§ The eating of asafoetida before a meal exposes one to serious skin disease. Immediate bathing in water may prevent it.

Chullin 59a

◆§ A test as to whether an animal had been bitten by a serpent was to put the meat on a fire in the stove. If the meat disintegrated, the animal had been bitten and poisoned.

Chullin 59a

◆§ The lion of the forest of Ilai was so powerful that when one roared at a distance of four hundred parasangs from Rome, the pregnant women had miscarriages, and the tower of Rome shook violently; at a distance of three hundred parasangs, the teeth of those who heard its roar fell out, and Caesar fell from his throne.

Chullin 59b

◆§ The men of Alexandria consulted Rabbi Joshua ben Chananyah on twelve points of law, coming under four categories. Three were questions of wisdom [*halacha,* meaning "rules of law"]; three were *haggadic* ["homilectics"]; three were nonsensical [ignorant]; three concerned practical everyday matters.

Niddah 69b

◄§ The concluding words of the Talmud indicate that not only is peace the ultimate blessing, but that peace and security depend on strength—a quotation from Psalm XXIX, 11: "The Lord will give strength to His people . . . the Lord will bless His people with peace."

End of Treatise Uktzin

20

GEMATRIAH

Interpretive Numerology

Among the most notable of Jewish curiosities is *Gematriah*.

This is a word derived from the Greek, either from *geometria*, from which the English word *geometry* comes, or from *gramma*, meaning *letter*. In Hebrew, however, it denotes and connotes far more than mere mathematical values—*Gematriah* actually refers to exegetical, hermeneutical, homiletical numerology, or, to put it more simply, the system of discovering the hidden sense or significance of a biblical text by interpreting it through the numerical value of its letters. In Hebrew there are no numerals (like the Arabic or Roman)—each letter of the alphabet is a different number:

ahlef	1	*hai*	5
beth	2	*vov*	6
gimmel	3	*zahyin*	7
dahleth	4	*cheth*	8

teth	9	*koof*	100
yood	10	*raish*	200
kahf (or *chaf*)	20	*shin* (or *sin*)	300
lahmed	30	*tov* (or *sov*)	400
mem	40	final *kahf* (or *chaf*)	500
noon	50	final *mem*	600
sahmech	60	final *noon*	700
ahyin	70	final *pai* (or *phai*)	800
pai (or *phai*)	80	final *tzaddi*	900
tzaddi	90		

To express numbers from 11 to 19, and other numbers in the decimal system (21 to 29, 31 to 39, etc.), the corresponding letter is added to each decimal unit. For example, 11 is *yood-ahlef* (10 and 1); 25 is *chaf-hai* (20 and 5). The only exceptions are 15 and 16, which are written *teth-vov* (9 plus 6) and *teth-zahyin* (9 plus 7) respectively, as the combination of the *yood* with the *hai* or *vov* forms God's Name and is therefore prohibited secularly.

Through *Gematriah* many novel and curious interpretations are achieved. The amazing thing is how often they coincide arithmetically with interpretations derived from tradition or logic.

For example, Genesis XIV, 14 speaks of the members of Abraham's household who accompanied him in his pursuit of Lot's captors: "the trained men in his house, 318 men." According to the Talmud (*Nedarim* 32a), these "men" were just one individual—Eliezer, Abraham's chief servant or steward. This is a tradition. Yet, strange though it may seem, the numerical value of the word, *Eliezer* (*ahlef, lahmed, yood, ahyin, zahyin, raish*—1 plus 30 plus 10 plus 70 plus 7 plus 200) is identical—318.

Another example is the first letter of the first six sentences of Deuteronomy XXXII—the "Farewell Song" of Moses. These six letters (*hai, yood, chaf, hai, shin, hai*) add up to 345, identical with the numerical value of the name, *Moses* (*Moshe*—

mem, shin, hai), the inference being that the spiritual doctrines contained in these verses epitomize the philosophy of the Lawgiver in his farewell address to his people.

There are many variations to the system of *Gematriah* aside from the normal numerical value of the letters of the alphabet. The minor value of the letters may be utilized, disregarding the ciphers. For example, the word, *Torah* (Bible), whose full numerical value is 611 (*tov, vov, raish, hai*—400, 6, 200, 5), by minor calculation becomes 17 (4 plus 6 plus 2 plus 5), which equals *good* (*Tov—teth, vov, beth*—9 plus 6 plus 2).

Then again, there may be permutation of letters, whereby the first letter of the alphabet (*ahlef*) is exchanged with the last letter (*tov*), and so on through the entire alphabet.

Another variation is the permissibility of adding or subtracting for the words themselves. For instance, if the total of two words in the Hebrew text equals 611, 2 may be added for the value of the two words themselves; if the total equals 615, 2 may be subtracted for the value of the words themselves. In addition, there are other more complicated variations, such as the square value of the letter or word, the multiple value, the cube value, to mention but a few.

For want of a more suitable or understandable term, *Gematriah* has been referred to above as "numerology." That, actually, is a misnomer, because numerology is a pseudo-science which has no authoritative standing. Yet since it is "the science of numbers," and since significant interpretations of biblical text are derived from the numerical value of its letters, *Gematriah* has its definite place in exegesis. To use a vernacular expression, some scholars swear by these numerical interpretations, others swear at them. In *Pirkei Ahvoth* (Chapters, or Ethics of the Fathers), the ninth treatise in the mishnaic Fourth Order (*Nezikin*—Damages, or Torts), we find the statement by Rabbi Elazar (ben) Chisma: "Astronomy and *Gematriah* are the after-courses of wisdom." (Incidentally, the word for "after-courses" (desserts) is, in Hebrew, *periph'ri'aoth,* evidently a direct derivation from the Greek and Latin roots of the English word, *periphery,* denoting that *Gematriah* is one of the outer or boundary sciences bordering on wisdom.)

In any event, it is fascinating to discover how many unique explanations can be arrived at through the alphabetical-numerical system of biblical interpretation. Every sentence, phrase, word, and even letter of the Torah has been subjected to the minute exploration of its numerical value.

There is one school of thought which asserts that everything that has occurred or will occur is contained in the Bible. A follower of that doctrine was once jocularly asked where prohibition in the United States of America is mentioned. In less than a minute, he replied: "Verse 9 of the 10th chapter of Leviticus . . . 'Drink no wine or strong drink.'" When it was pointed out to him that this could easily apply to any country in any epoch, he showed that the final letters of these four Hebrew words ("Yahyi*n* v'sheicha*r* a*l* taish*t*") have a numerical value of 680 (*noon, raish, lahmed, tov*)—and that it was in the year 680 of the fifth millennium (the Hebrew year 5680, corresponding to 1920) that the Volstead Act ordering prohibition went into effect! A curious "coincidence" indeed!

Closely linked with *Gematriah* is *Notarikon* (or *Notrikon*), derived from the Latin *notaricum* from *notarius,* a shorthand writer. This consists of simply abbreviating the words, or of writing only one letter of each word—a method claimed by some talmudic sages as having originated with Moses. Through this system, a word of say seven letters, for instance, may stand for seven complete words which interpret the original word itself. On the staff of Moses, according to tradition, there were three words engraved, consisting of a total of ten letters, which were, in consecutive order, the initial letters of the ten plagues visited upon the Egyptians before the Exodus, and which were brought about through Moses and his staff.

In addition, interpretations are often derived by taking the *Gematriah* (numerical value) of the initial letters (*rashei taivoth*) or final letters (*sof taivoth*) of the words in a phrase or sentence, or by anagrams—combining such letters into different words. A classic example is to be found in the Bible itself—in Genesis VI, 8: "And Noah found grace." The Hebrew letters of *Noah* (*noon, cheth*) when reversed, form the word, *grace* (*chain*). Hence the word itself corroborates the text.

Another example is contained in Genesis V, 23: "And all the days of Enoch were five and sixty years and three hundred years." The last letters of the words (five and sixty years and three) in Hebrew are *shin, mem, hai,* and *shin,* which in themselves form the word *ha'shemesh* (the sun), for Enoch lived as many years as there are days in the solar year—365.

Here are a few additional simple examples of *Gematriah.*

In the Talmud, we are told that the name of Pharaoh's daughter who rescued Moses from the river was Bathiah—a name not included in the biblical recital. In Exodus II, 5, she is referred to as *bath Pharaoh* (the daughter of Pharaoh). The numerical value of these two words is 757, identical to that of *shem Bathiah* ("Bathiah by name").

Numbers XVII, 25, telling of the rebellion of Korach, uses the term *Mehri* to describe his followers. *Mehri* is spelled *mem, raish, yood,* which total 250 (40 plus 200 plus 10), and strangely enough, this is the exact total of the number of rebels who accompanied Korach (Numbers XVI, 2). "And they rose up in face of Moses, with certain of the children of Israel—250 men."

Deuteronomy V, 2 states, "The Lord our God made a covenant with us." The word for *made* in this sentence is, in Hebrew, *korath,* which also means *cut.* Its numerical value is 620 (*kahf, raish, sov*—20 plus 200 plus 400). This refers to the 620 letters which are contained in the Ten Commandments, cut in stone by the Almighty. It also denotes the 620 main commandments emanating therefrom—the 613 of the Torah, plus the 7 rabbinical ones.

In Deuteronomy VI, 7, we find the phrase, "And thou shalt speak of them." The Hebrew word meaning "of them," or "in them" (*bum*), is composed of two letters, *beth* and *mem,* representing that which should be spoken of. It is indeed interesting to note that the *beth* stands for *B'reishith,* the first word of the written Torah, meaning "In the beginning," and the *mem* stands for *Mei'eimsai* ("From when"), which is the first word of the oral Torah.

As a final example of *Notarikon,* in Deuteronomy XXXIV, 1, we have the phrase, *"el har n'voh"* ("to the mountain of Nebo"). The Hebrew letters, rearranged, form the word, *L'har'uvein* ("in that of Reuben"). Mount Nebo was situated in the portion of the Promised Land allotted to the Tribe of Reuben, as mentioned in Numbers XXXII.

Some numerical values are fantastic, some possibly contrived. Yet many are simple and logical. It would require a separate volume to cite the thousands of interpretations derived therefrom. The few instances given in the preceding paragraphs give an inkling, however, of this fascinating area of Jewish curiosities.

BIBLIOGRAPHY

Ahvoth d'Rab Nathan. With Hebrew commentaries. Vilna, 1833.

The Apocrypha. Edgar J. Goodspeed translation, in *The Complete Bible, An American Translation,* Chicago: The University of Chicago Press, 1939.

The Bible (Torah, Prophets, Hagiographa). Hebrew editions with commentaries. For English, see Isaac Leeser translation, Philadelphia: Sherman and Company, 1853; also *The Complete Bible, An American Translation,* Chicago: The University of Chicago Press, 1939.

Cohen, A., *Everyman's Talmud.* London: J. M. Dent and Sons, Ltd., 1934.

———— *The Teachings of Maimonides.* London: George Routledge and Sons, Ltd., 1927.

Daily and Holiday Prayer Books. Hebrew editions; also English translation and commentary by Joseph H. Hertz, New York: Bloch Publishing Company, 1948; D. A. DeSola translation, London: Shapiro, Vallentine and Company, 1929.

Ein Yaakob (Agada). Berlin: Choreb, 1927. See English translation by S. H. Glick, New York, 1916.

Encyclopedia of Jewish Knowledge, ed. Jacob De Haas. New York: Behrman's Jewish Book House, 1934.

Jastrow, Marcus, *A Dictionary of the Targumim, the Talmud Babli and Jerushalmi, and Midrashic Literature.* Berlin: Choreb, 1926.

The Jewish Encyclopedia. New York: Funk and Wagnalls Company, 1906.

Maimonides, Moses, *Mishneh Torah (Yad Ha'Chazakah).* With Hebrew commentaries. Vilna: Rosenkranz, 1928.

———— *Moreh Nebuchim (Guide for the Perplexed),* tr. Michael Friendlaender. New York: E. P. Dutton Company, 1910.

Midrash Ha'Refuah, ed. Moshe Perlman. Tel Aviv: D'vir, 1926.

Midrash Rabbah, Yalkut Shimoni, Midrash Tanchuma. Berlin:

Choreb, 1927. Also minor *Midrashim* in *Otzar Midrashim*, New York: J. D. Eisenstein, 1928.

The *Mishnah*. With Hebrew commentaries. Berlin: Choreb, 1924. For English, see Herbert Danby translation, Oxford: The Clarendon Press, 1933.

Otzar Yisroel (Hebrew Encyclopedia), ed. J. D. Eisenstein. New York, 1907.

Pirkei d'Rabbi Eliezer, tr. Gerald Friedlander. London: Kegan Paul, Trench, Trubner and Company, Ltd., 1916.

Sefer Ha'Agadah, ed. Bialik and Ravnitzky. Tel Aviv: D'vir, 1933.

Strack, Hermann L., *Introduction to the Talmud and Midrash.* Philadelphia: Jewish Publication Society of America, 1931.

Talmud Babli. With Hebrew commentaries. Berlin: Choreb, 1925.

Talmud Jerushalmi. With Hebrew commentaries. Berlin: Choreb, 1929.

Vallentine's Jewish Encyclopedia. London: Shapiro, Vallentine and Company, 1938.

The Works of Josephus, tr. William Whiston. Boston and New York: The C. T. Brainard Publishing Company, n.d.

The Works of Philo Judaeus, tr. C. D. Yonge. London: Henry G. Bohn, 1854.

Wright, Dudley, *The Talmud.* London: Williams and Norgate, Ltd., 1932.

Zabara, Joseph ben Meir, *Sefer Shaashu'im.* Ed. Israel Davidson. New York: Jewish Theological Seminary of America, 1914.

INDEX